Acclaim for Louis Uchitelle's

The Disposable American

"Compelling, relevant and emotionally wrenching. If you wonder how the American dream became the American nightmare, read this book."
—*Tucson Citizen*

"Skewering the mythology, *The Disposable American* draws heartfelt portraits of a handful of Americans whose plights illuminate a festering national crisis."
—*The Oregonian*

"Impressively researched, [and] clearly written.... A book with a refreshingly angry tone, as a talented investigative journalist sets out the irrefutable evidence that layoffs damage society at large."
—*Milwaukee Journal Sentinel*

"Vivid. . . . Uchitelle digs deeper than most, to show the devastating effects of this paradigm of failure on the affected workers, on the corporate life of the companies involved, on communities where the shrinking companies are located, and on the American economy and culture."
—*The Seattle Times*

"Most impressive.... Moves seamlessly from the story of the personal trials of laid-off American workers to the macroeconomic and political history that has led to their individual suffering."
—*The San Diego Union-Tribune*

"A quiet, thoughtful screed against the phenomenon of mass layoffs. *The Disposable American* is at once a narrative history of American layoffs, with profiles of workers bearing the brunt of the trend, and a broader polemic against job cuts and the politics that offer them no resistance."
—*Orlando Weekly*

Louis Uchitelle

The Disposable American

Louis Uchitelle has covered economics for *The New York Times* since 1987, focusing on labor and business issues and traveling widely in the United States. He shared a George Polk Award for a series of seven articles, "The Downsizing of America," published in *The Times* in 1996, that explored the layoff phenomenon. He was a visiting scholar at the Russell Sage Foundation in New York from 2002 to 2003, and he taught journalism for many years at Columbia University's School of General Studies. Before joining *The Times*, Mr. Uchitelle worked for the *Associated Press* as a reporter, editor, and foreign correspondent in Latin America. He and his wife, Joan Uchitelle, live in Scarsdale, New York. They have two grown daughters.

The Disposable American

The Disposable American

LAYOFFS AND THEIR CONSEQUENCES

Louis Uchitelle

VINTAGE BOOKS

A DIVISION OF RANDOM HOUSE, INC.

NEW YORK

The Library of Congress has cataloged the Knopf edition as follows:
Uchitelle, Louis.
The disposable American : layoffs and their consequences / by Louis Uchitelle—1st ed.
p. cm.
Includes bibliographical references and index.
1. Employees—dismissal of—United States. 2. Displaced workers—United States.
3. Unemployed—United States. 4. Downsizing of organizations—United States.
5. Plant shutdowns—United States. I. Title
HD5708.55.U6 U34 2006
331.13'73'0973—dc22
2005044423

Vintage ISBN: 978-1-4000-3433-8

Author photograph © Fred R. Conrad
Book design by Wesley Gott

www.vintagebooks.com

Printed in the United States of America
10 9 8 7 6 5 4 3 2 1

For my brother Bob,
   who set me on this path

CONTENTS

Myths That Blind

More than two decades have passed since the modern layoff first appeared as a mass phenomenon in American life. Until that happened, companies tried to avoid layoffs. They were a sign of corporate failure and a violation of acceptable business behavior. Over the years, however, the permanent separation of people from their jobs, abruptly and against their wishes, gradually became standard management practice, and in the late 1990s we finally acquiesced. Acquiescence means giving up, seeing no alternative; we bowed to layoffs as the way things have to be. Now we justify them as an unfortunate necessity.

Three myths help us do that. The first myth promises a payoff. In exchange for so many painful layoffs—at least 30 million full-time workers have lost their jobs since the early 1980s—a revitalized corporate America will emerge, once again offering job security, full employment, and rising incomes. Be patient, this myth goes. Every significant shift in the nature of a market economy since Adam Smith's day has entailed a period of hardship and disruption followed by a new equilibrium. The current cycle is no exception. Rebirth and stability will surely follow the current destruction.

But the promised payoff is not on the horizon. The layoffs continue unabated. Some are inevitable as American companies adjust to the growing competition from abroad. But there has been no return to the old stability. If there is a new equilibrium today, it is one that, benefiting from the acquiescence, perversely produces many more layoffs than the changing economy requires. What started as a legitimate response to America's declining hegemony has become an unending, debilitating condition.

The second myth holds that the laid-off must save themselves. They lost their jobs, this myth argues, because their value to their employers was less than their cost in wages and benefits. So they must raise their value. They must acquire the necessary education and training to qualify for the work that is in demand in the new economy. If they fail to land good jobs in a reasonable period of time, then that in itself is evidence that they did not take the right actions and are to blame for their own demise.

Education is without doubt a good thing. But there are not enough good jobs for the college educated, and neither the private sector nor government offers much help. The burden is on the workers themselves. What has taken place is a massive shift from a shared, we're-in-it-together way of thinking to a go-it-alone world of personal responsibility.

The third myth holds that the pros and cons of layoffs are entirely measurable in dollars and cents, the relevant standard for a market system. In this framework, savings in labor costs can seem to justify layoffs. I found this myth hard to challenge until I encountered and documented a layer of human damage that is difficult to quantify, but is alarmingly destructive, so much so that it sets back companies that are supposed to thrive through the freewheeling use of layoffs.

Neither the companies nor the victims easily recognize the damage that layoffs inflict on them. For the victims, a layoff is an emotional blow from which very few fully recover, as you will learn from the men and women you meet in the following pages. The laid-off are cut loose from their moorings and rarely achieve in their next jobs a new and satisfactory sense of themselves. Psychiatrists and psychologists know this; they run across it regularly in the treatment of patients who have been laid off and who suffer from depression and from a neurotic reluctance to return to challenging work and risk being disposed of again.

The mental health profession, however, does not raise an alarm, although the damage from this loss of self-esteem and identity, multiplied millions of times, undermines public health. In addition, layoffs damage companies by undermining the productivity of those who survive but feel vulnerable, as well as the productivity of those who are laid off and get jobs again. All lose some of the commitment, trust, and collegial behavior that stable employment or the expectation of stable employment normally engenders. Various studies bear this out, and some of the nation's most successful companies—Southwest Airlines and Harley-Davidson, for example—refrain from layoffs or limit them, openly recognizing that people who feel secure in their jobs work better.

The myths blind us to these realities, particularly the mythical promise that in the end, when the new equilibrium finally arrives, the layoffs will cease or greatly diminish, and America will flourish at the high end of innovation and production, which is its rightful and inevitable perch in the new economy.

While waiting for this nirvana, the country has deteriorated. Without the easy and frequent use of layoffs, there would not have been so many wasteful mergers, or so much outsourcing or ceding of production to foreign competitors and to the overseas subsidiaries of American companies. Over the last couple of decades, sensible resistance to the shedding of workers would have acted as a brake, sifting out at least some of the unnecessary layoffs. Union power, as a result, would not have been so indiscriminately undermined and wage stagnation would not have become so entrenched. More subtly, the acquiescence to layoffs facilitates the dismantling of company-paid health insurance and fixed monthly pensions. If we have no value as employees beyond what we can produce in a day or a week or a year of work, why preserve the trappings that go with careers?

And they are not being preserved—not by our employers or our politicians, neither the Democrats nor the Republicans. Faced with layoffs, one president after another, starting with Jimmy Carter and running through George W. Bush, has either facilitated layoffs or acquiesced to them, or both. There is no loyal opposition. I set out to tell the story of our acquiescence and in doing so ran into a festering national crisis. Until we recognize it, an effective opposition cannot form.

The Disposable American

CHAPTER ONE

The Stanley Works

Several years ago, Donald W. Davis stopped making regular visits back to New Britain, Connecticut. He felt shame for what had happened to the Stanley Works, the city's largest employer, which he had led from 1966 to 1988—from its best days to the beginning of the layoffs and plant closings that, after he was gone, finally reduced Stanley's presence in New Britain to a collection of mostly empty factory buildings and reproachful former workers.

Davis by then no longer lived in New Britain. He had sold his Dutch Colonial home, which he had painted a bright and optimistic yellow, and had moved with his wife to Martha's Vineyard, where their summer house on seven acres of rolling lawn became their main residence. It was an entirely different setting, but the trip back to New Britain for visits was easy enough—less than four hours by ferry and car—and Davis at first made it often. Like many chief executives of his era, he had been deeply involved in the life of the city that, in his day, had supplied thousands of Stanley's workers. He had served on the board of education for many years and was its president for a while. The six Davis children attended the public elementary schools.

But in the late 1990s, the visits home became infrequent. Meeting former Stanley employees on the streets, in restaurants, at the YMCA, where Davis still went to exercise, was too painful. "They just moaned about what was happening to this great company," Davis told me. He had tried to share their sadness, to distinguish his stewardship from the accelerated pace of layoffs and the disregard for New Britain that had become so striking after he was gone—as if he were a victim too. But he wasn't really. The people he encountered had lost their jobs against their wishes, while he had retired on schedule, a wealthy man. And he had, after all, initiated the layoffs. No one blamed him, Davis maintained. But the encounters with former Stanley workers became, as Davis put it, "much too personal." So he stayed away.

When we renewed our acquaintance a few years into his self-exile, I found a restless, often passionate man, unable to put behind him his final years as chief executive. At eighty-one, still stocky and agile, he was grateful for good health so late in life. Age showed only in his hair, which was pure white, and in his eyes, which became tired and bloodshot in the late afternoon, although when I suggested that we take a break in our conversation, which had started in the morning and had continued through lunch at a noisy seafood restaurant, he waved me off, intent on his recollections. He no longer bothered with the suits and sports jackets of his CEO days, but he did have on a white button-down shirt. He was running a leadership seminar twice a week during the fall semester at the Massachusetts Institute of Technology, where he shared a small, cluttered office with two other instructors.

Davis rarely canceled a class; the seminar he led became a last connection to his former business world, a final public platform. Sitting in on a class in the late afternoon, listening to him draw on his experiences from his Stanley days, I imagined that beyond the nineteen young people seated in the room, he was speaking to all those he knew back home, explaining that he had done as well as any executive could, in a very changed world, to preserve Stanley as it was. And that could not be done.

The Stanley Works illustrates, as well as any Fortune 1000 company, the accelerating deterioration of job security in America over three generations of chief executives, a deterioration that Davis and his counterparts in the first generation resisted for a while, reluctant to let go of the expiring norms. So did their workers. For almost ninety years, from the 1890s until the late 1970s, the thrust of American labor practices had been toward lasting attachments of employers to workers and vice versa. There were lapses and backsliding in those decades. Descriptions of labor practices during the 1921–22 recession, for example, are remarkably similar to labor practices today. But the direction was toward job security, not away from it. Efficiency seemed to require it. So did union power, government policies, community expectations, and social norms. Even the Depression, with its mass unemployment, produced in reaction labor laws that in the post–World War II years strengthened job security. We had decided as a people—managers, politicians, and workers—that job security had value, and in pursuit of that value, we lifted ourselves out of insecurity. And then, starting about 1977, midway through Davis's twenty-one-year term as chief executive, there was a U-turn.

Over the next twenty years, the achieved job security disintegrated in the United States. Layoffs were the medium. Each step in the disintegration was a novelty and a shock. But the layoffs continued, and in 1984 the Bureau of Labor Statistics began to count "worker displacement." By 2004, the bureau had counted at least 30 million full-time workers who had been permanently separated from their jobs and their paychecks against their wishes. Huge as that number was, it did not include the millions more who had been forced into early retirement or had suffered some other form of disguised layoff, masking the magnitude of the problem. A more comprehensive survey would very probably have found that 7 or 8 percent of the nation's full-time workers had been laid off annually on average—nearly double the recognized layoff rate. And the percentages crept higher as the years passed.

Davis remembers vividly the circumstances that brought on the U-turn. The experience was, in his word, "traumatic." He awoke in 1979 to find that customers for Stanley's hand tools were defecting in alarming numbers. The lure was Asian tools. Once-shoddy socket wrenches, screwdrivers, claw hammers, saws, levels, chisels, pliers, and measuring tapes imported from Asia had gradually become indistinguishable in quality from Stanley's offerings, and at 60 percent of the price—a feat Davis and his counterparts in many other industries had not anticipated.

Scrambling to respond, they cut prices and, hoping to preserve profits, they began to cut labor costs, at first through attrition and then through layoffs. Hundreds of other companies were caught in a similar experience. From then on, job security unwound in America. Layoffs became the measure of our national retreat from the dignity that had been gradually bestowed on American workers over the previous ninety years. What started as a necessary response to the intrusion of foreign manufacturers into the American marketplace got out of hand. By the late 1990s, getting rid of workers had become normal practice, ingrained behavior, just as job security had been twenty-five years earlier.

That did not happen without resistance, particularly in the 1980s and early 1990s. Community groups, for example, tried to purchase and reopen shut factories, the goal being to reemploy the working people who gave the community its existence. The Roman Catholic Church joined in this endeavor, and issued two pastoral letters in the 1980s opposing job destruction. But then the church fell silent, as did the communities, which disintegrated without the steady jobs that had sustained them. Government regulation had protected the jobs of nearly 13 percent of the workforce, those employed in airlines, trucking, public utilities, telephones, banking, and railroads. And then deregulation, starting with President Jimmy Carter, precipitated endless reorganizations in those industries, and endless layoffs to accommodate the reorganizations, until reorganization and layoff finally became the norm. Organized labor also protested, but union membership and power were already in decline, and after 1981, when President Ronald Reagan fired and then replaced the nation's striking air traffic controllers, strike activity in support of job security—or in support of any other demand, for that matter—declined precipitously. The old assumption that a worker out on strike had his job waiting once the strike ended was gone.

Just as layoffs began to be a source of national anxiety, mainstream economic theory completed an about-face that in effect endorsed layoffs and diminished the pressure on the nation's presidents and on Congress to preserve job security. The dethroned way of thinking had recognized a central role for government in protecting workers in a free market economy. Entrepreneurial, hard-driving managers were essential to keep the economy vibrant and growing. But they ran roughshod over workers unless they were restrained by government rules and regulations, including rules that strengthened labor's bargaining power. The marketplace would not provide job security without pressure from government. That way of thinking, born in the New Deal in the 1930s and greatly expanded over the next three decades, died in the 1970s.

The new intellectual framework took the opposite view, and in so doing validated what was already beginning to happen. Companies were freeing themselves from the many obligations to their employees that had accumulated over the years, and now mainstream economics blessed that endeavor. In the process, government was depicted as an obstacle to prosperity. Unfettered enterprises, the argument now went, would expand more rapidly and, over the long run, share their rising profits with their workers, doing so voluntarily through job creation and raises. If that did not happen—and it did not happen for tens of millions of people who lost their jobs—well, that was the fault of the job losers themselves. They had failed to acquire the necessary skills and education to qualify for the increasingly sophisticated jobs that were available. They lacked value as workers. And the argument took hold. Sanford M. Jacoby, the economic historian, citing a study typical of this period, noted that "workers with at least some college education were more likely than less educated workers to view fairness as 'recognition of individual abilities' instead of 'equal treatment for all.' "

The new economic theory, making each worker responsible for his or her own job security, interacted fatally with the actual layoff experience. Layoffs, we were told, do not happen to people who improve their skills and are flexible, innovative, congenial, and hardworking. The layoff says you have failed in these endeavors, no matter how hard you tried to follow the prescription. You are an inferior worker. The damage to self-esteem from this message is enduring. It shows up frequently in people who have been laid off, whether or not they work again, and yet it is ignored in the political debate. Job creation and full employment are held up by Democrats and Republicans, and nearly all the experts who advise them on policy, as sufficient antidote. Putting the laid-off back to work in new jobs solves the problem. There is income again and even prosperity, or the potential for it. But mental health is not easily restored.

Psychologists and psychiatrists are just beginning to recognize that layoffs chip away at human capital by eating at self-esteem on a mass scale. It is like acid rain eroding the environment, according to Dr. Theodore J. Jacobs, a professor of psychiatry at Albert Einstein College of Medicine and New York University School of Medicine in New York. He says: "Even if a person is accurate in saying, 'I did a really good job, and I can see that the company is in a bad way and they have to lay off a lot of people and it is really not about me,' there is seldom an escape from the inner sense of 'Why me?' In other words, one has some sense that one has failed and the outside world has made that judgment. And that self-perception dovetails with existing inadequacies that many people feel about themselves."

The Great Depression was less damaging. Millions of people lost their jobs then, but the majority blamed flaws in the market system, not in themselves. They demanded that government fix the flaws. That collective response, which helped to produce the New Deal, is missing today. Implicit in self-blame is acquiescence to layoffs, now the American condition.

All this was still well in the future when Don Davis became chief executive of the Stanley Works in 1968. Job insecurity in those days—at the Stanley Works and most other manufacturers—went no further than the temporary furloughing of blue-collar workers when sales weakened. The white-collar staff—clerks, secretaries, salespeople—were not touched. "We thought of them as part of management," Davis said. But at the factory level, some workers would be told to stay home until production picked up again, which it always did in those truly prosperous years. Seniority dictated who was furloughed first, and in what order they would be recalled, which they always were. "That was a very important thing, that recall; it made people feel they still had this connection with Stanley," Davis said. Seniority rights continued to accrue during the stay-at-home period, and health insurance remained in effect. These were Stanley's ways, and the ways of many American companies.

The onslaught of imports starting in the late 1970s changed those ways. As customers defected, sales plummeted and failed to bounce back. Nowhere was that more on display than in the auto industry's struggle with Japanese imports. But nearly every manufacturer was hit, and the steep recession in 1981 and 1982 compounded the damage. The old world has never returned. Visit the tools department at Home Depot, which is Stanley's biggest single customer, purchasing 12 percent of its annual output in 2004, and the array of products shows Stanley painfully struggling to stand out. The company's yellow and black colors still dominate the shelves where measuring tapes are stacked, the clip-to-the-belt models whose steel blades spool out across a room and quickly retract into stubby cassettes at the click of a lever. Many of the claw hammers bear Stanley's name, and also the scraper blades, the linoleum-cutting knives, and every variety of saw—hacksaws, wood saws, keyhole saws, compass saws, pull saws. But even on these shelves, the colorful tools of other companies are well represented. And the Stanley label no longer dominates the displays of socket wrenches, screwdrivers, adjustable squeeze-handle pliers, levels, wood planes, counter punches, chisels, and bolt cutters. What all the tools have in common, including Stanley's, is origin: the great majority are made outside the United States, particularly in Asia.

Shifting manufacturing abroad was not in Davis's thinking in the late 1970s and early 1980s. Struggling to prevent the imports from gaining a foothold, he tried at first to bring down labor costs by shrinking the previously sacrosanct white-collar staff, not through layoffs—that would not happen to America's white-collar workers for a few more years—but by attrition. He froze hiring and decreed that as white-collar workers resigned or retired, those who remained would have to pick up the work of their departed colleagues in addition to their own. "Wearing two hats," he called it. The goal was a reduction of six hundred employees over two years, or 15 percent of the white-collar staff—a mild cutback by later standards, but worthy then of a display of anguish. Davis and his second in command, the chief operating officer, engaged in an exhausting tour of Stanley's plants, concentrated then in the Northeast and Midwest. They divided them up, and at each stop, one or the other explained to the assembled workers how the company's survival had become the issue. "We had a meeting of all the employees, salaried, white-collar, blue-collar, management, everybody," Davis said, "and where that was too big a crowd, we'd break it up into two or three groups. Then we'd have the night shift in another group. And he or I spoke to each one of these groups about the revolution that had taken place in competition, and how we had to respond to it if we were going to survive as a major player."

The attrition worked. The white-collar staff shrank as planned. But it was not enough cost-cutting and Davis turned to his factory workers. For the first time, he went beyond temporary furloughs into outright dismissal. He also began—reluctantly, he insisted in old age—to shift some operations from New Britain to lower-wage cities. As he did so, he figured out a system, by trial and error, for handling layoffs with a minimum of backlash. He even reduced the procedure to a checklist, and on the day I sat listening in his classroom at MIT, he introduced that checklist to his nineteen seminar students, all selected because they seemed to have the potential to become chief executives themselves.

"Let's say you are a plant manager of four hundred people and you are not going to need most of them because of automation," Davis explained. "Your boss tells you that the new machinery will arrive in three months and the switchover has to be made without a breakdown in production. Your job as leader of this group is to minimize the outcry and keep production going. What do you do?"

Several students raised their hands. Be honest with the workers about what you are doing, one suggested. "Of course you explain to the workers," Davis replied, impatiently, "but what about the politicians, the editor of the newspaper, the union officials, the mayor—all the people who can accuse you of messing up the town? You need a game plan for telling them, in just the right order in advance of the public announcement, so that when they hear the news later, they can say, Yes, we knew. It takes the sting out of layoffs." And he illustrated the point. You wait until just after the newspaper's deadline to tell the editors, he explained, so they know in advance but can't break the news to their readers ahead of the public announcement. "Stanley had a whole timeline of people who had to be notified and explained to if we had a significant layoff."

For all his regrets, Davis by the mid-1980s had clearly become skilled at layoffs. He had bitten into the apple, if you will. "I was forced to get used to layoffs," he told me. What he had begun, his handpicked successor, Richard H. Ayers, an industrial engineer with a bent for efficiency, accelerated. Ayers closed a huge distribution center in New Britain and reopened it in Charlotte, North Carolina—away from unions. Other operations also moved south, or overseas. Under Ayers, the merchandise Stanley sold in America was increasingly not made in America. Sledge-hammers and crowbars now came from a Stanley plant in Mexico, socket wrenches from a company purchased in Taiwan, a trickle of door hinges and latches from China, the result of a new joint venture. Under pressure from Ayers, two hundred workers who made hinges for kitchen stoves accepted a wage cut of $2 an hour as a condition for keeping the operation in New Britain. "I looked at this process as being evolutionary," he said.

But Stanley's directors weren't satisfied. Ayers, they felt, was not moving fast enough. So in 1997 they hired an outsider, John M. Trani, as chief executive, luring Trani away from General Electric with a signing bonus of one million Stanley stock options and a seven-figure annual salary package two to three times greater than either Davis or Ayers had ever earned. And Trani, who had won a name for himself at GE, excelling at the company that invented the modern American layoff, did move faster. Over the next six years, he closed forty-three of Stanley's eighty-three factories. The total payroll plummeted to 13,500 people from nearly 19,000. Some work was outsourced to contractors; other operations were combined in one factory. New Britain was a big loser in this shuffle. By the fall of 2002, the payroll there had dwindled to 900 employees, a far cry from the 7,000 people who had worked for Stanley in multistory brick factory buildings that dominated the downtown when Davis joined the company in 1948 as a twenty-seven-year-old junior executive, freshly graduated from Harvard Business School, which he had attended on the GI Bill.

Not much besides the headquarters building is left in New Britain. That building, strangely, is new, a modernistic, three-story structure put up by Davis in 1985 in a wooded industrial park as a last, futile gesture of loyalty to the city of Stanley's birth. In the fall of 2002, if you stepped out of the elevator on the third floor, where Trani and his top executives had their offices, against the opposite wall stood a wooden rolltop desk, beautifully restored, a desk once used by Frederick T. Stanley, who founded the company in 1843 in a workshop at the rear of his home in what was then a rural village. Along another wall, portrait paintings of eight earlier chief executives, each ornately framed, each man a stalwart in the civic life of the growing industrial city, paid tribute to the illustrious past. The eight paintings were lined up opposite the entrance to the chief executive's office, and as Trani came and went, those long-gone chiefs peered out at him. Elsewhere along the quiet carpeted halls were black-and-white drawings, in Norman Rockwell style, of fathers and sons, circa 1930s, working serenely together at home, fixing things with Stanley tools.

All this Trani made a point of ignoring, as if he had chosen corny, anachronistic adornments so he could snub them, which he certainly did. He is a chubby, tall, tightly scheduled man. He had an hour available in mid-November that year, his administrative assistant had told me, and if that did not work, January or February was the next available slot. I took the hour in November and drove to New Britain. We met alone in a conference room next to his office, sitting across from each other at a round, barren table. He answered my questions fully. Nothing I asked fazed him. He was very pleasant. But he did not permit our conversation to veer into a discussion of alternatives to layoffs. There were no alternatives, he insisted. "People who basically look at reality as it exists, without hoping for it to change, and deal with the hand they are dealt, so to speak, they are the successful ones," he said.

Reality for Trani at the outset of his stewardship meant sales revenue per factory. As Trani tells the story, the first thing he did when he took over in 1997 was to divide the total annual sales revenue ($2.6 billion that year) by the number of factories. The outcome, $31 million in average sales per factory, was too low, much lower than his main competitors. So he closed factories left and right, particularly the ones with the highest wages—i.e., in the United States—and by 2002 sales per factory were approaching $55 million, even though sales revenue, the numerator in the Trani equation, was still stuck at $2.6 billion. Too many competitors were offering too many hand tools at cutthroat prices. Cost-cutting, which meant mainly labor cost-cutting, was the only way out. "Layoffs and plant closings," Trani explained, "are not such a rare event anymore that one generally makes a big deal out of them."

He was equally casual about New Britain. He kept the headquarters there, he said, only because a better opportunity elsewhere had not yet presented itself. He emphasized the "yet." Given the opportunity to disparage the hometown, Trani rose to the occasion, as if he wanted to burnish his image as a rootless executive. He had recently been vilified in newspaper editorials and media accounts for attempting to move Stanley's headquarters of record to a post office drop in Bermuda to avoid $30 million a year in U.S. taxes. The public exposure had forced him to cancel the plan, but he was still defiant. Several competitors had reorganized as Bermuda corporations and had gained a competitive advantage, he told me. They had not been challenged by local politicians as he was, one of the critics being Mayor Lucian Pawlak of New Britain. "I understand that he does not like globalization," Trani said, "but that's the way it is. The mayor thinks that Stanley owes New Britain forever. Forever! We have discussions all the time. Nice guy. Great guy. But he has a view that I think is so far from reality that it creates angst when it does not necessarily have to be that way."

Davis and Ayers would never have belittled the mayor, or New Britain, so openly. They see themselves, in hindsight, as incrementalists and Trani as a CEO who does things "by overnight fiat," as Davis put it. They also see themselves as more humane. They walked the factory floors, greeting workers by name, asking after their families. Trani rarely hobnobbed. Not surprisingly, he also abandoned the periodic dinners for workers celebrating twenty-five, thirty, and forty years with the company, dinners that Davis and Ayers made a point of attending. And yet, in the end, for all their disdain for Trani's ways and his unseemly speed, they were not in disagreement with the outcome. They accepted as probably healthy for Stanley's profitability the reduction in the workforce and in the number of factories. Trani, in effect, finished what they had started.

Ayers in particular felt this. He noted, for example, that while Trani moved most of the production of Stanley's retractable clip-to-the-belt tape rulers from New Britain to a factory in Thailand, it was he, Ayers, who had acquired the Thai factory in the first place. The same was true for steel door hinges and latches. A staple of the Stanley product line, they were once manufactured in a great variety of shapes and sizes only in New Britain—and under Trani only in Xiolan, China, near Shanghai. Ayers started up the Chinese joint venture that Trani embraced with unnerving speed, employing a thousand people in Xiolan. In doing so, Trani closed a decades-old hinge factory in downtown New Britain—the five-story building is still shuttered—and laid off five hundred workers. He also shut a newer, smaller hinge factory in Richmond, Virginia, that Ayers had started up. Ayers, like Trani, had sought to lower labor costs, but more gradually. The nonunion Richmond factory was an interim step.

Ayers, a slightly built, courteous, patient man, had moved more slowly, he said, because for him a social norm existed that kept him in check, a norm that disappeared on Trani's watch. The Thai factory, in the Ayers strategy, would have made steel measuring tapes only for the Asian market, not for American consumers. Selling those tapes in the United States, he felt, would have offended customers, many of them carpenters and construction workers who belonged to unions that campaigned against purchasing merchandise not made in America. Hammers manufactured in China might be acceptable to these workers, but not the retractable steel measuring tapes, a signature Stanley product. "We had a very high user base in the unions," Ayers said, "and there was still resistance on their part in the mid-1990s to imported products." By the late nineties, however, the Made in America sentiment had dissipated. Americans had become focused on quality and price, and uninterested in origin. That a product was made abroad ceased to be a negative.

But even if Ayers had enjoyed a freer hand, he still would have held back on layoffs. He simply did not have the stomach, he said, for the upheaval that Trani thrived on. Much later, that was the justification he offered for his early departure from Stanley in 1997 at age fifty-five, still in his prime, only three years older than Trani, his replacement. Soon Ayers, in retirement, was shuttling between a summer home on a New Hampshire lake and a winter one in Florida, devoting considerable energy to Habitat for Humanity, the philanthropy whose volunteers, Jimmy Carter among them, build housing for the poor with their own hands. Of his decision to retire, he insisted that it was not Stanley's board of directors that threw him out, but his own distaste for the work ahead. "I disliked the difficult decisions you had to make in terms of their impact on people and I knew there was more of that coming," Ayers said. "I decided that it was time for someone else to do it. I could not."

Davis to Ayers to Trani—the dismantling of Stanley's workforce through three generations of chief executives finally got to Diane Sirois. After twenty-five years she still worked for the company at its last factory in New Britain of any consequence, an elongated, two-story building where Stanley once made all of the retractable measuring tapes that it sold in the United States, millions of them each year. In 1995, Ayers had taken a stab at keeping most of this manufacture in New Britain. He had spent millions on machinery to automate the assembly process. When I visited that year, Diane was a curly-haired thirty-nine-year-old climbing over the new machinery, which resembled a Lilliputian railroad, the tracks only a few inches apart.

Small pallets, the Lilliputian equivalent of railroad flat cars, moved slowly along the tracks, each bearing a partly assembled measuring tape. The pallets halted briefly at automated stations to receive components: a black plastic cap was welded to a reel at one stop, the spooled metal blade was inserted at another, an outer casing was added at a third, the belt clip at still another. There were several of these railroads. Each could be reprogrammed to produce different models: the 30-footer, the 25-footer, the 16-footer. Only a handful of workers was needed to keep the machines running. In 1995, however, men and women seated at work-stations still assembled many of the measuring tapes by hand. But Ayers assured me that more railroads would be installed, as soon as funds were available to invest in the contraptions.

As they arrived, hand assembly would be phased out. Production would remain in America, but not as many jobs. The survivors would be those with enough gumption to train for the automated assembly lines and then staff them, responding like emergency workers when the various red beacon lights installed along the lines flashed on, signaling a break-down. Diane had decided to be among the survivors. She liked new ventures, and the automated railroad system required greater skill and ingenuity than sitting at a worktable repetitively assembling steel and plastic parts into measuring tapes. While we talked she gestured disdain-fully at a group of assemblers seated nearby. They were doomed, she said. But she was not. She had spotted a way to immunize herself against lay-off. Under Stanley's labor agreement with the International Association of Machinists and Aerospace Workers, those employees with the least seniority had to go first in a layoff, even if they performed essential tasks. As they departed, colleagues with more seniority were reassigned to their jobs. Sirois, with eighteen years at Stanley then, was vulnerable. One of those expressionless assemblers she had just belittled could bump her. But the contract had an out. While others balked at the training needed to operate the new machinery, she had jumped at the opportunity, knowing that, under the contract, she could be bumped by a colleague with greater seniority only if that colleague could learn her job in a week. Diane had needed three months of training to master the skills required to fine-tune and troubleshoot the railroad. She did not think anyone could do it in less time. "Job security is why I bid for this job," she told me then.

Visiting the tape factory seven years later, I walked through a build-ing that was a ghost of its former self. The second floor was almost deserted and soon to be closed off entirely. In the mid-1990s it had bustled with workers assembling tape measures by hand. So much was gone that Stanley no longer invited Boy Scouts and civic groups to tour the plant. The tours would be an embarrassment, Terry Christensen, the plant manager, explained. Downstairs, not a nickel had been spent on more automation. The hand assembly had nearly disappeared, but the Lilliputian railroad system had not been expanded to replace the assemblers. That system had turned out to be more breakdown-prone and less efficient than Ayers anticipated. But rather than invest in better technology—better automation—John Trani eliminated jobs in New Britain and shifted to hand assembly in Thailand, which now was the focus of expansion.*

Now only the most sophisticated, high-end models came off the aging railroad, those used by skilled carpenters and other professionals—the FatMax, for example, featuring a thirty-five-foot-long, one-and-a-half-inch-wide tape, the steel specially treated so that the ruler can arc out eleven feet, like the tongue of a lizard, without cracking. Several of the features in the FatMax were still patent-protected, Trani said, and by keeping production in New Britain, at least for the time being, he reduced the risk of theft and foreign knockoffs. Manufacture of the numerous handyman models, however, the sort that a family keeps in a kitchen drawer or in a toolbox in the basement, had migrated to Thailand.

As the work departed, Diane Sirois gradually lost her faith in the seniority and the special training that she had counted on to preserve her job. She still threw herself into her work, enthusiasm being in her nature. She had even risen to shift leader. And by her reckoning, she had greater seniority than nearly all of the 120 other workers assigned to the four automated assembly lines, so that when one line shut down on a particular shift, as one recently had for lack of enough work, and nine or ten peo-

---

*For the Stanley Works and for many other manufacturers, going overseas to a country like Thailand is on balance less expensive than staying put and investing in automation. More workers are required, but with Asian labor so cheap, the company can invest in less expensive, semiautomated equipment and still come out ahead, says Daniel Luria, an economist at the Michigan Manufacturing Technology Center. That calculation, however, does not take into account damage to the community where the company's facilities were located. Nor does it measure the value lost in the withering of satellite companies that supported the manufacturing operation: accountants, materials suppliers, and truckers, for example.

ple were laid off, she was untouched. So was her husband, Dennis, who also worked on the automated assembly lines, on the same evening schedule as his wife. He had worked for Stanley for thirty years. She had been a waitress when they married in 1978, and he soon discovered, to his annoyance, that when he had vacation time at Stanley, she had to work. "I said, 'That's it,' and I got her into Stanley," he said. They were inseparable. Both had been raised in small Maine towns along the Canadian border, the children of French Canadian immigrants. They had met at a French club when she was twenty-two and he twenty-four. Their marriage was childless.

What frightened them now was their growing realization that if the aging automated equipment malfunctioned too often and performance in New Britain deteriorated, then Trani would shift all of the measuring tape assembly to Thailand. Everyone would be laid off and the factory closed. Their seniority wouldn't matter. That was not an abstraction. Every week, Christensen, the plant manager, posted on a bulletin board on the shop floor a chart that compared wage rates, output per worker, material costs, and other measures of performance in Stanley's various plants. The comparison with Thailand mattered most. "I cannot understand," Diane Sirois said, "why a company would want to hire a man like Trani. He does not care if we are an American company. He looks at us and says, What are we doing in America?"

The optimism that animated her when Ayers introduced automation seven years earlier had deteriorated into a tenuous hope that somehow the Lilliputian railroads would continue to operate until she and Dennis were sixty and could retire with full pensions. That was still twelve years away for him and fourteen for her. They did not think their plant would last that long; too much had already disappeared in the six years of Trani's rule. They would be forced to find other work, almost certainly at far less than the $32 an hour they earned between them at Stanley. Each would probably have to take on two jobs to match the lost pay. But that day had not yet come, and until it did, they carried on their lives as if Davis still ran the Stanley Works, in the days before the trauma of global competition ended job security. The Siroises never manifested grief, self-pity, or desperation at the coming downturn in their incomes. They were angry at Trani, but otherwise in a good mood. "If he closes the factory, I'll have to go look for a job somewhere else," Dennis said. They didn't know what job they would pursue or where they would look. "But we would not sit there and pout," Diane said. "We would look somewhere else." And Dennis finished the thought: "You have control over your life."

They don't, of course. No one does entirely, and certainly not assembly-line workers in a factory whose production is gradually being shifted elsewhere. But until the plant finally closed and everyone was laid off, they refused to give up the semblance of control over their lives that so many years at Stanley had bred in them. "We have five weeks' paid vacation," Dennis said. "Where else would we get that much? I have thirty years' seniority, and why would I give that up before we absolutely have to? We have too many years invested in Stanley to quit and go somewhere else."

On a rainy Saturday morning in late February 2003, on one of my visits to New Britain, I met the Siroises at a roadside restaurant called Kisl's, near their home, where Diane and Dennis ate breakfast three or four times a week. Arriving first, I took a booth big enough for six people, so we could spread out comfortably and talk. The place was packed, but the owner did not seem to mind. He was extremely hospitable, and Diane later introduced me to him. If John Trani, their nemesis, proclaimed his indifference to the community, Diane and Dennis Sirois made a point of belonging.

They are stocky, compact people and careful eaters, not feeling obliged to finish the abundant portions that came. Diane had changed very little, except for the color of her dark hair, now strawberry blond. Dennis was amiable, but also blunt and hurt. "When Davis and Ayers were there," he said, "they used to treat us like people, like employees. They walked the floor and talked to us, but this guy Trani, I've never seen him on the floor. I was at a meeting with him once, where he told us that if we called in sick or took a day off during the week and then worked Saturday we should not get time-and-a-half for Saturday. He figured that if you lost a day during the week, you should work Saturday at straight pay to make your forty hours."

The Siroises explained in some detail their experiences with the Lilliputian railroad. It had not produced the efficiencies that Ayers had expected. The complicated mechanisms broke down too often, increasing labor costs. For example, a breakdown at the station where the coiled steel measuring blade is inserted in the reel meant that a worker had to be hastily placed at this station to do the insertion by hand until repairs were made. Otherwise the line would have to halt, suspending production. Similarly, an automated conveyor system that carried the completed measuring tapes from the railroad lines to the packing and shipping area had broken down so frequently that Stanley dismantled it and substituted manual labor. Finally, there was line speed. Trani had decreed that production on any given day would be limited to the number of tape measures sold the day before; there would be no excess output for inventory, or as little as possible. Slowing the line deprived the automated system of the increased profitability that comes from economies of scale. The output per worker declined, which provided still another reason to shift production to the lower-cost labor in Thailand.

Faced with all these signs that their factory was in its death throes, the Siroises nevertheless refused to cut back in their personal lives. "Let's not go down that road," Diane responded to a question about their savings. Dennis acknowledged that they had managed to put away over the years "less than six figures," including their 401(k) accounts. Although they commuted to work together and were companions in almost everything else they did, they maintained two SUVs: a 1994 GMC and a 2001 Tahoe, which they had purchased new for more than $30,000. They had no credit card debt, but they did owe money for the newer SUV and there was still a mortgage on their three-bedroom ranch house, which they had modernized and redecorated over the years. Their annual vacation is often two or three weeks on a cruise ship, the most recent to Hawaii in May 2002 to celebrate their twenty-third wedding anniversary.

Still, they had begun to trim some expenses in anticipation of contract negotiations in the spring of 2003. Stanley's three-year contract with Local Lodge 1433 of the Machinists, which represented the 442 factory workers still left in the New Britain area, came up for renewal three months after our breakfast. What worried the Siroises was the possibility that Trani would simply close their plant in the midst of the negotiations. That would be his response to demands from Local 1433 for wage increases or a job-security clause. In a plant closing, their seniority would be meaningless and their union helpless. "We feel," said Diane, "that John Trani—

not him but CEOs in general—if they decide to close the doors, they will do that."

In the end, the Siroises found themselves caught up in a strike that neither their union leaders nor Trani had anticipated. "The membership struck because we failed to bring back what we went in to get," said Everett Corey, the union's business representative. The union had sought a job preservation clause in the new contract, one in which the company promised to maintain the 442 remaining jobs at the tape measure factory and a smaller factory in nearby Farmington where electronically controlled entrance doors were manufactured. If there was no job preservation, then the union wanted a richer severance package for those laid off.

Trani rejected job preservation out of hand. He would keep the factories going for now, he said, but would make no promises. He also rejected the local's proposal that a laid-off worker get, as severance, one week's pay for each year worked, with no cap on the number of years. Yet the strike ended after ten days. "They were afraid that if they stayed out any longer they would lose their jobs," Corey said. So the membership accepted a contract in which severance remained capped at twenty-six weeks, although most of the workers had more than twenty-six years at Stanley. The only concessions were tokens: a minuscule $2 increase in the monthly pension for each year worked, and minor improvements in pay. As a final humiliation, Trani insisted, successfully, that the unionized workers take vacation time during the traditional Christmas shutdown. Those who had used up their vacation time would have to collect unemployment insurance during that period. "That was nasty," Diane said.

Trani also announced, in the midst of the strike, that he would retire at the end of the year. The workers proclaimed that their unanticipated walkout had jolted Trani into early retirement. They were wrong. He had given no ground at all on any significant issue. "That strike was a pimple," Trani says. In his announcement, he had said that he would continue to be the chairman and chief executive during the seven remaining months until year's end, and then would depart, with the blessing of the board of directors, which rewarded him handsomely—an $8 million bonus and an annual pension of $1.3 million. He had nearly completed the process of transforming the Stanley Works into a moneymaking machine, indifferent to its employees. It was time, he told me, to move on to some new application of the tactics that he had learned at General Electric and had applied at the Stanley Works.

That was the explanation he offered when we met in January 2004, a few days after he stepped down as CEO. He had installed himself in smaller quarters in an office building in downtown New Britain, where Stanley housed some engineering staff. He was dressed casually in a red crewneck sweater and dark slacks, and he guided me down several corridors to a sunny cafeteria overlooking a paved courtyard surrounded on two sides by shuttered factory buildings. Over a lunch of sandwiches and soft drinks, he recounted his tactics as chief executive, and justified them.

The just-completed fourth quarter, Trani informed me, would be the best in years, which it was. Revenues and net income were finally rising, and so was the stock price. He had left behind three top executives whom he had hired, all of them molded at General Electric in the years when Jack Welch ran the company. Welch's disciples had fanned out to top corporate jobs across the United States, and Trani, as one of these missionaries, saw no other salvation for the Stanley Works than the methods he had learned from his old boss.

What set Welch apart from so many chief executives of his generation was his skill and tenacity in devising ways to multiply demand for the products that GE sold while shrinking, disposing of, or relocating operations where demand could not be bolstered and costs had to be cut. Trani had applied the shrinking–relocating–cost-cutting to the Stanley Works and then had moved on to multiplying demand, a skill that he had acquired as chief of GE Medical Systems. There he had not only sold sophisticated diagnostic equipment, but had signed contracts to service what he sold. He leveraged his way from there. "We branched out from servicing our equipment to servicing all of the diagnostic imaging equipment in a hospital," Trani explained. "Then we moved to servicing all of the biomedical equipment, and finally to servicing all the equipment in a hospital. So you are migrating, but you are still servicing the same customer and you've got a big, big presence there. And then they can't get you out." It was that tactic, multiplying demand through open-ended service contracts, that Trani applied to the Stanley Works in his final two years as chairman. And at each step of the way there were layoffs.

"I call it favored markets," Trani said. Selling hand tools was not a favored market. The tools were sold to a wholesaler or a retailer and that was the end of it. Automatic entrance doors, like the sliding, swinging, folding, and revolving doors that Stanley made in the small Farmington factory, were a different matter. The initial selling was no different than the selling of spooled tape measures or carpenter's levels. What set the doors apart was the need to service the various electronic components that opened, closed, and locked these doors. They were security devices and, in Trani's mind, the heightened fear of terrorism after 9/11 multiplied the demand to keep security systems in good working order. By 2002, Trani had organized a new Security Solutions division within Stanley, and soon he set about expanding it. As his first acquisition, he purchased Best Access Systems in Indianapolis, a manufacturer of high-quality door locks and other security products. "They were the people who invented the cylindrical core coming out of a lock," Trani said, "so you replace the core without having to replace the lock." Best made not only the locks but the replacement cores, multiplying demand, in the Trani jargon. It was also involved in card key locks, the electronic locking devices on hotel and dormitory rooms. These require regular servicing.

That was one payoff from the Best acquisition. The other came from layoffs. "On day one of the Best acquisition, we took out 23 percent of the people," Trani said. That meant three hundred workers laid off, including some doing administrative tasks henceforth taken over by Stanley's headquarters staff in New Britain. The money gained from this shedding of workers helped to reimburse Stanley for the $310 million it had paid to acquire Best, and once that debt was paid, the money went to the bottom line.

Best was the first acquisition in the expansion of Stanley's Security Solutions division. Over the next seven months, until he left as CEO, Trani negotiated the acquisition of three more companies for the new division. In each case, a mass layoff like the one at Best was the first order of business. And the man chosen to be Trani's successor—John F. Lundgren, an outsider like Trani, who was hired away from the Georgia Pacific Corporation, where he had been president of the European consumer group—continued this strategy, particularly the foray into security solutions.

By 2004, the new division accounted for 23 percent of Stanley's sales revenue and 37 percent of its operating profit, up from 5 percent and 7 percent, respectively, just three years earlier. The tools group was still the biggest Stanley operation, but Security Solutions now grew much faster than tools or any other division. This was a sea change for the Stanley Works, Trani said, but a necessary sea change if the company was to survive and prosper—and that justified the layoffs. "In every stage of the process, you've got layoffs," Trani said. "That is just the way it is. And now it is like novocaine; we're numb. . . . If every day it is raining, pretty soon you don't think rain is a bad thing, it is just part of life. The human condition is to adapt, and people adapt."

Thus did John Trani bury Donald Davis's job security and Richard Ayers's gradualism.

CHAPTER TWO

The Rise of Steady Work

When I was young, job security was tangible, so tangible that it could be conferred on people, and it was. My turn came in September 1957. I had been hired four months earlier by the Associated Press as a probationary reporter and sent to the New Haven, Connecticut, bureau to fill in for regulars away on vacation. I was told that if I did well that summer, I would be made permanent. Employers actually used that word in those days. Permanent meant paid vacations, health insurance, overtime pay, a pension plan, annual wage increases. Getting fired required acts of flagrant incompetence or laziness—not just one such act, but several. The word "layoff" seldom popped up in daily conversation and never with today's meaning. Dictionaries defined it as a temporary interruption in steady employment.*

A union, the Newspaper Guild, negotiated my job security. In those days, 35 percent of the nation's workforce belonged to unions. But non-union employers also encouraged tenure. Before working at the AP, I had broken in as a reporter at a small family-owned newspaper, the *Daily Argus* in Mount Vernon, New York, and while it offered neither health insurance nor a pension plan, nor formal guarantees of any sort, the message to me, over and over, was *stay*. Most of the fifteen or so editors and reporters had been employed for twenty years or more at the *Argus* or at one of the sister newspapers owned by the same family in neighboring towns in Westchester County.

---

*As recently as 1989, the *Oxford English Dictionary*, second edition, defined layoff as "a spell of relaxation; a period during which a workman is temporarily dismissed or allowed to leave his work."

They were wonderful teachers for a young man recently out of college, and they possessed a knowledge of the community that enriched the daily coverage. The city hall reporter had covered the various mayors and city council members for nearly thirty years, and though his prose was less than animated, the people of Mount Vernon knew on a daily basis, and accurately, what their elected officials were up to. The police reporter, who grew up in Mount Vernon, had attended high school with several of the top brass in the police department and also with two or three of the better-known thieves who, in the days before legal state lotteries, ran illegal numbers operations that the police periodically raided, and between raids permitted. The education reporter had been covering the public schools for nearly a decade, and in detailed stories that appeared two or three times a week, she gave the community valuable, evenhanded, informed coverage.

I left after two and a half years to join the AP, which represented for me a step up into big-time journalism. My former *Argus* colleagues did not consider AP journalism better than their own. There were always three or four slots on the *Argus* for beginners, who either failed or moved on. That pattern of a few transients among a dozen skilled, experienced journalists well enough paid to be middle class endured until 1964, when the Gannett Company purchased the *Argus* and the seven other dailies in the chain and took them step by step into the age of cost-cutting, consolidation, and layoffs. The *Argus* itself is now gone, as is detailed daily coverage of local issues and events.

Without knowing it, I had entered the workforce in the final decades of a truly remarkable ninety-year period in American history. Over those decades, until the mid-1970s, job security in the United States rose to an extraordinary level, becoming standard practice. That was not true for poor people, many of them black, who were stuck in insecure, low-wage jobs, if they could get work at all. Many women did not have access to steady work either. But the great majority of the nation's employees held long-term jobs as we entered the 1970s. If they switched, as I did, or quit, it was their choice. And then, having ingrained job stability in our lives to such an extent that most Americans felt invulnerable to layoffs, we dismantled a system that had taken so long to construct and had contributed so much to the nation's prowess.

The layoffs started because a mainstay of job stability—robust economic growth—disappeared. The prosperity that had paid the bill diminished in the mid-1970s. Since then, the economy has grown, on average, at a noticeably slower pace than it did over the previous 120 years, even allowing for the Great Depression. During that long stretch of powerful expansion, employers gradually shifted from an attitude of indifference to their workers to commitment to them, and the workers returned the commitment, benefiting both sides. That was particularly the case in the aftermath of World War II, when the austerity and sacrifice of the war years gave way to a craving for the output of America's industries, not just among Americans but in Europe and Asia, too. There was not yet any competition. To satisfy this surge in demand, not only did companies hire more people, but each employee, new and old, produced more. A company with one hundred workers in 1953, for example, added ten more in 1954 and simultaneously the output of each worker rose from 1 item an hour in 1953 to 1.03 items the following year, and so on up the productivity ladder year after year. Innovation and new technologies made this possible, as well as investment in new equipment, but so did the attachment that workers had to their companies. The steady improvement in productivity required ingenuity and energy on the part of the workers, and commitment. Job stability fostered these qualities, and as productivity rose so did the loyalties that bound workers and employers to one another.

Peter F. Drucker, the management guru, recognized the importance of this loyalty in his classic work, *The Practice of Management,* published in 1954, one of the first books to set forth guidelines for executives, and among the most influential. To raise output year after year, Drucker declared, the enterprise "must demand something much bigger than a fair day's labor. It must demand, over and above fairness, willing dedication. It cannot aim at acquiescence. It must aim at building aggressive *esprit de corps.*" That only happens when workers feel secure in their jobs, Drucker said, conferring significant recognition on stable employment as an essential ingredient in the achievement of rising output per worker. Drucker cited IBM as compelling evidence. IBM had embraced stable employment early in the Depression, he noted, and the output of its workers had risen every year since then, even in years when "large wage increases could not prevent [output from] slipping in most other industries."

How far we had climbed in the space of a lifetime. "Job stability"—the long-term commitment of employers to workers and vice versa—barely existed as a concept in the late nineteenth century. Neither did "unemployment," for that matter, or "layoffs." Both occurred in abundance, of course. But they were thought to be the result of personal shortcomings, not flaws in the system. People lost their jobs because they were lazy, immoral, intellectually defective. Not until the 1890s did the recurring boom-to-bust-to-boom-to-bust business cycles bring public recognition that downturns in the economy, not personal shortcomings, had cost many workers their jobs. The evidence was unmistakable. Too many victims were obviously energetic, capable, hardworking people, eager to hold a job, but they were thrown into unemployment and poverty anyway. Faced with this evidence, prominent organizations like the New York Association for Improving the Condition of the Poor acknowledged, for the first time, that being out of work was in some cases "not due usually to moral or intellectual defects," but to "economic causes over which they [those who lost their jobs] could have no control." To capture this new awareness, the word "unemployment" came into use in the 1890s, although Alfred Marshall, the great British economist, called it "inconstancy of employment" in his classic work *Principles of Economics*, published in 1890. He still considered full employment the norm in a capitalist market system and anything less a temporary deviation.

But if unemployment gradually gained recognition as a shortcoming of a capitalist market system, the layoff went unrecognized as a separate, damaging phenomenon. In those days it was not yet all that damaging, at least not in the United States. The frontier was still moving west, promising opportunity. In addition, the waves of immigration from Europe, starting in 1870 and not letting up until 1920, injected into the labor force hundreds of thousands of men and women with very little attachment to particular jobs. "People moved around a lot and there was not a big social consequence," Sanford M. Jacoby, the economic historian, explained. "You got laid off and you moved on. And workers were wont to quit just as employers were quick to lay off."

As World War I approached, however, there was growing recognition that job tenure mattered; that is, keeping a job rather than going from one job to another with layoffs in between. A changing society helped to foster the shift. The economic historian Robert A. Margo pointed out that as the country became less agricultural and people switched from self-employment on farms to wage labor in cities, they became more vulnerable to downturns in the business cycle and pressed for more job security. The closing of the frontier also raised in importance the negative consequences of losing a job. Men who had once been called "pioneers" and "adventurers" when they were laid off or left a job, presumably to seek opportunity in the West, began to be called "vagrants" and "tramps," and a first attempt was made to count them—a forerunner of today's monthly employment reports. Going west no longer substituted for keeping a job. And in the East, the children of immigrants settled into communities and into steady work.

Their jobs were often blue-collar, but these first-generation Americans began to feel entitled; they claimed for themselves norms of treatment and security until then reserved for the relatively small cadre of white-collar workers. The layoff was no longer the casual occurrence it had been for their parents. Unions also made a contribution, asserting in effect that their members had a stake in their jobs and involuntary layoffs eroded that stake. Membership in unions rose in the first twenty years of the new century, reinforcing the demand for job security—protection, that is, not only from unemployment but also from layoff. With steady work, these blue-collar workers hoped to rise into white-collar life, and if they did not make it their children would.

Still, none of this would have brought the desired long-term employment if not for another development. Giant corporations had come on the scene, large enough to operate in the new national marketplace, which had been knitted together by railroads and the telegraph, both of which rapidly expanded after the Civil War. By the late 1880s, companies could communicate quickly with retailers and get merchandise to them in a matter of days. The world's first mass market had come into existence and the population inhabiting that marketplace, their incomes rising, sought to purchase the goods and services of the nation's industries. Demand surged and companies hustled to keep up. There were setbacks, of course, notably depressions in the 1890s and the 1930s. But there were also extraordinary bursts in demand, particularly after each world war—demand increasingly financed with credit, which intensified the demand.

For nearly a century, then, ending in the 1970s, American enterprises grew, added workers and found ways to increase each worker's output to take advantage of the economies of scale that mass marketing made possible. The giant corporations that resulted were an American invention. And as they took root, so did the realization that employee well-being mattered in developing managers and subordinates who could master the complexities of these new entities. "A crucial skill was understanding the organization's systems and procedures, a skill that could be developed only by means of long-term service to the corporation," Peter Cappelli, a business historian, wrote. The long-term service produced, in turn, loyalty and commitment and encouraged ambition. These were especially important motivators because in large, complex corporations it was difficult to monitor individual performance. With so many lightly supervised employees spread across a corporate network, self-motivation counted, and getting it was not that costly. "The possibility of moving up the ladder provided powerful motivation at relatively little cost," Cappelli said, "since few employees could ever make it to the top."

The railroads were the first giant corporations formed in the United States and the first to embrace job security as good management practice. The New York Central System and the Pennsylvania Railroad, the two main trunk lines, emerged in the 1880s from federations that smaller railroads had formed to keep a lid on ruinous competition. So did a dozen other major railroads, each capitalized at $15 million or more—three times the capitalization of the largest manufacturer of the day, Carnegie Steel. These railroads soon recognized the value of managerial skill and experience in coordinating the complicated flow of train traffic. Never mind that financiers and investment bankers controlled ownership of the railroads and used that control to siphon off huge wealth for themselves and to gouge midwestern farmers with extortionist freight rates. The financiers and bankers put the actual running of the railroads, getting trains from point A to point B quickly, efficiently, and safely, into the hands of professional managers, and the managers recognized the usefulness of job stability as an incentive for their subordinates, not to mention themselves.

Other giant corporations in other industries—Eastman Kodak; Sears, Roebuck; U.S. Steel; National Cash Register; International Harvester—required other skills, initiative, and experience, and in each case job stability helped to bring these out. A company was not just hiring a worker but "the whole man," Drucker explained in *The Practice of Management*. One must consider "the human resource as human beings having, unlike any other resource, personality, citizenship, control over whether they work, how much and how well, and thus requiring motivation, participation, satisfactions, incentives and rewards, leadership, status and function."

How quaint and toothless that classic formulation has become fifty years later. Drucker himself switched horses late in his long life. By the 1990s, "knowledge workers," by which he meant skilled and educated people who made their living manipulating information, had become his new interest. He even coined the label. Their numbers were multiplying in the final years of the twentieth century and they were much more mobile, much less tied to companies than their fathers and grandfathers, the factory and office workers who had thrived on job stability, Drucker decided. The products and services the fathers and grandfathers produced in America will shift increasingly to workers in developing countries, he now proclaimed, blandly acknowledging what was in fact happening. Here in America, he wrote, "the psychology of the workforce—especially the knowledge workforce—will largely be determined by the large minority who are not employees" of the organizations they serve.

The job stability that Drucker praised in the 1950s and dismissed in the 1990s appeared first in the late nineteenth century among managers and other white-collar employees and spread thereafter to the much larger blue-collar workforce. The extension was partly to inhibit the growth of unions and to discourage government intervention on behalf of these workers, but also to encourage the same productivity valued in the white-collar ranks. No industrial nation suppressed organized labor with more success than the United States, or with more brutality. But along with suppression, the savviest managers saw the value in good treatment of their blue-collar workers, in order to reduce the "prodigious" turnover rate, cut the cost of constantly having to train new people, and benefit from the rise in experience and skill that job stability made possible. Personnel departments made their appearance in this period, and by 1920 more than half the companies with 5,000 or more workers had them, as well as 25 percent of those with 250 or more employees. The personnel departments gradually established promotion ladders, administered seniority, restrained dismissals, and took control of hiring, replacing a system that had relied on powerful foremen to hire and fire, offering no job security to the workers they chose and just as easily shed.

What the foremen did was one element in the hodgepodge of practices that manufacturers in particular relied on to avoid or minimize what they considered the costly commitment that came with direct employment of factory workers. In addition to all-powerful foremen, the owners turned for labor to contractors who recruited workers and brought them into the factories as their own employees. But there were frictions. The contract workers, for example, resisted productivity improvements that required them to work harder. Wages differed among groups of contract workers and between contract workers and those hired by foremen. These differences produced still more friction. And the high turnover rate that resulted from the makeshift systems interfered with the efforts of employers to increase output to satisfy the constantly rising demand.

The solution, adopted slowly and reluctantly, lay in direct employment of all workers, a process administered by the new personnel departments and by a cadre of other professional middle managers. "The objectives of this search for order were higher productivity, lower costs, and reduced levels of conflict," Howell John Harris, a historian, wrote in *The Right to Manage*. "Its promise was that the outcome would satisfy workers as well as managers. Employees would become more efficient, more tractable, and more contented."

The new system grew and flourished, overcoming setbacks, until the 1970s, and along the way various adornments increased the payoff to employees for remaining with an employer. Profit sharing appeared in these early years, as a supplement to wage increases, not a substitute for them. The goal was to encourage employees to tie their well-being to that of the company, and to remain on the payroll to collect this extra compensation, which was often deferred until a worker was older. Company-funded pensions—fixed monthly payments in retirement—came into use too, first among the railroads and then among banks, public utilities, manufacturers, insurance companies, department stores, and mail-order houses. By 1916, more than 50 percent of all railroad employees had pension coverage—the main proviso being that to collect a pension, a worker had to remain with an employer until age sixty-five or seventy. In 1921, the

Metropolitan Life Insurance Company offered the first group annuities, in effect giving companies the means to offer pension coverage to more workers while reducing administrative costs.

These early plans, which proliferated between 1880 and 1930, were still a fraction of what they later became. Employers rarely felt compelled to provide pension benefits to workers who left before retirement or to the spouses of employees who died before retiring. And they retained the right to modify or cancel the plans at will. Still, they were an incentive for workers to stay put and develop skills valuable to their employers, and then depart in old age as their effectiveness declined. The new railroad pensions in particular encouraged people to develop the necessary skills over a career and to work in "close coordination" with all the other specialists in a railroad system to keep the trains moving, Steven A. Sass explained in *The Promise of Private Pensions*. And then in old age the pensions became an incentive to retire, with dignity. Timely retirement was important. Or as Sass put it: "The services provided by all these employees were essentially complementary, with the output of any one worker tied closely to the output of co-workers." One inefficient aging man "thus degraded an entire group's performance." Train wrecks could result, and did.

Procter & Gamble fielded one of the earliest profit-sharing plans and, in time, one of the most generous and idiosyncratic. Concerned that labor unrest elsewhere in the country would spread to his workers, William Cooper Procter, grandson of the founder, decided in 1887 to use profit sharing as a means of keeping his growing staff satisfied and loyal. The fifty-year-old company had started as a soap and candle maker in Cincinnati and was just beginning to market Ivory soap nationwide. With production multiplying, efficiency and docility seemed essential, and in pursuit of this goal Procter, in October 1887, distributed a bonus equal to 13 percent of each worker's annual wage, and repeated the bonus each year. But Procter worried that his workers viewed it as a short-term incentive, not as a reason to stay with the company, linking their careers to Procter & Gamble's success. So in 1903 he began to offer $4 in Procter stock each year for every dollar of stock purchased that year by a worker, with the proviso that the worker would not get control of the growing portfolio until he or she left the company, hopefully in retirement.

Forty years later, in 1944, Procter & Gamble sweetened this nest egg and pitched it as a richly endowed pension plan for those who stayed until retirement. The employees no longer had to contribute. Instead, the company gave its employees an annual profit-sharing bonus equal to a percentage of their salary. The bonus, at first a mixture of cash and company stock and later entirely company stock, started at 5 percent of annual salary for new employees and rose to 23 percent for twenty-year veterans. Employees had to stay at least that long to reach the maximum 23 percent, and then keep working and collecting the 23 percent each year until age fifty-five. Only then could they take control of these savings upon leaving the company without paying a penalty. The scheme worked, mainly because Procter's stock price rose through most of the twentieth century. By the 1960s, Procter employees had fallen into the pattern of electing to retire in their late fifties or early sixties, in many cases with nest eggs in excess of $500,000. By the late 1990s, it was $1 million or more.

World War I solidified the corporate foray into long-term employment, which came to be known as welfare capitalism. With civilian workers in short supply because of the war, employers found themselves increasingly offering pensions and profit sharing as a hiring lure and then to keep experienced workers from jumping ship. There was no mistaking anymore the thrust toward the attachment of employers to their workers and vice versa. "Before the war, management had made a commitment to labor and it was somewhat reciprocal," said Alfred D. Chandler Jr., the economic historian. "What really made it work was the war and the postwar boom in the 1920s, the first big boom in modern capitalism." Put another way, strong demand for the output of the nation's industries and stable profits made welfare capitalism affordable as well as useful.

These were the years that the average workweek fell to 49.9 hours (in 1923) from 55.5 (in 1914) and U.S. Steel abolished the seven-day week, partly in response to public pressure stirred up by muckraking journalists. General Electric's top executive, Owen D. Young, declared that managers were no longer representatives just of stockholders: they were trustees of an institution and labor was also a beneficiary of that institution. Patriotic fervor among workers during World War I had stimulated production. Managers saw the connection between incentive and output. And after the war, they used job stability as an incentive to raise productivity. Promotions served the same goal. They recognized good behavior and ability, and also enhanced an employer's control over his workers by raising the cost to workers of leaving a company; each promotion reduced the odds of finding another job with similar pay and status. Finally, bolstering a worker's spirits, encouraging workers through training to feel skilled and valued, became an antidote for the repetitive assembly-line techniques that Frederick W. Taylor had popularized—an antidote that hopefully would make workers less class-conscious and less interested in unions. By the 1920s, a low turnover rate had become "an index of the effectiveness of a company's labor program," the historian David Brody wrote. And union membership declined.

The giant corporations in the forefront of this movement employed only a small percentage of the nation's total workforce; the rest remained vulnerable to the whims of their bosses, who were more concerned about ridding themselves of costly workers when production slacked off. But the giants set standards that others gradually emulated. The march toward job security would continue into the 1970s, pushed along if not by employers then by unions and government. It would gather steam after World War II, so much so that William H. Whyte warned in *The Organization Man* that job security had gone too far.

His best-selling book, published in 1956, argued that middle-class workers were becoming captives of the organizations that employed them, losing their individuality and their entrepreneurial spirit. But what Whyte described as captivity others saw as entitlement to one's job at a decent wage, a combination essential to the maintenance of the very individuality and independent thinking that Whyte saw disappearing. It was the stripping away of this entitlement that made the waves of layoffs at the end of the twentieth century so destructive, not only to the victims but to the democratic process. "In political debate in the public arena," Michael J. Sandel, a political scientist at Harvard University, argues, "people have to have a certain economic security, otherwise they are likely to feel adrift, anxious and victims of circumstances beyond their control." As a largely rural nation of independent farmers who owned their own land and earned a sufficient living from it, people had that sense of control. But off the farm they lost it for a while in the urban industrial centers of the early twentieth century.

In *The New Deal at Work,* Peter Cappelli opens the second chapter with a description of labor practices in those years. Cappelli does not tell you right away that he is describing the early 1900s. He just goes on for a page or two relating conditions that seem very much like what is happening today. Employers routinely warn workers that their only source of job security is their own "employability"; that is, their willingness to acquire enough skills to land the next job when they are laid off from the one they have. Union membership weakens. Companies rely on temporary workers who are easily dispensed with in slack times. Entire departments are routinely outsourced to contractors. And so on.

The difference between then and now, however, is fundamental. In the early 1900s, no one knew any better. The upward march toward a sense of belonging to a job was still in its early stages. The presumption of invulnerability to layoffs that became the American version of lifetime employment would not come into full blossom for five more decades. What has been happening since the late 1970s, on the other hand, is a long and dismaying fall back toward the early days of the twentieth century, and the tragedy is that people know what they are losing and that the loss damages them. "People feel as if they are being thrown away; the layoff negates their sense of skill," says Richard H. Price, a professor of psychology at the University of Michigan, one of the few psychologists in the United States doing research into the psychological damage from layoffs.

Even the Depression, for all its horrendous unemployment, produced in the end more job security, not less—indeed, considerably more. Employers no longer set the pace, as they had in the 1920s, when welfare capitalism flourished. On the contrary, they shed employees by the tens of thousands, unable to afford them. Because workers had taken welfare capitalism to heart, they felt all the more abandoned by their employers when the Depression struck, Lizabeth Cohen, an economic historian, found. But instead of dying, the initiative for job security shifted to government and unions. For the first time in American history, employment at will—the employer's will—was legally curtailed. Laid-off workers, for example, won the right to petition for reinstatement in their jobs. The National Labor Relations Act of 1935, also known as the Wagner Act, guaranteed workers the all-important right to organize unions and bargain collectively, and it specified that employees facing dismissal must be given time to improve their performance and thus save their jobs.

The Norris–La Guardia Act gave workers the legal right to strike. The minimum wage and the forty-hour week came into existence, the latter forcing employers to curtail layoffs so they would have enough employees to staff their operations now that each employee worked a shorter week. The labor movement also flourished, mainly through the rise of militant unions representing unskilled workers. Union membership, as a result, grew from less than 3 million in 1933 to 10.5 million in 1941. By the start of the war one out of every three manufacturing workers was a union member. And President Franklin Roosevelt was on record as having declared, in 1935, that if he were a worker, he would belong to a union.

The war years added more job security. In exchange for a no-strike pledge and a ceiling on wage increases, the War Labor Board authorized the union shop: workers in unionized companies automatically became union members unless they chose to opt out in their first fifteen days of employment. Few did, and union membership took another spurt upward, reaching nearly 15 million in the war years, or 40 percent of the workforce in the private sector, the highest percentage ever reached in the United States. Company-funded pensions and health insurance spread, further tying workers to their jobs. Unions led in negotiating these benefits, but companies were active participants. In part, corporate managers wanted to fend off further incursions by unions and government, and in part they saw in job security a means of encouraging employees to push for greater productivity—a revival, in effect, of welfare capitalism. Sometimes unions "did nothing more than formalize existing procedures by writing them into their contracts," Sanford Jacoby wrote.

Managers, union leaders, and government officials all seemed to move in the same general direction in the late forties and fifties. Circumstances pushed them along. The Cold War competition with the Soviet Union was a prod; American workers in a market economy had to be better off than their Soviet counterparts in a government-run system, and they were, with an assist from government. Nearly 20 percent of the workforce in the fifties and sixties worked at companies with enough monopoly power to pay for rising labor costs by increasing prices, not eliminating jobs. Telephone companies, banks, trucking companies, auto manufacturers, electric utilities, airlines, railroads, and insurance companies all operated as monopolies, either by virtue of government regulation or, as in the case of the Big Three automakers and IBM, for lack of significant competitors.

Through regulation, the airlines, for example, could charge fares that covered costs plus a profit equal to, say, 10 percent of total revenue. Many economists insisted that regulation stifled incentive and innovation, and discouraged price-cutting. Their views helped to justify the dismantling of regulation in the last twenty-five years of the twentieth century. But even in regulated industries, incentive existed to drive down costs through innovation and efficiencies. The incentive worked this way in the airline industry: as costs fell at a particularly innovative airline, it lowered fares below what the government permitted. The lower fares attracted more travelers to the airline and, as a result, total passenger revenue rose. Dollar profits also rose, despite the regulated 10 percent profit ceiling. Ten percent of $100 million in total passenger revenue was greater than 10 percent of, say, $80 million in passenger revenue, before innovation made possible lower fares. Fares, in fact, did fall at a steady pace in the years before the start of airline deregulation in 1978.

There was another prod toward long-term employment. Memories of the Depression made job security a priority that companies as well as unions and government felt compelled to address. Eastman Kodak; Sears, Roebuck; DuPont; IBM; Hewlett-Packard; Procter & Gamble; TRW—all hugely successful corporations with few or no unions—presented themselves as loyal and benevolent to their employees. That was important, not only for people who had come of age during the Depression but for their children, born in the 1930s and 1940s and affected by their parents' experience. Better that companies took the lead in funding pensions and health insurance, generous raises and promotions, the reasoning went, than let unions or government decide these matters in response to pressure from workers and the public.

In this world, paid vacations ranging up to four weeks for long-term employees became a norm. Incomes rose at a faster pace from 1950 to 1970 than in any two decades since 1900. That happened without people having to work more hours, although the optimistic predictions of fewer hours and more vacation at the same pay never panned out. By the early seventies, company-sponsored defined-benefit pension plans, guaranteeing fixed monthly payments in retirement, covered nearly 40 percent of the workforce at medium-size and large companies, up from 25 percent in 1950. The companies themselves funded 90 percent of the cost, and the biggest pensions went to those who spent their careers at a single company.

Still, there were bitter struggles. While managers and union leaders agreed that job stability should be maintained, they fought endlessly over working conditions, safety, speed-ups, and seniority—particularly seniority. Both sides acknowledged its value in determining a worker's slot on the wage scale and in shielding long-term employees from temporary furloughs during periodic cutbacks in production as demand fluctuated. But how should seniority be defined?

Donald Davis, the chairman and chief executive of the Stanley Works, spent years in disputes over this issue. He had joined Stanley in 1948, right out of Harvard's Graduate School of Business, and for the next decade he was Stanley's director of industrial relations, in charge of negotiating the contracts that covered blue-collar workers. Nearly every factory had a separate contract, and not necessarily with the same union. In each case, when it came to job security, no clause was more important than the one defining seniority. Would it be plantwide, as the unions demanded, or departmental seniority, which Davis tried to impose, sometimes succeeding, sometimes not? With plantwide seniority, a furlough could be very expensive for the company. It meant that if work slackened among, say, assemblers of clip-on measuring tapes in New Britain and the assemblers happened to have the most seniority at the plant, they could not be furloughed. Workers with less seniority in, say, the maintenance department would be sent home first, and if maintenance was still a busy operation, then idle assemblers would be transferred temporarily to maintenance and trained hastily to do this work. The contracts allowed Stanley to break seniority if this interim training took more than three days. "But the fact remained that departing from seniority was hemmed in by all kinds of judgmental calls that were the basis for all kinds of grievances," Davis said. "And when you have a grievance and you can't settle it, it goes to arbitration. And if you lost the arbitration case you had to pay back pay. These were all major deterrents to furloughing people."

But some of the ingredients were already in place for the permanent layoffs that would later sweep the country. The Taft-Hartley Act, enacted in 1947, was one. With the Depression over, employers chafed at restrictions imposed on them by New Deal labor laws. Taft-Hartley amended or qualified some of this earlier legislation and in doing so pushed job security into quicksand. It placed a restriction on the right to strike in cases involving "national emergency," and it gave employers a tool to use against strikers. Elaborating on a Supreme Court ruling in the late 1930s, the new law authorized companies to hire replacements for regular employees out on strike—a provision that corporate executives did not invoke for more than thirty years. Firing strikers and then replacing them with nonunion workers ran counter to acceptable workplace behavior until 1981, when Ronald Reagan replaced thousands of striking air traffic controllers, and in doing so gave formal, very explicit notice that the federal government would not only tolerate but encourage a U-turn away from job security.

Taft-Hartley made labor agreements enforceable as binding contracts. For the first time, unions could be sued if locals walked out in wildcat actions before the expiration of a contract. Gradually these local uprisings were specifically outlawed in master agreements, curtailing a once powerful, often tumultuous grassroots means of squeezing concessions from management. Perhaps the most damaging aspect of Taft-Hartley was the opening it gave to state governments to enact what became known as right-to-work laws, which meant that workers in states that enacted such laws could no longer be compelled to join unions. Southern states in particular took this route. In many cases, they did so just as unions were making their first organizing efforts in the South. The organizing efforts failed, brought down in part by Taft-Hartley, which also became a means of legally decertifying existing unions. Thirty-five years later, when companies were scrambling to cut their labor costs in response to foreign competition, the low-wage, nonunion status of southern workers offered opportunity. Manufacturers in particular shifted operations en masse from the Northeast and Midwest to the less expensive South and Southwest, laying off hundreds of thousands of unionized northern workers as they migrated. And service companies followed suit. Companies had migrated before from North to South, but not at the stepped-up pace that would develop in the 1980s and 1990s.

"In a sense," wrote Thomas Geoghegan, a pro-union labor lawyer and labor historian, "Taft-Hartley gave employers a license to break the Wagner Act, but it took employers 20 years to realize, at last, how far they could go."

Even before Taft-Hartley, another cloud had formed over job security. The New Deal itself was the source of this cloud. The New Deal actually was two sets of policies. The first set, abandoned as a failure by 1938, gave labor and government bigger roles in running the economy than they had ever had before. This first New Deal tried to lift the country out of the Depression through various interventionist policies. The Tennessee Valley Authority's dams and power plants, built by government, were an intervention. For the first time government provided electric power in sufficient abundance to bring down prices charged by private power companies. That made the operation of household appliances practical; the cost of the electricity was now within a family's budget.

During the Depression, however, people did not have the wherewithal to purchase the electric refrigerators, electric stoves, and electric water heaters that the new power supply now made practical. So government intervened here, too. President Roosevelt created the Electric Home and Farm Authority, which made consumer credit available on easy terms. The EHFA pioneered installment purchases in America. As appliance sales rose, the Roosevelt administration pressured General Electric and other manufacturers of household appliances to lower prices. That stimulated more sales. Production rose and so did employment as people went back to work to make appliances and sell them. "As EHFA grew more national in scope, the City of Austin, Texas, put flyers into utility bills that depicted Uncle Sam declaring, 'I'll carry your appliance purchases,' " Jordan A. Schwarz wrote in *The New Dealers: Power Politics in the Age of Roosevelt*.

John Steinbeck caught the spirit of the interventionism, or at least the hopes it aroused, in his novel *Grapes of Wrath*. In the movie version, Robert Margo, the economic historian, notes, men and women wait in a long line for the opportunity to pick apples at 5 cents a bushel. The harshness of their plight in the private sector gives way in the next scene to the orderliness, safety, and relative comfort of a government-run camp in which cabins are furnished and meals provided. "In the Depression," Margo says, "the government is seen as a savior, pressuring the private sector to be more humane; that is the message of 'The Grapes of Wrath.' "

In this more planned economy, the Roosevelt administration tested schemes for setting prices and production levels in the private sector. Such interventionism outraged corporate executives, but a considerable faction among the president's advisers was eager to give government a role in management. The nation's executives, after all, were unable on their own to undo the Depression. So with government loosely supervising the process, companies in chosen industries were permitted by the National Recovery Administration (NRA) to set common prices and to agree on industry-wide production levels without concern for anti-trust prohibitions. In exchange, the companies would commit themselves to minimum wages and full-time hours, recognize labor unions, and negotiate labor contracts, thus preserving jobs and incomes. The hope was that through a harmony of government, business, and labor, production could be brought back into line with demand, without resort to severe price-cutting or layoffs.

The harmony foundered, however. Managers and labor leaders bickered constantly, and within the Roosevelt administration support eroded for the production and pricing agreements even before the Supreme Court invalidated the practice in 1935. The final blow to interventionism came in 1937 with the sudden plunge in stock prices and in economic growth, after nearly four years of a steadily improving economy. The nation seemed to be climbing out of the Depression, and suddenly it fell back into it.

With the reversal came an unwinding of the public's faith in the Roosevelt administration's efforts to sustain jobs by intervening in business management. Caught by surprise, casting about for ways to get the recovery back on track, Roosevelt turned away from interventionism and toward Keynesianism, finally embracing the view that public spending on the construction of roads, dams, and buildings, for example, could provide the necessary support for economic expansion. Until then, public spending had been relatively small scale and mostly for relief. But in 1937, Roosevelt, shifting course, authorized vast amounts for public projects as a substitute for the missing spending by consumers and by business. Some of this money went to the Work Projects Administration, which at its peak in the late 1930s had 3.5 million people on its payroll—artists, writers, and actors as well as ordinary workers. But most of the financing went through the private sector, which did the majority of the actual work under contract, and in doing so distributed the federal spending in wages, in the purchase of materials and equipment, and in investment. Soon the accelerated public spending melded with the huge outlays for World War II and the Depression finally ended.

So did the foray into statism, and with it a precedent for government intervention that could have stopped, or limited, the layoffs that started up forty years later. The business community, and workers and consumers, too, "expressed their desire for the government to establish policies, programs, and institutions that would guard against shortfalls in income. But they were not willing to endorse fully centralized systems of planning," Michael A. Bernstein, a Princeton University historian, wrote in *The Great Depression*. The Keynesian spending would sustain incomes by revving up the private sector so that it would hire again. There would also be government regulation to require companies to behave in the public's interest, but no intervention in management.

The unions signed on to this arrangement by allying themselves in effect to the Democratic Party. They gave up aspirations to become a political force in their own right, through the formation of a labor party that could insist on interventionist policies intended to preserve jobs and field candidates who supported these policies. Forty-five years later, when corporate managers were closing plants and shifting investment to lower-wage cities, organized labor played no role in the decision-making beyond the restrictions that might be written into particular collective bargaining agreements, although the decisions were devastating for labor. The opportunity that the first New Deal offered to give labor a voice in corporate management and make this standard practice had been lost, and the attempt to recoup years later through support for employee stock ownership plans was marginal at best.

The policy switch came to be known as the second New Deal. The federal government certainly intervened during World War II, in the construction, for example, of factories for war production at little cost to the companies that took them over, and in wage and price controls. But essentially spending was counted on to provide prosperity and full employment. If private spending was insufficient to do this, then the government would step in with public spending to cover the shortfall. In the high-spending economy that would result, the steady demand for workers would minimize unemployment. The full employment, in turn, would generate enough income for consumption to rise and maintain the full employment—a virtuous circle.

That became not only Roosevelt's view but also Republican policy. In the 1944 presidential campaign, Thomas E. Dewey, the GOP candidate, referring to Keynesian policies, declared: "If at any time there are not sufficient jobs in private employment to go around, then government can and must create additional job opportunities because there must be jobs for all in this country of ours."

But Congress refused to bring the second New Deal to its logical conclusion. It watered down a bill that would have required the government to estimate the number of jobs needed for full employment in a given year, and if private sector spending and investment did not create the specified number of jobs, then the government would be required to step in with loans and public project spending, or outright job creation in the public sector, to fill the gap and achieve the desired full employment. After much debate, Congress enacted the Employment Act of 1946, which embodied the concept, but left out the teeth to make the government spending and job creation automatic. The new law gave the federal government broad responsibility to encourage economic expansion through corporate growth. That would be the aim of numerous government activities, and the resulting growth would generate full employment. But if that did not happen, nothing in the Employment Act of 1946 required government to be the employer of last resort, in effect granting every adult able to work and seeking work a legal right to a job. Instead of full employment, the concept was watered down to "maximum employment."

Who really cared then? Private spending along with military spending were more than enough to sustain robust employment and rising wages during the first three decades after World War II. Consumer demand surged. The devastated world needed America's output and the

Marshall Plan gave Western Europe in particular the wherewithal to rebuild, using machinery and merchandise purchased in the United States with American loans. Without foreign competition, profits surged. So did business investment and government spending on infrastructure, notably interstate highways and airports, not to supplement private-sector job creation, but simply because the country needed the infrastructure and the population wanted it. Recruiting enough workers became a concern, not layoffs. And the outpouring of government research, in response to the Soviet Union's launching of Sputnik in 1957, resulted in spin-off technologies and products that gave consumer spending yet another lift, along with job stability.

Histories of this period, as well as surveys and case studies, bear out how entrenched job security had become. There were layoffs in the modern sense from time to time, but they were dealt with as exceptions, not the norm, shocks to be avoided or ameliorated as quickly as possible. In their classic work, *The Dynamics of a Labor Market*, Charles A. Myers and George P. Shultz, both MIT economists, studied a New England town, Nashua, New Hampshire, after its biggest employer, a textile company, announced unexpectedly in 1948 that two of its mills would be closed and 3,500 employees permanently laid off. In response, the Textile Workers Union of America demanded and got a Senate subcommittee investigation, after which the company scaled back its original decision, agreeing to keep open one of the mills, thus preserving 1,500 of the 3,500 jobs. In addition, the mayor and state officials pushed to attract new employers, with partial success: eight companies, mainly manufacturers, set up in the town in this period. Finally, the upturn in the economy in late 1949, after a year of recession, generated enough manufacturing work in Nashua to absorb most of those who were laid off and still wanted work. Some people suffered hardship and some were forced into lower-paying, less-skilled jobs, Myers and Shultz found. But the mass layoff, for all its initial shock, did not cow workers. Quite the contrary, Myers and Shultz warned, "the management that relies on the threat of unemployment as a primary means of motivating its workforce may find itself handicapped when economic conditions improve. . . . The employer may find himself with what he calls an 'uncooperative' workforce."

Optimism and confidence flourished among workers, and corporate

America catered to it. A group of social scientists caught the mood in a study titled *Labor Mobility in Six Cities,* published in 1954. "A substantial portion of those making [job] changes obtained higher earnings or 'better jobs' as a result," they found. That happened whether the worker quit or was laid off. Quitting was the norm; layoffs were an infrequent occurrence, and yet they had the same happy ending. "The kind of job shifts made after layoffs did not differ substantially from the kinds of changes made voluntarily," the study found.

J.-J. Servan-Schreiber, a French journalist, caught the hubris of the times in *The American Challenge,* which became a best-seller in the United States as well as in Europe in 1968. Servan-Schreiber warned that the American industrial juggernaut—in which "the government official, the industrial manager, the economics professor, the engineer and the scientist have joined forces" in the interest of technological innovation and economic growth—would soon reduce Europe to a colony of the American economy, if Europe did not wake up and react. The launching of Sputnik a decade earlier had set off a great, coordinated American response. But even before that, the Bretton Woods agreement in 1944 had facilitated American corporate investment in Europe by forcing European central banks to purchase large quantities of dollars, thus giving American companies a pool of francs, marks, and other currencies to invest in Europe. And this they did, purchasing factories and machinery as well as distribution centers and offices to produce and market merchandise to European consumers. The expansion abroad took place without cutting back investment and expansion at home—the exact opposite of the shifting of production overseas that would become the situation less than two decades later, draining away jobs at home.

I had gone abroad as a foreign correspondent in 1964 and was AP's bureau chief in Buenos Aires, Argentina, when *The American Challenge* appeared. Servan-Schreiber was right: there was an American juggernaut, in Europe undoubtedly, but also in Argentina. These were the juggernaut's final years, but that was not evident then. Trying to barricade itself against American intrusion, Argentina, like other Latin American nations, erected high tariff walls to protect native-owned industries. Tariffs, however, did not stop the juggernaut. Numerous American companies set up shop behind those walls, and then proceeded to draw on production back home to run their operations in Argentina. General Motors, Ford, and Chrysler were experts at this practice. All three operated big assembly plants in Córdoba, the Argentine Detroit, or in Buenos Aires. But new cars assembled in those factories were essentially the same models as those that had been assembled in the United States several years earlier.

The machinery and tooling were first used in Detroit and then shipped south, tariff-free. How else could the Argentine plant function without this "investment"? Rather than manufacture sophisticated engine components in Argentina, it imported them from the United States, also tariff-free. The finished steel came from America, and when an Argentine consortium tried to get financing abroad to build a local steel mill, it met with considerable opposition from the U.S. Steel Corporation, whose representative made his case with journalists like me. The Argentines could not match U.S. Steel's technological prowess, the representative argued, or the cost savings that came from the economies of scale embedded in America's mass production economy. And the steel mill project failed.

No wonder, then, that America's overwhelming productive might and the demand for its output generated so many secure jobs. In only eight of the years from 1945 through 1970 did the average annual unemployment rate rise above 5 percent. Sure of their jobs in so tight a labor market, unionized workers often staged spectacular, frequently successful strikes. They wanted a bigger share of the growing pie in wages, benefits, cost-of-living payments, and working conditions while their employers wanted as little disruption as possible during a period of unprecedented expansion and profitability, at home and abroad. Some regions of the country got less of this prosperity than others. The rural South and Appalachia were notable examples of startling poverty. So were urban ghettos. But while poverty and pockets of unemployment were much debated, layoffs were not a public issue. Job security was affordable as long as economic growth surged and American companies dominated not only their home market but those abroad as well. When that domination began to come apart in the 1970s so did job security.

Several things undid the hegemony. Fixed exchange rates collapsed in 1971, bringing down the Bretton Woods currency arrangement that favored American exports and American investment abroad, particularly in Western Europe. The OPEC oil embargo in 1973 deprived the country of cheap energy, and the sharp increase in oil prices persisted, draining money away from profits and wages. Rising budget deficits inhibited public spending. But above all, the United States lost its hold on the marketplace, not just at home but gradually across the industrial world.

The Japanese were the immediate cause. Having finally secured their domestic markets, they went after ours. They did so with an array of sophisticated products often developed from American technology that the Japanese had licensed, first to mimic American merchandise but in time to export to the United States the mimicked merchandise, much enhanced. Fast ocean transport in giant cargo ships gave Japanese companies, and also Western European manufacturers, the means to supply U.S. consumers en masse, and thus employ the economies of scale that had given American corporations such an edge in pricing and profitability for so long.

While America's best engineers and scientists had put much of their energy into the nation's military industries, their counterparts in Europe and Japan, without this distraction, concentrated on becoming masters of production for civilian purposes. The Japanese in particular adopted quality controls developed in America in the 1930s and widely ignored in the mushrooming affluence of the postwar years. By the 1970s, they had achieved levels of efficiency and quality that surpassed those of the United States. Faced with this unforeseen superiority, forced to share the marketplace with foreign competitors, the sustained, robust expansion that had lasted for nearly thirty years after World War II came to an end in the mid-1970s, and with it the momentum that supported job stability.

At the Stanley Works, Donald Davis, the chairman, taken by surprise, made a Don Quixote–like attempt to shame wholesalers and retailers out of stocking what he and his executives trumpeted as Asian knockoffs of Stanley's tools. He ordered his people to purchase piles of the Asian tools from retailers in Los Angeles and San Francisco, the main ports of entry. "We took them into a parking lot in Los Angeles," Davis recalled. "We invited the press. We invited our wholesale customers. We got a steamroller and we crushed them. We did the same thing in San Francisco, but in that case we used cargo nets with helicopters and we dumped them in the bay, with the press there."

The drumbeat against knockoffs had some momentary effect, but soon it was clear that the Asian hand tools could not be dismissed as mere knockoffs. Swinging in the wind, Davis tried another tactic. He told retailers that Stanley would cut prices by 35 percent, to get within 15 percent of the Asian prices. All a retailer had to do in exchange was to give up the no-charge extras that the Stanley Works traditionally furnished: fast order filling, for example, "missionary salesmen" who set up store displays, first crack at new products for the best customers. That tactic helped, but not enough. Nothing stopped the onslaught of imports, and the severe recession in 1981 and 1982 made matters worse, turning a bad dream into a prolonged nightmare. So Davis cut costs. So did everyone else, and before long that meant layoffs. The juggernaut that Servan-Shreiber had described with such alarm in *The American Challenge* in 1968 evaporated, and a new juggernaut, one that thrived on layoffs, took its place.

CHAPTER THREE

Retraining the Mechanics—But for What?

The speaker, Jo Goodrum, a thin, energetic woman older than her audience of aircraft mechanics—old enough in appearance to be their mother—got their attention with a single, unexpected sentence, which she inserted early in her presentation. Her husband, she said, had been laid off six times since the late 1980s. And yet here she was, standing before them, in one piece, cheerful, apparently okay, giving survival instructions to the mechanics, who would be laid off themselves in ten days.

They were in nearly every case family men in their thirties and forties who had worked for United Airlines since the mid-1990s. Summoned by their union, they had gathered in the carpeted conference room at the Days Inn next to the Indianapolis airport, not far from the giant maintenance center that United operated on the far side of the runways, a building so big and spread out that twelve airliners could be housed in it and overhauled simultaneously. That no longer happened. Most of the repair bays were routinely empty now. The airline was cutting back operations and the sixty mechanics at the meeting were in the fourth group to be let go.

They were moving on submissively. An attempt at confrontation had brought on the layoffs. Influenced by a militant faction of their union local, Hoosier Air Transport Lodge 2294, International Association of Machinists, the two thousand mechanics at the maintenance center had engaged in a work slowdown and then a refusal to work overtime—a resistance that had lasted many months. But rather than give ground, United had responded by outsourcing. It brought fewer of its airliners to Indianapolis for the periodic overhauls, known as heavy maintenance, that are required by the Federal Aviation Administration. Instead, the planes went to nonunion contractors elsewhere in the country, and as the work disappeared from Indianapolis there were layoffs. That finally scared the mechanics. Rather than respond with more militancy, they quieted down and, in effect, authorized the leaders of Lodge 2294 to make peace. Their hope was that if they cooperated, United would ease up on the layoffs and eventually revive operations, or at least maintain them on a reduced scale. After all, no airline in the United States had a more efficient high-tech maintenance center for overhauling Boeing 737s, Airbus 319s and 320s, and similar midsized, narrow-bodied airliners.

In this state of mind, the union leadership was helping to usher the sixty laid-off mechanics quietly away. It had rented the hotel's conference room on this cold January evening in 2003 to introduce the men to what amounted to a boot camp for recycling laid-off workers back into new, usually lower-paying lines of work. Similar federally subsidized boot camps, organized by state and local governments, often in league with unions, have proliferated in the United States since the 1980s, and now many cities have them. Unable to stop layoffs, government has taken on the task of refitting the victims for "alternate careers," the goal being to get them back to work before their severance pay and unemployment benefits run out. In deciding as a nation to send laid-off workers through boot camps that would somehow rejuvenate them as workers, we put in place a system, however unrealistic, that implicitly acknowledged layoffs as a legitimate practice. In a few days there would be workshops for the mechanics in résumé writing and interviewing skills, personality evaluations, job counseling, and, for a lucky few, tuition grants to go back to school for a semester or two. The mechanics were being "counseled out" of their well-paying trade, as some of them wryly put it, and Jo Goodrum was the lead-off speaker in this endeavor.

She presented herself as one of them. Her husband's wage had slid from $25 an hour in his heyday as a factory worker in the 1980s to $10 an hour in his latest job, as a clerk in a watch-repair store. To supplement that falling income, she had taken part-time work as an "education presenter" for the Consumer Credit Counseling Service of Central Indiana. In this capacity, it was her task to explain how easy it would be for the departing mechanics—separated from salaries of $55,000 a year and up—

to sink deeply into debt if they failed to adopt her belt-tightening measures. The glimpse that she offered of her husband's downfall suggested that she had learned these lessons in her own hard life.

Distinguish, she said, between needs and wants. Rent, food, insurance premiums—those are needs. Cable television is a want; cancel it. Day care can be a want or a need. It's a need for parents with jobs, but a want for the soon-to-be-laid-off mechanics who would now have more time to watch their children themselves; canceling day care at least part of the week meant saving money. New sneakers for teenagers are another mix of need and want. And here she dipped back into her own life. Soon after her husband's first layoff, their teenage son needed new sneakers for basketball; his had worn out. He got them—that was a need. But he did not get the expensive, high-end variety that he wanted. The Goodrums could not afford the extra cost, and they resisted this want, as the mechanics now had to.

Some of the doomed mechanics had come to the meeting after finishing a shift at the maintenance center; others had made a special trip from their homes. They did not talk to one another, which seemed strange for men who had worked together for so long. Many sat alone, separated by several seats from the next nearest mechanic in the spacious hotel conference room, filled for this occasion with folding metal chairs arranged in rows before a long, bare wooden table, a sort of dais at the front of the room. Four had come with their wives, who sat close to their husbands, arms and shoulders touching, listening as intently as the men, sharing the apprehension of the loss and uncertainty descending upon them.

In the blue-collar world, aircraft mechanics are at the top. They are the highly skilled people who repair and overhaul the airliners in which we fly. Each mechanic in the room had completed two years of college-like schooling to qualify for this work. Several compared their role proudly to that of a pilot. Like the pilots, the mechanics log their work, signing for each repair they make and every part they replace, and they claim as much credit as the pilots for the safety of air travel. "Our name follows the part we put in until it is changed," a mechanic told me, "so if it ever goes wrong or fails, you are going to get a knock on your door. If you are neglectful, you can be prosecuted for a felony."

Now the mechanics were falling out of this high-level world, in most cases for good. They were unlikely to match or come close in their next jobs to the $26 an hour or more in pay that would cease on Friday of the following week, their last day. They would be newcomers again in the workforce. They must learn how to get their foot in the door, the speakers that evening unceremoniously told them. Their careers were gone and the grief at this loss must be absorbed in order to move on. Recognizing their vulnerability, Goodrum spoke to the mechanics in the simplified, encouraging language that a skilled teacher uses to instruct children just learning to read, or a speech therapist adopts to guide stroke victims struggling to speak again.

Did the mechanics realize, she said, that credit card companies and mortgage lenders give special consideration to laid-off workers? And she held up a form letter, a "sample letter to a creditor," in which the writer announces his layoff, states confidently that he expects to be working again in three months, and proposes to reduce his installment payments for those three months, the exact amounts of the reductions to be filled in by the mechanics. "It is very important that you negotiate now," Goodrum admonished, "and not when you are sixty days behind on a debt."

As she spoke, she displayed pages from a packet of instructions that she had passed out to the mechanics—each page a different color, each laying out in step-by-step detail a different survival strategy, which she hastily summarized, hurrying to stay within her allotted twelve minutes. She segued from debt relief into a brief discussion of debt collection practices, holding up a green sheet on which were listed the debtor's rights in dealing with collectors. The latter are prohibited by law from threatening debtors, addressing them in obscene language, publicizing the debt, harassing the debtor with repetitive phone calls. The list covered both sides of the page. From her folder also came tips on "saving your home from foreclosure" (beige paper), avoiding "vehicle repossession" (blue), and the hidden traps in "payday loans" (yellow). Avoid these loans, she warned. They hide drastically high interest rates. Also avoid secured loans, particularly home equity loans; you can lose your home for nonpayment. "If you have to borrow, do it against a credit card," she instructed.

When she had finished, Ben Nunnally, the overweight, bearded forty-four-year-old president of Lodge 2294, rose and without coming from behind the head table inserted into the proceedings some impromptu advice, exercising his authority one last time as their union leader. While he had the mechanics in one room, Nunnally said, he wanted to caution them about the unemployment checks they would soon be getting from the government. If they were not careful, they could waste two weeks in getting that first check. In detail, as if he were a company spokesman rather than a union leader outraged by the layoffs, he explained how United Airlines would phase them off the payroll.

Their last day would be January 25, and they would be eligible to begin collecting unemployment five days later, if they applied for it promptly on the twenty-fifth. They should not wait until their last paycheck reached them from United two weeks after that final day of work. Even if the unemployment checks arrived on time, they would be little enough: $336 a week for twenty-six weeks, way below the nearly $1,100 a week or more that the mechanics had been earning at United, in jobs they had counted on to last. Nunnally made no mention of either amount. They were moving on; that was the purpose of this session, to move them on, not dwell on the loss. "We have no choice but to offer as little conflict as possible with United and hope that will avoid more layoffs," Nunnally told me.

It was a wasted hope. Three months later, in April 2003, United Airlines abruptly laid off the 1,100 remaining mechanics, including Nunnally, who had been working a regular shift in addition to his nonsalaried union duties, and on May 4, the airline announced that it was walking away from the giant maintenance center. Outsourcing had won, hands down, and although Nunnally stayed on as the president of Lodge 2294, now a shadow of its former self, he too applied for unemployment pay. To get by, he became a partner in a window-washing business that had been organized by another former mechanic. Most of their customers were suburban homeowners whom they recruited by distributing flyers in prosperous neighborhoods and by making cold calls. On a good day, when it was not raining or too cold, Nunnally and his partner could each do three houses, at $150 a house. He worked with a younger assistant because he was too overweight to climb ladders easily himself. "I do a lot of the inside work," he said, "and I do climb some, but then my knees start to hurt." When he could string together five good days a week, and he was doing that often in the spring of 2004, he pocketed about $650, or two-thirds of his weekly take-home pay as a mechanic. The window-washing income did not include health insurance, which he and his wife and their twenty-year-old son no longer had, although his wife, who had gone back to work for the first time since their son was born, hoped to get it if the temporary job she held turned into a permanent one. "I have moments when I really get concerned," Nunnally said.

He clung to the union presidency because he liked the prestige it still conferred and the access it gave him to the city's politicians, although that access was fading. Before United closed the maintenance center, he had consulted often with Mayor Bart Peterson of Indianapolis during the mayor's attempts to persuade the airline to stay and to stop the lay-offs. When that failed, Nunnally played a role for a while in the mayor's efforts to find a new tenant for the maintenance center, which the city partly owned, having subsidized, along with the state, more than half of the $600 million it cost to build. But after a while, the mayor and his aides stopped calling. None of the potential tenants—Boeing, for example, or one of the contractors that the airlines now used to do heavy maintenance—wanted to employ union mechanics. The mechanics them-selves no longer stopped by Lodge 2294's small suite of offices upstairs in a two-story building on the airport grounds to socialize and to commiser-ate with one another. Nunnally still came, of course, spending an hour or two in the late afternoons after washing windows.

In April 2004, a year after the maintenance center closed, he explained to me what he would do if the window washing failed to grow into a larger, more lucrative enterprise, one that he and his partner could preside over while others "washed the windows or cleaned the carpets or whatever else we decide to do." The Nunnallys would sell their four-bedroom home on nearly seven acres of land and return to Birmingham, Alabama, where they were born and raised. There he would take a job as an aircraft mechanic with Pemco Aeroplex, one of the companies the air-lines now used to outsource heavy maintenance. Pemco was constantly advertising for sheet metal mechanics to work on an aircraft's outer skin. That was Nunnally's specialty. At Pemco, he would earn $16.50 an hour, half his pay at United, but "not bad money in Alabama," he reasoned. "I would be crawling over airplanes again, probably on the midnight shift. But there would be health insurance, and they are represented by the United Auto Workers, which I wouldn't have any heartburn with. I could even get involved again down there."

I had met Nunnally for the first time on the morning of the Days Inn meeting. Window washing was not remotely on his mind. Neither did he imagine that the closing of the maintenance center was just three months away. He thought then that his considerable seniority would protect him from layoff indefinitely. He had been president of the Machinists local for a year and he saw in a writer's visit an opportunity for yet another appeal to the airline to reverse the layoffs and restore the maintenance center to its former glory.

Nunnally had experienced the glory days. He had joined United in 1989 as a thirty-year-old mechanic in San Francisco and had transferred to Indianapolis in 1994, drawn by the much lower cost of living. The maintenance center itself was an attraction. It had just opened and it was, in the eyes of aircraft experts, the most efficient in the world for overhauling narrow-bodied airliners. Nunnally explained to me how the mechanics had exploited that efficiency to United's advantage. With morale high in the 1990s and the mechanics willing to work hard, they had put airliners through their periodic overhauls in record time. They worked mostly on 737s, but as United gradually expanded the center—opening more repair bays, hiring more mechanics, and extending the legs of the L-shaped building until each leg was nearly half a mile long—they also overhauled Airbus 319s and 320s and the larger Boeing 757s and 767s. The stem-to-stern refurbishing of a 737 normally required twenty-two days. That had been the best time at other maintenance centers. The mechanics at Indianapolis cut that to eleven days for a 737 going through its first heavy maintenance and to less than twenty days for older planes. "We had overhaul bays that kind of competed in a friendly way to see who could do the best," said Frederick L. Mohr, general manager of the Indianapolis center from 1997 until 2002.

For United, the rapid turnaround meant an infusion of passenger revenue from the additional days the plane was in service. The extra revenue, in turn, justified the mechanics' pay of $26 an hour in the late 1990s.

Still, some executives at United's headquarters in Chicago were leery about sending too much work to Indianapolis, of becoming too dependent on this union shop. They had pushed for the use of outside contractors to overhaul the A319s and A320s that United had leased in the early 1990s as it expanded its fleet of narrow-bodied jets in those salad days for the airline industry. The Airbuses were coming up for their first heavy maintenance, as the stem-to-stern overhauls every five years were called. But Andrew P. Studdert, the airline's chief of maintenance and later its chief operating officer, insisted on bringing the Airbuses to Indianapolis. He saw in the expansion of operations there a further boost in the morale of the mechanics and thus in their efficiency. "The mechanics loved the expansion," he said. "If you are working the midnight shift and the base is expanding with new guys, your seniority gets you off the midnight shift and gives you other choices."

Capitalizing on the growing productivity, United itself got into outsourcing as a means of keeping the giant center busy during slack periods in United's own operations. America West was sending 737s and 757s to Indianapolis for heavy maintenance, and by the spring of 1999 the workforce had grown to 2,400 mechanics, from fewer than 250 when Nunnally arrived in 1994. The rapid turnaround time and the reliable work justified the relatively high fees that United charged, and America West shifted maintenance to Indianapolis from a private, less expensive contractor in Portland, Oregon, whose mechanics earned less. It was outsourcing in reverse. "We had people visiting us from Europe to see what we were doing," Mohr said. "We were negotiating with Lufthansa for a while, but that deal never came about."

What these visitors saw as they approached the maintenance center along an asphalt highway that circled the airport's outer rim was a strikingly futuristic light gray structure, trimmed jauntily in blue, that had risen in the rolling, grassy fields on the far side of the runways. The soaring entrance hall, designed to suggest a giant airliner cabin without seats, struck me at first as extravagant and surrealistic, but in fact it reflected the efficiencies that were built into nearly every aspect of the building. The mechanics came and went through this hall; there was no other way in and out for them. And here in one place, before or after a shift or during a meal break, they took care of nonproductive chores. Doors along the walls of the entrance hall, where cabin windows would have been, opened into rooms and offices that housed a credit union, a cafeteria, a nurse's station, a personnel office, a small store. David Doucey, the maintenance center's operations manager, pointed this out as he walked me through the center just two weeks before the closing, explaining its features, several of which he had helped to develop. The majority of Doucey's working years since graduation from Southern Illinois University in 1983 had been dedicated to the center. Having failed to become a pilot because of an eye problem, he had joined United as a mechanic in San Francisco in 1987 and two years later he was chosen as one of thirteen team leaders for the Indianapolis project, then in the design stage. He had helped to build and then run the place and had honed many of its efficiencies. Soon he would be put in charge of mothballing the hangar bays, which we looked down on from a height of nearly three stories, moving along an indoor boardwalk from one giant pit to the next.

On the eve of the closing, only Hangar 1A was active. A 737 was parked there, nose toward us on the boardwalk, its interior already gutted. It was the last airliner that United would recondition in Indianapolis, and Doucey told me, matter-of-factly, that although the mechanics had already received their layoff notices, they would finish the job seven or eight days faster than any other maintenance center could do the work. Parts from the dismantled interior were spread out before us on an unpainted wooden floor, a mezzanine that fit snugly around the plane just below the wings and stretched out two hundred feet on either side. The servicing of many components removed from the cabin and cockpit took place right there on the mezzanine, eliminating the time and manpower required to send them to workshops elsewhere and then bring them back—the practice at other maintenance centers. This efficiency is wasted, however, without a constant flow of planes cycling quickly through the maintenance center and back into service. When that does not happen, the payoff is not enough to justify the huge investment required to construct and operate so sophisticated a maintenance operation.

The time-saving features at the United center in Indianapolis are numerous and Doucey pointed them out. Sixty minutes after an airliner enters the hangar, hydraulic devices have pulled the wooden mezzanine into place and also a metal scaffold that gives the mechanics quick and easy access to the outer skin and tail. In other shops, bulkier scaffolding takes four hours to erect—half a shift, as Doucey put it—and there are no mezzanines. Parts delivery is also fast. Less than thirty minutes after a mechanic punches in a parts order on one of the computers in each bay, black plastic tote bins, large enough for a five-year-old to bathe in, bring the parts along thirteen miles of miniature railroad, from an automated central depot to stations in each hangar bay. From start to finish, the delivery is six times faster than in other maintenance centers, Doucey said, and no human hand touches a part until a mechanic lifts it from the black tote bin. At other maintenance centers, parts are loaded by hand onto motorized carts or they arrive in oversized baskets mounted on bicycles.

The lighting in the Indianapolis maintenance center is several times brighter than in other shops, a trick borrowed from gambling casinos, Doucey said. People seem to work harder at night if it seems like day. An elaborate heating and air-conditioning system keeps temperature and humidity at constant levels throughout the huge building, a form of climate control that permits the mechanics to work with fiberglass or graphite composites in patching the outer skin of a wing aileron or a tail elevator, for example. Lacking this climate control, as virtually every other maintenance center does, these sections have to be removed from a plane and taken to special shops, stretching out a task that takes two to three hours in Indianapolis to two to three shifts elsewhere.

Large black hoses in each bay force heated air into the fuel tanks, dispersing kerosene vapors so mechanics can enter the giant tanks much sooner than in other maintenance facilities, where hangar doors are kept open to disperse the vapors. Once the tanks are ready for use again, a fueling system fills them so accurately that cockpit gauges can be calibrated. "I do not know of any other place in the country where you can safely fuel a plane in a hangar bay," Doucey said. Everywhere else the potential for fire is too great.

What drove away America West and stopped Lufthansa from negotiating an agreement with United to overhaul its aircraft in Indianapolis was the labor trouble that erupted over the July 4 weekend in 1999 and then mushroomed into a prolonged slowdown. In retrospect, that weekend was the turning point, the moment when the remarkable efficiencies that had been achieved at Indianapolis began to unwind, and labor-management tensions that had been accumulating suddenly asserted themselves. In an earlier era, the two sides would have tried to settle their differences through negotiation and would probably have succeeded. There was really no other alternative. The outsourcing of maintenance did not exist before the 1980s; airlines did their own maintenance. But now layoffs and outsourcing had become too easy and too acceptable an option.

The incident that started United down that road seemed so minor. During the trusting years, when the work was getting done in fine form, the foremen had relaxed the restrictions on the number of mechanics who could take vacation days at the same time. For the July 4 weekend in 1999, more than a hundred mechanics had been granted time off—ten times the prescribed number. Fred Mohr, the general manager, was himself on vacation in the days leading up to the weekend, and he called the office to remind his lieutenants to be careful about allowing too many mechanics to be away. Somehow that became a wholesale, last-minute cancellation of vacation time, outraging the mechanics. "To this day, they get upset when they talk about what happened that weekend," Doucey said.

The uproar over vacations stirred up other resentments—what Mohr and Nunnally both describe as the coming together of a perfect storm. United had gradually gotten tough about sick days. Management had also withdrawn the leeway that allowed mechanics to come in an hour or so late and work an hour or so beyond the end of a shift to accommodate those who took classes or had some other personal need. And United substituted an eight-hour shift for the ten-hour one that permitted three- and four-day weekends, which the mechanics preferred. "Once the vacation thing happened, that ignited a lot of small fires," Nunnally said. The militants in Nunnally's local fanned those fires. They were partisans of the Aircraft Mechanics Fraternal Association, a rival union that was trying to displace the International Association of Machinists as the bargaining agent for United's mechanics in every city. AMFA, as it is known, argued that the mechanics, because of their unique skills, were special people, essential to airline safety, and United should be forced to recognize their value, giving them more money and job security. They should not be lumped in with customer service agents and baggage handlers, as the IAM did in its various locals, including Lodge 2294.

Mohr resisted this logic. "Anything we had to do to respond to the business environment was seized upon by the mechanics as something negative," he said. Nunnally, who was then chairman of the lodge's grievance committee, was caught between management and his members, his leadership challenged by the militants, who numbered nearly three hundred mechanics. "I said to Mohr, 'I have to have some wins, too; I can't be beaten in every grievance and do nothing,' " Nunnally told me. "I practically begged him to cooperate and he could not do that." By the early fall of 1999, the mechanics were clearly engaged in a slowdown. That is not difficult when airline safety is an issue. Inspectors, drawn from the ranks of the mechanics, have to sign off on all maintenance. If an inspector finds fault with a newly refurbished wing flap assembly, for example, he writes up a ticket reporting the flaw or a potential malfunction; even if there isn't a problem, time has to be spent to determine this to the satisfaction of the Federal Aviation Administration. "In heavy maintenance," Mohr explained, "there is an inspection of each hull and of systems on the hull and as this is done there are nonroutine write-ups. And what we saw, the number of nonroutine write-ups essentially doubled."

The slowdown produced the damage to efficiency that the mechanics had sought. Turnaround time inched up, soon reaching fifteen days and eventually more than twenty days for the 737. America West stopped sending planes to Indianapolis for heavy maintenance. The mechanics had sought just such a withdrawal. To regain the lost business, they expected United to restore some of the lost perquisites and thus win back the mechanics' cooperation. Jobs would be preserved, and on the mechanics' terms. That did not happen, and as the slowdown dragged on, work backed up on United's own airliners. For the first time, planes were parked on the tarmac outside the maintenance center, out of service and awaiting overhaul.

Then in July 2000 the mechanics slowed work even more by voting to withhold overtime—to protest what the militants viewed as management's recalcitrance in negotiating a new labor agreement to replace the one that had just expired. In the days leading up to the vote, Nunnally, as grievance chairman, spoke against withholding overtime, and worked it himself, in defiance of his militant members, but his point of view did not prevail.

Soon after, the outsourcing began. In the early fall of 2000, United diverted work from Indianapolis to private contractors in Alabama and North Carolina, contractors who employed nonunion mechanics, in most cases, at lower wages and with fewer benefits, and had large enough hangars and repair bays to accommodate narrow-bodied jet airliners. "The outsourcing was a business decision," Mohr said. "The cycle time had gotten to the point that if we did not outsource, we would have aircraft continuously parked, waiting for maintenance."

There were problems at first. The contractors had to be brought up to acceptable standards. Inspectors from the airline and the FAA were in constant attendance, but in time the quality of the work rose to an adequate level, although the contractors never got close to the turnaround times achieved in Indianapolis. When United and the union finally signed a new labor agreement in March 2002—twenty months after the old one had expired—and the mechanics in Lodge 2294 lifted their ban on overtime, United continued to outsource maintenance anyway, gradually shrinking the operation in Indianapolis.

Under the new agreement, the combined value of wages and benefits rose to more than $60 an hour for the mechanics, an increase of roughly $20. True, that was the first increase in five years. But it was double the labor cost of the nonunion contractors, too big a spread for the mechanics in Indianapolis to overcome—unless they got back to the record turnarounds achieved in the late 1990s. The old efficiency did not return. Even if it had, the outsourcing would not have stopped for a reason quite apart from labor costs. United would not submit again to the leverage over maintenance operations that the mechanics in Indianapolis had exercised for nearly three years, starting with the slowdown that had begun in July 1999. Outsourcing had become too easy an alternative, and the airline crisis that resulted from the terrorist attacks on September 11, 2001, only encouraged the practice. In the contract negotiations, the IAM, bent on preserving jobs, had gotten United to agree to limit the outsourcing of maintenance to 20 percent of the total amount spent by the airline for this function. But fifteen months after 9/11, United filed for bankruptcy protection, and the bankruptcy court lifted the restriction on outside maintenance.

Even before the court acted, United kept pushing the limit. What had started as an escape from a unionized, often militant workforce took on a second function after 9/11. The outsourcing of heavy maintenance became a means for the beleaguered airlines to cut costs, and nearly every major airline, not just United, gradually moved that way. In an earlier era, before layoffs and outsourcing were acceptable options, United might have weathered the crisis by taking in work from other airlines, as it had once done with America West. But layoffs and outsourcing were now standard practice, and rather than economies of scale, United sought heavy maintenance at the lowest immediate cost. As work shifted away from Indianapolis, the layoffs multiplied.

The sixty mechanics gathered at the Days Inn that January evening were in the fourth wave to lose their jobs, bringing the total to twelve hundred. The recycling of ex-mechanics into new lines of work was now in full swing, and Nunnally, when he had finished speaking about the importance of filing promptly for unemployment benefits, introduced Tori E. Bucko. She turned out to be the main speaker, the chief of the boot camp the mechanics were being encouraged to enter.

Bucko seemed out of place—a tall, stylish woman with bobbed blond hair, festively dressed in a white turtleneck blouse under a bright red blazer with large buttons. As she spoke, a delicate gold neck chain and pendant swayed gently against the backdrop of her blouse, in the V formed by the buttoned blazer. Given her responsibilities, she was surprisingly young, only thirty. But as the manager of a federally subsidized program for processing laid-off airline workers in Indianapolis, she would in the weeks ahead play a more important role in the lives of many of the mechanics than the portly Nunnally or the union they were leaving behind.

Like Goodrum she knew her lines by heart and she rattled them off, but unlike Goodrum she did not personalize her message. Mildly annoyed that Nunnally had cut into her time, she was rushing through her presentation, offering no digression into her personal experience to get the mechanics' attention and arouse their sympathies. When I pointed this out to Bucko later, she reacted with surprise. She had shortened her talk so as not to drag out the meeting, she explained, and in doing so had left out her own layoff. In her frequent presentations, she usually mentioned that painful experience, using it as a selling point for the boot camp she directed. "Normally I say to these people, 'If these programs had been available to me, I would have used them.' "

The program Bucko directed was sponsored by the Indianapolis Private Industry Council, a coalition of companies, unions, government, and civic groups. Virtually all of the meager funding for these programs comes from Washington, which sends less than $7 billion a year to the states to recycle laid-off workers back into jobs. In Indiana's case, the state distributes its share of the federal money to sixteen regional workforce investment boards. The Indianapolis Private Industry Council is one of these boards, and the council in turn paid a private, nonprofit company, Goodwill Industries of Central Indiana, to do the actual work. Goodwill employed Bucko as the manager in charge of the recycling program for laid-off airline workers in Marion County, whose boundaries encompass the city of Indianapolis. Goodwill also recycled men and women laid off in other industries in Marion County, recruiting them as they signed up for unemployment benefits at state-run offices. But in the winter of 2003, outcast airline employees, two-thirds of them United's mechanics, were still getting special attention. Soon after September 11, 2001, a special $3.1 million federal grant went to Marion County to recycle people who had lost their airline jobs. Henceforth they would be separated from the laid-off in other industries and given special treatment at the AIR Project, the acronym for the Airline Industry Re-Careerment Project, a title that suggests just how awkward and difficult recycling is.

Bucko's task, in this initial presentation at the Days Inn, was to encourage the sixty mechanics to take the next step. There would be no help for them if they failed to show up at the AIR Project's center, which had been set up in a single-story brick office building on the main street of an industrial park not far from the airport. There they would be asked to fill out a detailed enrollment application and submit to a series of workshops and evaluations. What Bucko did not mention was the pressure on her employer, Goodwill Industries, and on herself, to meet the employment goals specified in the federal grant—to get a majority of the mechanics re-employed at 90 percent of their previous wage. Meeting this goal was a condition for getting more federal money once the initial grant expired in two years. In the end, Goodwill managed to put together enough additional money from Washington to string out the AIR Project for nearly four years. But the employment goals were not met; they could not be met because they were too optimistic, mythically optimistic.

The myth—promoted by economists, educators, business executives, and nearly all of the nation's political leaders, Democrats and Republicans alike—holds that in America's vibrant and flexible economy there is work, at good pay, for the educated and skilled. The unemployed need only to get themselves educated and skilled and the work will materialize. Education and training create the jobs, according to this way of thinking. Or, put another way, a job materializes for every trained or educated worker, a job commensurate with his or her skills for which he or she is appropriately paid. If the workers were already trained, as the mechanics certainly were, then what they needed was additional training and counseling, in programs like Bucko's, to transition to well-paying, unfilled jobs in other industries. If the transition failed to function as advertised, well, that was the fault of the workers themselves. Their failure to land good jobs was due to personality defects or a resistance to acquiring new skills or a reluctance to move to where the good jobs were. Ronald Reagan made this point bluntly in the early years of his administration. The newspapers he read were filled with help-wanted ads, the president said. What better evidence was there that good jobs go begging for lack of qualified workers?

That was the myth. It evaporated in practice for the aircraft mechanics, whose hourly pay ranged up to $31. Not enough job openings exist at $31 an hour—or at $16 an hour, for that matter—to meet the demand for them. Jobs don't just materialize at cost-conscious companies to absorb all the qualified people who want them. You cannot be an engineer or an accountant without degrees in those fields; in that sense, education and training certainly do count. Furthermore, in the competition for the jobs that do exist, the educated and trained have an edge. That advantage shows up regularly in wage comparisons. But you cannot earn an engineer's or an accountant's typical pay if companies are not hiring engineers and accountants, or are hiring relatively few and can dictate the wage, chipping away at it. Bucko knew that as she struggled to meet the unrealistic standard set by the federal government in granting the $3.1 million for the AIR Project. Carolyn Brown, vice president of the Indianapolis Private Industry Council, the agency that picked Goodwill Industries to run the project, also understood the futility of the endeavor. "When large numbers of people are laid off, there just isn't any occupational cluster that is waiting out there to receive them," Brown said.

Job training, as a result, becomes a channeling process, channeling the unemployed into the unfilled jobs that do exist, with a veneer of training along the way. Most of the unfilled jobs have paid less than $10 or $11 an hour in recent years, barely enough to keep a family out of poverty, whatever the jobholder's skills. Yet job training rather than job creation is central to employment policy. It has been since 1982, when Congress passed the Job Training Partnership Act (JTPA) at the urging of the Reagan administration. That was a turning point. Until then, the federal government had taken on the obligation of creating at least some jobs as a supplement to private sector employment.

The vehicle for doing this was the Comprehensive Employment and Training Act, enacted in 1973. CETA, as it was called, was hardly a means of achieving full employment. But thanks to CETA, city and state governments, along with various nonprofit community organizations, created 750,000 full-time jobs for adults at the height of the program in 1978, at a cost of more than $5.5 billion annually in federally subsidized wages. Most of the jobs were civil service office work or in social services. CETA also paid to train people for work, in addition to outright job creation, recognition that the former is of limited value without the latter. JTPA, which replaced CETA, paid only for training.

The mistaken assumption in the training-only approach is that the wages workers earn are primarily determined by the skills they bring to a job. Employers are indeed hungry for skilled workers and will pay good wages to obtain their skills. But the good pay happens only if one or two applicants show up for every three or four job openings, forcing employers to compete for qualified applicants. For most of the years since the mid-1970s, however, the opposite has been true: too many applicants, not enough jobs. Yet job training has been the reigning policy for twenty-five years, embraced first by Republicans, then gradually by congressional Democrats and finally by the Clinton administration, often in response to relentless lobbying from business organizations. Marching to this tune, Clinton took job training even further than Reagan had. In 1998, the Workforce Investment Act replaced JTPA and this time training became available to higher-income workers—including the aircraft mechanics in Indianapolis—not just the low-wage, entry-level people that were the focus of JTPA. Saying we should solve the skills shortage through education and training became part of nearly every politician's stump speech, a relatively innocuous way to address the politics of unemployment without strengthening either the bargaining leverage of workers or the federal government's role in bolstering labor markets.

But training for what? The reality, as the aircraft mechanics discovered, is painfully different from the reigning thesis. Rather than a skills shortage, millions of American workers have more skills than their jobs require. That is particularly true of the college educated, who make up 30 percent of the population today, up from 10 percent in the 1960s. They often find themselves working as salespeople and office administrators, taking jobs in hotels and restaurants, or becoming carpenters, flight attendants, and word processors to make a living. The number of jobs that require a bachelor's degree has indeed been growing, but more slowly than the number of graduates, according to the Labor Department, and that trend is likely to continue through this decade. "The average college graduate is doing very well," says Lawrence Katz, a labor economist at Harvard. "But on the margin, college graduates appear to be more vulnerable than in the past."

The Labor Department's Bureau of Labor Statistics offers a rough estimate of the imbalance in the demand for jobs as opposed to the supply. Each month since December 2000 the bureau has surveyed the number of job vacancies across the country and has compared these openings to the number of unemployed job seekers. On average, there were 2.6 job seekers for every job opening over the first forty-one months of the survey. It would have been even higher, according to the bureau, if the calculation had included the millions of people who stopped looking for work because they did not believe they could get a decent job.

So the demand for jobs is considerably greater than the supply—at least 5 million greater than the supply, according to a study by Tim Bartik, a senior economist at the W. E. Upjohn Institute for Employment Research, and the existing supply of jobs is not what the reigning theory says it is. Most of the unfilled jobs pay low wages and require relatively little skill, often less than the jobholder has. From the spring of 2003 to the spring of 2004, for example, more than 55 percent of the hiring was at wages of $13.25 an hour or less: hotel and restaurant workers, health care employees, temporary workers, and the like. That trend is likely to continue. Seven of the ten occupations expected to grow the fastest from 2002 through 2012, according to the Labor Department, are in the below-$13.25-an-hour category: retail salespeople, customer service representatives, food service workers, cashiers, janitors, nurse's aides, and hospital orderlies.

The $13.25 is important. More than 45 percent of the nation's workers, whatever their skills, earned less than $13.25 an hour in 2004, or $27,600 a year for a full-time worker. That is roughly the income that a family of four must have in many parts of the country to maintain a standard of living minimally above the poverty level. Surely lack of skill and education does not hold down the wages of nearly half the workforce. Something quite different seems to be true: the oversupply of skilled workers is driving people into jobs beneath their skills and driving down the pay of jobs equal to their skills. Both happened to the aircraft mechanics laid off by United Airlines.

Bucko's results in recycling workers into new jobs were as good as any in the country. Hers was a showcase program, better financed than most, and in the aircraft mechanics she had skilled people who urgently wanted to get back to their previous income levels. By the spring of 2004, however, out of more than 800 mechanics from United who had gone through her program or were still going through it, only 185 were working again. Despite their skill, 33 of those 185, or 18 percent, were earning less than $13.25 an hour working in warehouses, on construction jobs, in restaurants, and in retailing. Some were "throwing boxes," as the mechanics put it, for Federal Express, which paid them only $10 an hour at its shipping center in Indianapolis. They took the demeaning work, which entailed loading and unloading air freight packages, for two reasons: FedEx offered them company-paid health insurance, which some of the mechanics desperately wanted, and they saw in the job a gamble worth the hardship, given the glum alternatives. After a year on the payroll they would qualify as insiders to bid for an aircraft mechanic's slot at FedEx, when one came open. Although the company is nonunion, it paid its mechanics $25 an hour or more in Indianapolis, roughly comparable to what the mechanics had earned at United.

Earning the old level of pay once again was rare. Of the 185 mechanics back at work in the spring of 2004, the majority earned $14 to $20 an hour repairing heating and air-conditioning units, or in auto repair, or in computer maintenance, or as freight train conductors (CSX happened to be hiring), or as cross-country tractor-trailer drivers, having graduated from a two-week driver-training course offered by Bucko's people. The relatively high number of mechanics who became truck drivers angered Ben Nunnally, the union leader. "Here's a guy who fixed planes and now he is encouraged to be a truck driver and at first he is offended that they would even suggest that he become a professional truck driver," Nunnally told me. "But from the point of view of the people in Tori Bucko's operation, who have seen guys with families run out of severance pay and unemployment benefits, from their point of view, it is how do you get these guys back into the job market as quickly as possible." Bucko put it more succinctly: "They see it as a quick fix," she said. "Send me to two weeks' truck driving school, they say. I'll get my CDL [commercial driver's license]. I'll hit the road. And many have done that."

Only fifteen of the reemployed mechanics had regained their United wage level or exceeded it, and eight of those fifteen achieved this by becoming aircraft mechanics again. Several of the mechanics, stifling reluctance and resentment, had migrated from Indianapolis to do what Nunnally was thinking of doing. They had gone to work for the companies that United and other airlines were using to outsource heavy aircraft maintenance. They were mostly younger mechanics with relatively little seniority when United laid them off and for that reason were still low on the wage scale, earning $19 or $20 an hour, which is what the outsourcers also paid them. For the outsourcers, however, $19 or $20 an hour was top pay. Two of the eight had earned $30 an hour or more at United, and they did just as well in their postlayoff lives. They were the lucky exceptions. One became a maintenance supervisor at another airline; the other a visiting instructor in aircraft mechanics at Purdue University.

The wage loss from layoffs is now a pattern that shows up not only in individual cases, like that of the United mechanics, but in national surveys as well. Two years after a layoff, two-thirds of the victims say they are working again. Of those two-thirds, only 40 percent, on average, are making as much as they had in the old job, a less drastic result than the aircraft mechanics, but the same general breakdown. The rest are making less, often much less. Out of a hundred laid-off workers, then, twenty-seven are making their old salary again, or more, and seventy-three are making less, or are not working at all. That downward pull contributes mightily to the wage stagnation that has persisted, with only occasional relief, since the early seventies.

Bucko's recycling program was wasted on the eight workers who went back to their old trade. Given the limited funding, the goal is to screen out those who won't make use of the training, even before the scarcity of well-paying jobs imposes a screening of its own. The process is like a funnel: wide at one end where all the laid-off workers go in and narrow at the other, where a limited number gradually emerge into retraining and, if they are lucky, new jobs at decent pay. Mark Crouch, a professor of labor studies at Indiana University, calls the recycling of laid-off workers a "burial program."

Bucko's presentation to the sixty mechanics gathered at the Days Inn was a crucial first step in the funneling process, and she went at it bluntly, encouraging the mechanics to sign up but also dousing them with a demeaning reality. They must start from scratch in their search for a job, she told them, and she offered workshops in résumé writing and in how to behave in job interviews. When searching for work in other fields, they will find themselves subject to entry-level tests that more and more employers require of job applicants. In preparation for those tests, Bucko's center offered training in algebra—mainly fractions and decimals—and in spelling. Mistakes in these basic skills can mean rejection for a job, she explained.

The mechanics listened in utter silence as she canceled out their past. "We will do career assessment," she explained, "to bring out the skills that you have, not just skill in the work you think you want, but skills you don't realize you have. If you are a coach on your son's or daughter's team, that is a transferable skill." Discouraged by such talk, many of the mechanics did not show up at the AIR Project center to enroll in Bucko's boot camp. For those who did come, there was a further winnowing out. Sit in on an enrollment session, and the obstacles thrown up by Bucko's staff are obvious.

When Cheryl Anderson, a Goodwill staffer, began her presentation to twenty-seven newly laid-off mechanics, they had already gone through one of the Days Inn orientations and were seated at narrow tables arranged in rows. Each had been given an eight-page enrollment application. Facing them from the front of the room, Anderson was describing the various workshops—in résumé writing, interviewing skills, and job-hunting techniques—that they would have to attend before their applications for training subsidies would even be considered. "In the interviewing workshop," she explained, "two people will interview you just as if you were applying for a job. They will ask thirty-four questions commonly asked at job interviews and the session will be taped so you can see your performance."

The mechanics would also be required to submit to an evaluation of their personalities and skills, including a psychological test that would determine, among other things, whether they were introverts or extroverts. It would be pointless, Anderson explained, to steer introverts to jobs better suited for extroverts and vice versa. All these requirements would take three to four weeks to complete and only then would the mechanics have access to counselors. The counselors, in turn, were the ones who would authorize, or deny, funds for training and tuition. They would be more favorably disposed toward those mechanics who, in addition to doing well in the workshops and evaluations, had energetically hunted for jobs during the three- to four-week period, and could demonstrate this by submitting to the counselors a written log of each contact with a potential employer. Goodwill, in sum, wanted to gamble its limited funding only on those ex-mechanics most likely to land one of the jobs that paid at least $13.25 an hour and were in such short supply. The rest were invited in effect to make whatever use they could of the classroom instruction in job-search techniques. "They are valuable in themselves," Anderson said.

That was not what the mechanics wanted to hear, and when she finished her thirty-five-minute presentation they went at her. "Most of us are here for retraining," one said. "Must we look for jobs for three or four weeks before we can get it?" Yes, Anderson replied. How much of the funding goes to administrative costs and salaries, another mechanic wanted to know. Goodwill employed nine people in the AIR Project, Anderson informed him. Although she did not say so, salaries were consuming less than 10 percent of the $3.1 million grant. A mechanic with a stay-at-home wife wondered about income support for his family if he were to qualify for a tuition grant that kept him in school for a couple of semesters. There is no income support beyond the standard twenty-six weeks of unemployment benefits, Anderson said. "The mechanic and his counselor must make sure a family has money for food before a tuition subsidy is authorized," she explained. Still another mechanic asked if he could start school at his own expense and then, if a counselor subsequently approved a tuition grant, get retroactive reimbursement. No, Anderson replied. That last answer raised a murmur among the mechanics. "We are losing jobs that are very hard to replace," one responded.

That was true, but because of the scarcity of openings for good jobs, everyone wanted training, thinking that would gain them entry. The federal funding for that training, however, fell far short of the demand. The only way to stretch the money was to put up obstacles, as Anderson did. In response, ten of the twenty-seven mechanics at her session would drop out before they got to a counselor. That was the pattern. Bucko was not surprised. "I've worked with many populations of laid-off workers and it is the same fear, the same stress," she said.

She herself was an exception to the normal pattern. She had gone up the income ladder despite having been laid off once and almost laid off a second time. Her story, leaving out the pain, makes her seem like a poster woman for the numerous economists, personnel experts, management consultants, and authors of best-selling self-help books who popularize a second myth, a companion to the myth that good jobs go begging for lack of properly educated and skilled applicants. This second myth holds that layoffs can be a blessing. The career coaches who push this view argue that layoffs force people to find new work that in the long run makes them happier or better off or both. Tori Bucko, earning $50,000 at Goodwill Industries—double her prelayoff pay—is a rare example of someone who, forced to find new work, ended up earning more, but without the satisfaction that is supposed to have resulted from her perseverance.

The layoff she experienced—and the near layoff from another job five years later—still sours her thoughts. The first one occurred in 1993, when she was twenty-one. She had studied nursing for a while at Marian College in Indianapolis and then had gotten into day care, rising to director of a suburban community organization that minded the children of people who commuted to work in Indianapolis. That post lacked benefits or a career ladder, so she took a job in human resources with Pet Practice, a chain of veterinary hospitals, and eleven months after she arrived, Pet Practice was acquired by a competing chain. In the inevitable reorganization, her job was eliminated—a setback that for all her subsequent success sticks in her memory as cruel. Before the merger, she had been hiring personnel for twelve of the hospitals in Indiana. Henceforth, her new employers informed her, each hospital would hire its own people. "They told me that if I wanted to stay with the company, I could travel to Santa Monica and apply for a job at the headquarters there and I would get it," she said, "but the pay would be the same $23,000 that I earned in Indiana. I said no. I couldn't live on $23,000 in California. They laid me off."

She had been living with her parents in Lebanon, Indiana, commuting to Indianapolis, and she stayed on to keep down her expenses while she took night-school courses in business management and human resources. During the day, she freelanced, mainly in desktop publishing. Soon she hooked up with Interlocal Association, a nonprofit company that ran summer programs for disadvantaged young people in the seven counties surrounding Indianapolis and also worked with women in those counties who were moving into jobs from welfare. These were services offered by city and county agencies that contracted with Interlocal to provide the actual services. But with welfare-to-work funds winding down in 1999, Bucko faced another layoff. She had already been given a termination date, and just before it arrived, she jumped to Goodwill Industries as a $27,000-a-year case manager.

Goodwill was adding staff, having just been awarded the Indianapolis contract for laid-off workers. Bucko soon found herself rising in rank and in pay—first as director of the WorkOne recycling center serving the west side of Indianapolis and then, after 9/11, as chief of the AIR Project. Three years later, as the recycling of airline employees was winding down, Bucko evaluated for me what her team had achieved. She was pleased with the results, she said. Given the resistance from employers, the average wage of those who were working again, mechanics and non-mechanics alike, was a respectable 69 percent of what they had earned before they were laid off. That average had dropped from 73 percent six months earlier and would probably drop some more as additional people found work. But that was a positive sign, Bucko insisted. "It is an indicator that people are finally starting to accept what happened to them; to say, Okay, I've given up on $25 an hour and I'll take the $12 or $15."

After Bucko, two others spoke briefly to the sixty mechanics gathered that January evening at the Days Inn. A young woman, Elizabeth English, representing Morgan Stanley, made a pitch to them to roll over their 401(k) savings into Individual Retirement Accounts. She said nothing about Morgan Stanley as the agent in this process. But she had come early to the Days Inn meeting and had placed on each chair in the conference room a thin blue pamphlet entitled "The Morgan Stanley Rollover Resource Guide." The last page was a rollover application form addressed to Morgan Stanley, perforated along the inner edge for easy detachment and mailing.

Michael Barnes also spoke. Like Nunnally, he was part of the union movement. But while Nunnally had tried to persuade United to preserve the jobs at the maintenance center and was a reluctant participant in the transition to "alternate careers," Barnes was entirely engaged in transition. Not that he is against preserving jobs; he has worked hard to do so. But as the salaried director for Indiana of the Labor Institute for Training, an operation allied to the AFL-CIO that started up in the late 1980s, he measured success, as Bucko did, by the number of laid-off union members his institute placed in new jobs—any jobs, preferably unionized ones but nonunion if need be.

Advertising his successes, Barnes displayed on a wall of his office at the AFL-CIO's state headquarters building—a bleak one-story structure across the street from a fenced-in athletic field in a blue-collar neighborhood—three framed certificates of appreciation. They were thank-you notes in diploma-style lettering and format for his group's services in helping laid-off union workers adjust to their loss and move on. In each case, the Labor Institute for Training had supplied counseling, workshops in résumé writing, and help in searching for another job. The certificates were testimonials. But displaying them on a wall of his small, cluttered office, as if they were medical diplomas attesting to the skill of the doctor at the desk, seemed odd: organized labor was calling attention not to past battles and victories, but to its participation in the layoff process.

Barnes did not see himself as an agent of layoffs. The AFL-CIO, he insisted, had not slid from struggle against layoffs to "acquiescence." He hated my use of that word. But he agreed that starting in the late 1980s, the AFL-CIO had associated itself with organizations like Indiana's Labor Institute for Training and in doing so had become party to a process that accepted layoffs and sought to get the victims back into jobs.

Barnes is a well-groomed, slightly built man, courteous, even when angry, and cautious in describing his ticklish role in the union movement. When I first met him in 1998, on a visit to Indianapolis, he was the Labor Institute's forty-three-year-old deputy director, not yet having risen to the top job. Trained in psychology, he had worked for the state government for fifteen years, first as a leader of group-therapy sessions for families and also for drug addicts, then as a counselor in a state mental institution. He had taken a job with the Labor Institute in 1992, at age thirty-seven, as a program coordinator and later as deputy director.

Layoffs were proliferating in Indiana and, in response, the institute, which is better known by its acronym, LIFT, had quietly committed itself to a joint effort to get dislocated workers back into the workforce in other jobs. The city also was a partner and so, often, were the companies doing the layoffs. "The bad news is that LIFT has become a core activity of the AFL-CIO," Barnes had told me in 1998, speaking off the record, reluctant then to connect his name to so defeatist an admission. Nearly five years later, his reluctance had greatly diminished. Protest and resistance were still a priority, Barnes insisted, and both were ongoing. But their effectiveness had diminished. "They don't gain traction anymore in the community; there is not a lot of public sympathy," he said. "All we can do in that situation is address the transition needs of our members."

The United Airlines debacle now occupied much of his time. He had assigned one of his six full-time staffers to the case. She ran a "career connect" seminar at the AIR Project center at which speakers from various fields described possible job opportunities and then helped applicants follow up. Barnes himself was using his connections in the building-trades unions to get mechanics into the pipeline for construction jobs, once work on a new airport terminal in Indianapolis finally ratcheted up. He was also attempting to market the mechanics to DaimlerChrysler, which had opened a transmission plant in Kokomo, Indiana, thirty miles north of Indianapolis. But the application pool was huge and the competition fierce.

Barnes did not mention either of these long shots in his brief remarks to the sixty mechanics gathered at the Days Inn. Instead, he braced them for the hard times ahead, encouraging them to apply for free government health insurance for their children and for pregnant wives; the insurance would kick in once their coverage through United ceased four months after they were laid off. Aware of their anxiety about trying to make ends meet on unemployment pay, he warned the mechanics against turning too easily to a temporary help agency, even one that offered a high-paying job. While the mechanics worked as temps, their unemployment checks would be suspended. And when the assigned job ended, renewing the unemployment pay might not be so easy. The unemployment office could rule that a mechanic was still officially on the temp agency's staff, between temp assignments but not unemployed. "Buyer beware," Barnes cautioned. And the meeting was over.

· · ·

The United Airlines maintenance center remained empty for eighteen months, and then one of the contractor companies that did heavy maintenance for the airlines agreed to lease two of the twelve hangar bays and hire two hundred mechanics, promising to pay them at least $10.50 an hour, which was the average pay for all of Indiana's workforce.

The center had become a monument to a flimsy assumption in America: that cities and states, offering taxpayer-funded subsidies, can get companies like United Airlines to put operations within their borders, rather than in some other city or state, and the good jobs they bring will stay put. The bidding wars that have resulted from this expectation started in the 1970s and gradually escalated as the supply of skilled and semiskilled workers in so many communities outpaced the number of good jobs available for them. By 2004, municipal and state governments were spending more than $30 billion a year to get companies to put operations here rather than there. The money came in many forms: tax abatements, wage subsidies, gifts of public land, lowered income taxes, road construction at city or state expense, and outright cash payments. Whatever the form, from a national point of view, the $30 billion—enough to hire 400,000 schoolteachers at $50,000 each plus benefits, to cite just one alternative—was wasted. If the United Airlines maintenance center had not come to Indianapolis, it would have gone to Denver, or some other city. Subsidies or no, United still intended to build the maintenance center somewhere in the country. If the center had gone to Seattle, then employment in Indianapolis would have been less, but not employment in the nation as a whole.

The City of Indianapolis, with strong backing from the state government, won out over ninety-three other cities in the bidding war for the center. That was in 1991. An expanding United was adding flights within the country and building up a fleet of Boeing 737s and other midsized airliners to serve these routes. The maintenance center would keep the planes in the air, generating as much passenger revenue as possible, with a minimum of downtime for overhaul. That would be achieved through the construction of a superefficient center somewhere in America. To land this plum, the City of Indianapolis provided the land and jointly with the state paid $320 million toward construction, a sum that turned out to be more than half of the nearly $600 million actually invested in the cavernous center by the time United walked away, sticking the city and the state with $37.5 million a year in mortgage payments and maintenance for an empty building.

United had promised to bring the total investment to $800 million and to employ more than five thousand mechanics. "If it had paid the full cost of that maintenance center from its own pocket, or even all of the $600 million that was invested, it might not have walked away so quickly," Arthur Rolnick, the director of research at the Federal Reserve Bank of Minneapolis, argues. Rolnick has made a name for himself as a vociferous opponent of taxpayer-funded bidding wars. He believes that they distort the marketplace by making the companies that get the subsidies more footloose than they otherwise would be.

United has an answer. "I think the way this should be portrayed is that we built the facility on the basis of a fleet plan, and the fleet got lower, which made that amount of space no longer needed," Peter D. McDonald, United's executive vice president for operations, said. "Then, you know, as the market changed and outside providers were turning out heavy maintenance work at a much more competitive cost, we couldn't do it at that cost."

But what about the magnificent maintenance center, a jewel in America's industrial structure? Must it be abandoned or vastly under-utilized simply because "the market changed" and United Airlines, in response, revamped its business strategy, moving with the rest of the air-line industry to cheaper, less fastidious maintenance? Mark S. Moore, as the Indiana state government's director of public finance, was involved in the financing for the construction of the center and more recently in the effort to land a new tenant, or tenants, since no single occupant would be likely to generate enough maintenance volume to exploit the center's unique high-tech features. No one had a better grasp than Moore of the complicated public subsidies that United had received. "We are at the beginning of the 'condominiumization' of the maintenance center," he said, coining a word that reflected his distaste for what was happening. Moore had thought up what he considered a better strategy, not one likely to be adopted in a nation unwilling to deal with the inefficiencies of markets, but a better way. In the interest of aircraft safety and quality maintenance, he said, the FAA should require the airlines to do heavy maintenance at five or six designated facilities. These would be the finest in the country, and they would be staffed by licensed, well-paid mechanics.

The United Airlines center in Indianapolis would be the one desig-nated to overhaul narrow-bodied, midsized airliners. The volume of maintenance traffic would assure efficiency and profitability, but if the latter were a problem, the federal government could assign the center to another major airline. Or it could organize a consortium of airlines to run the facility. Or it could step in with subsidies to keep either the consor-tium or United afloat as the designated operator. After all, the city and the state had already paid out huge amounts on behalf of United. Why not make public subsidies pay off by mixing them with regulation? "I would say to the airlines," Moore said, "that we are going to care about where maintenance gets done, and make sure that people are appropri-ately incentivized through wages, benefits, and so on, and that it's good, safe stuff."

That is not what happened. The market, unfettered by rules, dictated that the next occupant or occupants should be the outsourcers who now did more and more of the maintenance. Mayor Bart Peterson finally landed one of these outsourcers, the AAR Corporation. While United had paid more than $14 million a year in maintenance during the heyday of its operation and $700,000 to lease the twelve hangar bays, AAR paid less than $1 million in total for two hangar bays, with an agreement to occupy eight more by 2009. The nearly empty center no longer required upward of $14 million a year in maintenance, but the government was forced to lay out close to $3.5 million annually to prevent deterioration of the underutilized facility.

While United had promised to employ five thousand mechanics and had actually employed nearly twenty-five hundred for a while, AAR agreed to hire only two hundred at the outset and six hundred more by the end of the decade. It was not much commitment on AAR's part, not for an outsourcer whose business was growing. But the city and state put up key money anyway, promising AAR up to $16 million in tax credits as jobs were added, plus a $2 million subsidy to purchase tools and $5 million more to spend on the building. AAR, after all, did not have much use for a high-volume, super-efficient maintenance center. Almost any unoccupied, reasonably equipped hanger space was sufficient, and there is plenty of that sort of space in this country. AAR had to be lured.

Nearly two thousand people seeking the two hundred mechanic jobs showed up for a job fair that AAR hosted in the maintenance center's great entrance hall. Company officials said nothing about wages or benefits. They simply asked people to fill out applications and told them they would be notified. The mechanics knew, of course, that at AAR's other maintenance centers, nearly all of them nonunion, mechanics' pay ranged from $12 an hour to just under $20 an hour, plus health insurance. Many of those at the job fair had belonged to Lodge 2294 of the Machinists, but the president of the nearly defunct lodge, Ben Nunnally, did not bother to show up. "The last guy they are going to pick up is the president of the local lodge," Nunnally said. "I think they'll hire a lot of people straight out of mechanics' school at $14 an hour, and a few experienced mechanics who have no association with labor unions. They are cheapening the jobs."

That was true. AAR later even brought in some mechanics through temp agencies—at $17 or $18 an hour—so that it would not have to put them initally on its payroll. But Mayor Peterson, caught up in the incessant bidding war for jobs, saw the AAR contract as a step forward. With

AAR in the bag, the city actively sought other tenants to do heavy maintenance or some other work related to aircraft repair—the condominiumization that concerned Mark Moore but not Mayor Peterson, at least not in his public statements. "This facility was a symbol of us being at the pinnacle of economic development," the mayor said, referring to the center's best days. Now to have AAR "come in here and begin the process of renewal I think is a good symbol for our state and for our city."

CHAPTER FOUR

The Shock, Part 1

I met Craig Imperio at the Days Inn that January evening in Indianapolis. He was among the sixty aircraft mechanics about to be laid off at United Airlines. Later Craig put me in touch with Tim Dewey, an older mechanic. Ben Nunnally gave me the names of other mechanics and that brought me to Erin Brown.*What is striking in their stories is that all three underestimated the damage they would suffer from the layoffs. They had been thrown out of their jobs, but in order of seniority, which diluted the debilitating message that they were selected because their work lacked value. Rather than blame themselves, they railed against outsourcing. "This may sound kind of corny," Imperio told me, more than once, "but it seems to me that America is what it is today for all the hard work and sweat of blue-collar workers, and now they take that away."

Still, the three men were confident they would soon be successful in new careers. They all maintained, in the early days of their layoffs, that in time they would have left United anyway, quitting in pursuit of more satisfying work. They never anticipated the odysseys that lay ahead of them. Imperio even considered his layoff a gentle shove in the right direction, a timely prod to finish college, and as the other mechanics left the Days Inn conference room, walking slowly toward the two double doors in the back, he headed in the opposite direction, toward the front of the room, to buttonhole Tori Bucko. She had taken questions after her talk, and his made him seem jauntier than the other mechanics in the audience. His buoyancy caught my attention and I introduced myself. Three days later I drove the sixteen miles from downtown Indianapolis to the two-bedroom ranch

---

*The last name has been changed by request.

house that Craig and Sarah Imperio had purchased for $119,000 the year before. It was located fancifully at the corner of Enchanted View Lane and Moonlight Court in a vast development of similar, neatly built homes spread across what must have been farmland five years earlier. Craig greeted me in the driveway. He is a sturdily built man, of medium height, with an open, friendly expression and dark brown hair. He was dressed in jeans, black sneakers, a nondescript dark woolen shirt. This was his son's second birthday, he explained, and his wife, who was five months pregnant with their second child, was inside preparing for a lunchtime party that Craig's parents would attend. She did not want us underfoot, so we drove to a restaurant along a nearby highway, ordered breakfast, and talked.

As soon as we started talking, Craig expressed his view that only those who had been laid off fully understood the emotions it aroused. "You have to be pretty stupid if you do not build up some type of defense mechanism from the experience," he said. I summarized for him the prevailing view of so many management gurus and economists—that a flexible workforce is an advantage for the American economy—and he responded in anger. "What if I get laid off from my next job," he said sarcastically. "How many times do I have to get laid off to satisfy the people who think it is good? Are two times enough for those professors who say it is good? Would they say that is enough?" He believed—mistakenly, as it turned out—that once he had his college degree, good jobs would open up for him, but he was angry that so few people who were laid off had enough savings or enough help from family to support them while they went back to school. He had both, and no debts, except the mortgage. "If education is going to be so necessary to work, then the government has to help much more than it does," he said, arguing in effect for a modern-day version of the GI Bill that sent so many World War II veterans through college and now should fund higher education for masses of people.

Craig had entered Fort Lewis College in Durango, Colorado, not far from the family home in Loveland, right out of high school. He had started as a biology major, then switched to mechanical engineering and, struggling with the hard course work, had dropped out with a year still to go. "Engineers look really smart," he remembered thinking, "and looking around the class I did not feel that I looked like an engineer."

At the suggestion of his father, a former New York City detective who had become an aircraft mechanic late in life, Craig got his mechanic's license, too. He joined United in San Francisco in 1997, shifted to the airline's Oakland maintenance base in 1999, and married Sarah that year. In the airline crisis after 9/11, United cut back at Oakland and Imperio was laid off. It was a furlough, really; he had enough seniority to bump someone in Indianapolis, where his parents and sister then lived, and he went there, never imagining that his job, and everyone else's, would soon disappear entirely.

Even before the layoffs, his wife had been after him to go back to college, get his degree, rise above mechanic. And in late December, the day after United sent him his layoff notification, he took the plunge, enrolling as a full-time student at Purdue University's campus in Indianapolis. "If I had not gotten laid off, I absolutely would have postponed finishing college," Imperio told me. The tuition and books for the spring semester came to $1,900 for four courses. He had not yet paid the bill. He wanted Bucko's organization to pay, and also to commit to paying the final semester's expenses, a total of $5,000. Her program was made for people like Imperio. He was only twenty-nine, with three years of college under his belt and only one to go to earn a bachelor of science degree—just the sort of short-term, job-oriented education that the meager, federally funded tuition grants were designed to finance.

Bucko did arrange for him to get the money. She liked his energy and boldness that night at the Days Inn and she helped him bypass the funneling process that weeded out so many others. Still, Imperio had to jump through some of the hoops. He had to register in person at Bucko's center for dislocated airline workers, and sit through four hours of workshops on how to interview for a job and how to search for one. Finally, he had to persuade three companies to write letters to Bucko, each stating that once Imperio had earned his BS degree in aeronautical technology, the company would consider hiring him. "Education is not the purpose of the tuition support I am getting," Imperio said, reciting to me an AIR Project credo. "They are not going to take some guy with no college and put him through four years, no way. They want you back working as soon as possible and before they give you any tuition money, they want evidence a job is probably out there for you."

In the spring of 2003 he had nearly completed the first semester of his resumed education, and he was getting As in each of his four courses. He was pleased with himself and playful as we talked. We were seated at the table in the Imperios' small dining alcove, which looked out through two sliding glass doors on a raised wooden patio. Sunlight flooded in through the door panels. Sarah, a month away from the birth of her second son, had just risen from an afternoon nap. She was relaxed. So was he. And yet the layoff, the finality of it, stayed unpleasantly in his mind, intruding in the conversation. "It is a humiliation," he said, his voice momentarily not playful and, to my surprise, edging toward tears. He looked straight at me and spoke slowly. "You are around your family and you are the laid-off one," he said. "You know they don't care, but if I were not going to school, I'd be going crazy. It gives me a sense of self-worth. The people who laid me off, they don't know who I am."

Sarah interjected. She was impatient with self-pity and saw no point in dwelling on the past. "All I care about is that he is getting a degree," she said sternly, redirecting the conversation. "The degree will give him an edge. He is going to Purdue, he is on the honor roll; who would not want that person?"

The second semester went as well as the first for Craig, but Sarah took a job in late summer to supplement her husband's unemployment benefits, which had nearly run out, and to get company-paid health insurance in place of the private coverage that the Imperios had been forced to buy, at a cost of $180 a month, when United's coverage stopped. Craig went to school in the late afternoon and early evening and cared for the children during the day, while she worked, earning $10 an hour plus commissions as a leasing agent for a new apartment-house complex.

He was just getting the baby up from an afternoon nap when I came by to see him during a trip to Indianapolis in late October, and we talked, seated again in the dining alcove, the baby cradled in Craig's left arm and the two-year-old playing on the dark linoleum floor near him. The children obviously adored their good-natured and affectionate father, but he was impatient to get back to a job. He had married Sarah in part because she wanted to be a stay-at-home mom while he worked, he said, and that was not happening. With graduation approaching, he was already job-hunting, and he was quickly discovering that while there were openings for aircraft mechanics or for truck drivers, he could not land a higher-level job that made use of his education, not even at the three companies that had written letters to Tori Bucko in support of Imperio's tuition grant. Those letters had been hypothetical, statements from the companies that if they were hiring for their engineering operations, they would hire someone with the sort of degree that Imperio would soon receive. They weren't hiring and more than ever, Craig blamed his predicament on corporate greed and outsourcing. He did not see the logic in United's saving money by laying him off while the country bore the cost of his unemployment insurance and his college tuition. Where were the savings for the nation as a whole, particularly when the hardship for himself and his wife was factored in?

The job Imperio finally took, four months out of school, was once again as an aircraft mechanic, this time for Pratt & Whitney in Columbus, Georgia, and that is where he brought his family. He had interviewed, in fact, for ten jobs as a mechanic, many of them openings in the South, at the very contractors who now did so much of the heavy maintenance for the nation's airlines. "I got offers for every job I interviewed for," Imperio said.

He had shunned working for a company that he considered an outsourcer. Like many of his former mates, he believed that these contractors cut corners on quality. They also used unlicensed mechanics, which Imperio considered unethical and a risk to safety, although the FAA allowed the practice. Pratt & Whitney, he decided, was a cut above the contractors, ethically and also in the job security that it seemed to offer. At its maintenance center in Columbus, P&W overhauled the engines it had manufactured in the first place, engines that were now installed in the aircraft of a dozen airlines. "That is not outsourcing," Imperio insisted soon after he started work, reasoning that Pratt & Whitney was simply servicing the engines it had built—among them engines that United just a few years earlier had serviced itself. As for job security, he reasoned that the Airbus 319 and the Airbus 320 were equipped with P&W engines, and given that airlines continued to acquire these aircraft, the 150 mechanics at the Columbus center were not likely to be laid off anytime soon for lack of enough engines to overhaul.

The trade-off in this arrangement was the wage, only $17 an hour, roughly 65 percent of what Craig had earned at United. The demand for mechanics had not declined after United closed down the maintenance center in Indianapolis. The nation's airliners still had to be serviced. Only the pay had fallen—stark evidence of the disconnect between skill and income. Craig's wage at Pratt & Whitney was so far below what he had anticipated earning that he was reluctant to tell me the amount, and when he did, he rationalized. He was actually averaging nearly $19 an hour, he explained, by regularly working ten-hour days, two of the hours at time-and-a-half. He had been told, when he signed on, that if he did well, he might in time be promoted to a job in the engineering department, one worthy of his BS degree. He had taken the job as a mechanic, he said, because it offered this opportunity for advancement. But even without the promotion, he would have to stay at Pratt & Whitney for at least a year. If he left sooner, he would be required to repay "the considerable sum" that Pratt & Whitney had laid out to move the Imperios to Columbus, where they lived in a rented two-bedroom apartment, having sold their house in Indianapolis. Their $900 monthly mortgage payment in Indianapolis became $900 a month in rent in Columbus.

"If someone had told me that night at Days Inn that I would be doing what I am doing now, I would have said, absolutely not," Craig said. He had not given up on education as the ticket to a higher position and more pay, or at least as much pay as he had once earned as a mechanic at United. He would go for a master's degree in his off hours; Pratt & Whitney had offered to pay the tuition. But this time it would be a master's in business administration or "something that does not have aviation or aeronautical in the title, so I have something to offer outside the industry."

He swallowed his disappointment about the pay at Pratt & Whitney. "You can't be picky," he said, "when you have been out of work for nearly a year."

•   •   •

Tim Dewey took a different, more impulsive route. Like Imperio, he had been laid off twice at United, but while Imperio slid quickly into a slot at the Indianapolis maintenance center, Dewey was out of work for twenty-two months after his first layoff. It happened in San Francisco in 1993, just as he and his wife were beginning to make ends meet on his salary, which was then $16 an hour in his fifth year at United. As their finances unwound, Dewey became despondent. Driving along a highway in this mood, with one of his children seated beside him in the car, he heard on the radio the chilling story of a man who had parked along a highway and, with his daughter in his arms, had stepped out into the oncoming traffic, intent on suicide. A truck had struck them, killing the child. The father had survived and in his grief he wanted to die, the newscaster reported.

That story sobered Dewey and stayed in his mind. Years later, he told it to his friend Craig Imperio as a cautionary tale. United finally recalled Dewey in 1995, assigning him to Oakland, and in 1997 he transferred voluntarily to the Indianapolis facility, seeking that city's lower cost of living. He lived for a while in a camper until his wife and two children joined him. He had done that in San Francisco, too, when he first joined United, and in the loneliness of that existence, he distracted himself by writing novels and short stories, a diversion he has continued to pursue as addictively as others watch television.

When we first spoke, he said he had completed seven novels and twelve short stories, and he had accumulated ninety rejection letters from publishers. He described most of his novels as adventures in which the protagonist converts a mundane life into a glamorous one. One of his novels, for example, is the tale of an aircraft mechanic who foils a complicated plot to set off a bomb on an airliner. His model was the movie *Romancing the Stone,* about a writer of romance novels caught up in a dangerous romantic adventure herself. Dewey tried to convert fantasy to reality. Recognizing that he was at risk of another bout of despondency, he plotted how he would save himself if he were laid off again. He knew he would be. United was shutting down too much of the maintenance work in Indianapolis and, sure enough, his turn came three months after Imperio lost his job.

The solution for Dewey, who was forty-three, was to never again leave himself vulnerable to a layoff by working as an employee. With that salvation in mind, he grasped at a way to achieve independence. On a vacation trip to the Florida panhandle the year before, he and his wife had run across a water taxi business in Destin Bay—actually a twenty-six-foot blue-and-yellow whale boat with an inboard engine and a yellow plastic canopy, fringed in blue-and-white stripes—that the owner used to ferry people for a fee to restaurants along the bay's three miles of shore or on a forty-minute sightseeing tour. The owner wanted to sell the water taxi and retire. Dewey kept in touch, and on the day he learned that he would be laid off, he called the owner and purchased the business over the phone for $54,000, which he borrowed against three of his credit cards. "After that first layoff, I waited desperately for my job to come back; I was not going to wait again," Dewey said.

We talked in early April, the afternoon before he departed for Destin Bay in the family motor home to take possession of his new business. Dewey is a short, nearly bald, fat man with a Ho Chi Minh beard that rests on his bloated chin, which in turn enfolds his neck. In his eyes, he had worked hard and made personal sacrifices for United, and the airline, in return, had betrayed him. The mirror image of these destructive emotions was the reckless hope that he invested in his new venture. "If I can work that water taxi and never work for anyone again," he said, "I'll die a happy man."

What should have bothered Dewey—indeed, everyone—was the damage he represented for the country. Here was a skilled and experienced aircraft mechanic who had opted to drive a launch around a bay, the sort of minimally skilled work that students do on summer vacations. He had migrated from industrial importance to the equivalent of roadside kiosk proprietor hawking boat rides to passing tourists. And no one noticed. In a nation that parcels out layoffs so easily, the mindless destruction of skill is an overlooked by-product. Dewey had dropped out to protect himself from the psychological damage and financial uncertainty of still another layoff, and in doing so had deprived the United States of his true value as a skilled worker. That was the real tragedy in his story, which spilled out of him with an intensity that struck me as anger. When I said that to Dewey, he offered an alternative description. "Insulted is the right word," he said.

Through the spring, he lived once again in the motor home, parked near the waterfront. His wife, Kelly, and their two children, a teenage son and daughter, had stayed behind while the kids finished the school year. By the time they visited in the summer, to look for a house, Dewey had to acknowledge, to himself and to his family, that the water taxi business, as he told me later, "was not going to make enough for them to survive."

Except for the big holiday weekends—Memorial Day, July 4, and

Labor Day—there were not enough customers, although Dewey put in twelve-hour days and, in his eagerness to get tourists aboard, often waived the charge for children ($5; adults $8). Having persuaded himself that the water taxi would give him financial independence, he managed not to recognize the obstacles until they overwhelmed him. He had taken customer demand for granted; tourists strolling along the waterfront would stand in line for rides. They didn't. He had not anticipated a delay in getting a captain's license, or the unusually rainy summer. And he had thought that the boat was in good shape. The transmission, however, needed major repair, at a cost of at least $1,000, a sum the Dewey family could not afford, living as they were on his severance pay and unemployment insurance, as well as Kelly's $10.75 an hour as a supervisor of cashiers at a Lowe's store in Indianapolis. So Dewey, the mechanic, made temporary fixes, but the transmission failed him partway through two of the three crucial weekends: Memorial Day and July 4.

The water taxi brought in a total of $6,000 in tourist revenue over the five months that Dewey ran it. That was barely enough to cover insurance, fuel, and other operating costs, and after Labor Day he returned to Indianapolis, having put the business up for sale through a broker for $45,000, which was $9,000 less than he had borrowed on his credit cards to purchase it. In Indianapolis Dewey was now pursuing a career in computers, and he was once again optimistic. But for all his determination to be successful in a career that combined income and independence, the story that he told me then was of a man losing ground and surrendering to the loss.

Less than a week after returning to Indianapolis, a friend told him that if he enrolled in Tori Bucko's AIR Project and got successfully through all the preliminaries, he might qualify for a $5,000 training grant, which would cover most of the $6,500 tuition required to get a certificate at a computer training center called New Horizons. Upon graduation, he would be a Microsoft-certified systems administrator, qualified to maintain a company's computer network. It was a skill billed as much in demand, and Dewey enrolled in the AIR Project. He spent four weeks working his way through the various requirements and finally got the federally funded grant. The classes at New Horizons were spread over the winter and spring, and, at the outset, Dewey propped himself up with the same optimistic certainty that had propelled him into the water taxi business. "If I go to work for one of those big places as a network guy, I won't be there very long," he explained to me. "Headhunters pluck these people right and left, and they move on to a better job at better pay. You're making $40,000 and you leverage that into more and more. I know several people involved in this and two of them do it as consultants; they have their own little business."

By early spring, he had completed three of the five courses and had passed certification exams that qualified him, he said, as a network programmer. But setbacks chipped away at Dewey's latest attempt to re-establish himself in the workforce. A heart condition, atrial fibrillation, flared up and he spent six days in a hospital getting his medications adjusted. His health insurance from United had expired, but he had served in the navy and he was treated at a Veterans Administration hospital. The hospital stay and two weeks at home dealing with the side effects of new medications delayed his course work, pushing back graduation into August. Through all of this, the family's debts became a critical problem. The Deweys could not maintain the payments on the motor home loan (they still owed $23,000) or on the $54,000 that he had borrowed to purchase the water taxi business, which a broker in Destin Bay had not been able to sell. So Tim and Kelly Dewey filed for personal bankruptcy, and while the court freed them of their debts, it took possession of many of their belongings, although not their home. The water taxi was finally gone, a relief, but so was their treasured motor home.

The big pay that Dewey first thought he would earn as a computer technician dwindled as he began to hunt for a job halfway through his schooling. His first job might pay only $10 to $12 an hour, he discovered. "I know I could get that much just manning a help desk at a call center," he said. "I mean you can go on any job search engine—Monster, CareerBuilder—and see what they have." He would take the low starting wage, but once he acquired real-world experience, he reasoned, he would be more in demand than veterans in the field who lacked his up-to-date training in the latest operating systems. Through a constant updating of his skills, getting new certifications every few years, he might even get back up to his final salary at United, $31 an hour. In the post-9/11 world, Dewey said, companies had become concerned about network security and that was an expertise he would acquire. "Once you are in the vein of the whole industry and you have your finger on the pulse and you know exactly what they are looking for, and you go into encryption and security and all the stuff that is going to be paramount in the days to come, you can write your own ticket."

He seemed unrealistically optimistic, but he was becoming realistic, too. For all his talk of big earnings and rising demand for his new computer skills, he had decided that in case his vision of success did not materialize, he and his family could be financially independent on a diminished scale, and he explained how. Dewey and his wife could support themselves indefinitely on her $10.75 an hour and his $10 to $12 an hour in a low-end computer maintenance job, the sort of work that in Dewey's view would always be available, although probably without health insurance. The bankruptcy had made this lower-level independence possible, by canceling the family's debts and the frightening monthly payments. "I'm absolved of all that," Dewey said. The judge had helped in another way, too. He had not seized a 1924 Model T Ford that Dewey had acquired from his mother and stepfather and had refurbished, and that he now valued at $7,000—a savings account of sorts. There would be health care for him through the Veterans Administration and through the family policy that his wife had at Lowe's, or that she would have at some future employer. Most important, the couple had gotten by since the bankruptcy on her salary and his unemployment insurance, which came to the equivalent of $8.40 an hour and, thanks to various extensions, had not yet run out. "The fact of the matter is we are making do on unemployment and my wife's wage and it can only go up from there," Dewey said. "So if this is as desolate as it would get, it would still be good."

• • • •

Erin Brown's decline took still another path. Money was not a problem. In five years as a United mechanic, most of them as a bachelor, he had put away big chunks of his salary, and by the time he was laid off, in January 2003, his savings and his wife's totaled $400,000 in cash and stocks, a cushion that set Erin apart in his own mind from the other mechanics. His wife, Stacy, a lawyer who earned well, had contributed considerably to the pot and their frugality, particularly Erin's, kept their savings intact. As a bachelor, he had spent next to nothing on vacations, autos, and entertainment. He rarely ate out and he shared rented homes with other young mechanics. Living this way, he had entered aircraft mechanics school in Denver, his hometown, after dropping out of the University of Colorado in his junior year. He had been on full scholarship at the university, seeking a bachelor's degree in engineering technology, but in his junior year, his grades had descended to Bs and Cs. He was in danger of losing the scholarship, and he quit before that could happen. "I was burned out, tired of theory and of Martian mathematics and physics," he told me. "I decided that it was time to see how things really worked, how they went together and really functioned in the world. My interest in airplanes drew me into an aircraft mechanics program."

During the two years of schooling in mechanics, he supported himself by working as a baggage handler at United Airlines. As soon as he received his license, in the summer of 1997, United sent him to its maintenance center in San Francisco. Eighteen months later he transferred to Indianapolis. "The Midwest was much more suited to my personality," Erin wrote in an autobiographical sketch that he e-mailed to me.

Erin Brown and Stacy had married on September 15, 2001, four days after 9/11. He was twenty-seven, a lanky, friendly man, and she five years older. Within a month, United Airlines, reeling from the crisis, offered a limited number of voluntary, unpaid furloughs until air travel revived. Erin took one, grateful for the respite. He would continue to accrue seniority and maintain his health insurance, but he would free himself from a particularly difficult situation, and he would have time to explore opportunities less narrow, as he put it, than being an aircraft mechanic.

His skills had won him a promotion to an inspector's slot at United in the fall of 2000. That was a notch above line mechanic, but his new duties made him a target of the airline's managers, who blamed inspectors for exacerbating the mechanics' slowdown, then in full swing. Inspectors, members of the Machinists like the line mechanics, jumped automatically to the top of the pay scale and had the power to slow production. If they faulted some aspect of the overhaul and pointed this out in writing, the shortcoming had to be corrected or the write-up challenged. Either alternative extended the time an aircraft was out of service. Erin did not write up nonexistent maintenance defects, he assured me. He wrote up real ones, but in a conscientious, well-documented manner, so that management could not easily override his reports. "I used to reference the maintenance manual or some other maintenance document," Erin said. "That made it very difficult for them to undo because if they were to sign off on the repair despite my report, then they were basically saying that the documents were incorrect."

There was another aspect of the skirmish with management that contributed to Erin's alienation. The 737 chronically suffered minor cracks along the forward bulkhead, a structural defect that showed up so frequently in the 737 fleet that Boeing eventually required every airline to fix it. But for a while the repair was made only when inspectors caught it, which Erin often did. "If you wrote it up, they asked why were you even in the front bulkhead," he said. "You had to kind of come up with another task that you were performing in the same area and say I was doing this and I saw the crack."

All this conflict came as Erin was pushing for still another promotion, this time to the engineering department at the maintenance center, capitalizing on the bachelor's in engineering technology that he had finally earned, taking classes in his off-hours at the Indianapolis campus of Purdue University. As an engineer, he would receive a fixed weekly salary, higher than his current earnings, and the work would be Monday through Friday, mostly nine to five. "The day before I was to be interviewed for an engineering position," he said, "I was called to one of my supervisors' offices. I was notified that he had placed a letter of concern in my employee record accusing me of participating in a slowdown. The accusation was baseless and the letter was later removed, but I couldn't obtain a position as an engineer."

Not that he was all that impressed with the people in the engineering department, which established the maintenance procedures that guided the mechanics. A few had formal engineering degrees, but most did not, Erin said. "They got in through the politics of the situation and they were reluctant to bring in someone who had more potential to move up faster than they could." The letter in his file, in any case, had closed off promotion to engineering, and his experiences as an inspector had left him angry and unhappy. Forced to take sides, he had sided with the mechanics, although not out of great loyalty to his colleagues. In the struggle that had erupted, he did not want management to get the upper hand. "If they're doing nothing but kicking you in the head, I don't think you want to turn around and help them," he said.

The voluntary furlough lasted fifteen months. He came back just days before he was permanently, and involuntarily, laid off. "They had to call me back so they could give me twenty days' official notice of the lay-off," Erin said. He seemed not to care. The leave had already distanced him from United; the layoff was more like an extension of the leave than a damaging rejection, or so he said. That was not the case, as Stacy eventually realized. Despite all the obstacles and the conflict that Erin had encountered at United, he intended to go back and make a success of himself at the airline. "He always knew that he was going to go back," Stacy said to me months later, "and then when that door was just closed on him, I don't know what went off in his mind." The arrival of their son, Kyle, hid the damage, apparently from Erin himself. For the next six months Erin, Stacy, and Kyle were home together; she on maternity leave and Erin in the early months of his layoff, optimistically planning his future.

While she nurtured the child, he began to remodel their home, with an eye to selling it at a handsome profit. The Browns lived in a gracious three-story Victorian house that Erin had purchased for $100,000 in 1999, while still a bachelor. It was in disrepair but situated in a promising downtown neighborhood of similar homes that had been inhabited four generations earlier by the city's wealthiest families. Young professionals and executives were moving in and a revival was under way. Erin was an early arrival and now, out of work, he talked of buying other homes in the neighborhood and renovating them with his own capable hands. His home had nearly doubled in value in the four years he had owned it, Erin figured, and his renovations would increase the value even more. A new second-floor bathroom was under construction when I met Erin and Stacy in the spring of 2003, and Erin had pulled open walls everywhere in the house so that insulation could be inserted prior to remodeling. The jewel of this project was a two-story carriage house, suitable for rental, that Erin was adding to the property. It rose from the concrete slab foundation of what had once been a carport fronting on an alley at the far end of the backyard. The construction was well along, although the exterior was still sheets of unpainted plywood awaiting another layer of siding, while inside the stud framing was entirely exposed.

Erin assured me then that the work was moving along quickly and would soon be done. He was getting plenty of encouragement from Stacy. They could rent the carriage house as a studio to one of the artists or artisans moving into the neighborhood, or they could use it as offices for their own ventures. He seemed confident that he could make a go in real estate, buying, renovating, and reselling homes while Stacy became a stay-at-home mom. Despite her success as a litigator, she had tired of the long hours. From the start of their marriage, they had agreed that one of them would always be present for the children they wanted to have; they would not employ a nanny or use day care. She would be the chief caregiver, once Erin earned a living again. Both being the children of divorced parents, they wanted to invest their energies in close family ties. "It's great to feel important and make a good income," Stacy said, "but at the end of the day, if you don't have a strong family, how happy are you going to be? So that's at least our philosophy about life and it is working for us."

One evening after dinner, which Erin cooked on a charcoal grill set up in the narrow side yard, he walked me down his street to show me two large houses that the neighborhood association had purchased at a foreclosure sale, one for $75,000, the other for $55,000. These had been resold to families, in each case for $15,000 markups, and without a nickel invested in improvements, Erin said. He had considered purchasing the less expensive home and converting it into three large apartments. "In this neighborhood, those apartments would have brought $700 apiece in monthly rent," he said. He regretted not having moved faster than the neighborhood association, a delay that in hindsight turned out to be an early signal of his reluctance to take risks, a side effect of the layoff. For an investment of only $100,000 to purchase the home and subdivide it into nicely appointed apartments, Erin would have enjoyed a huge return, 25 percent a year before expenses, he estimated. He would not miss the next opportunity, he said. Like Tim Dewey, he would fashion his own independence. But as the months passed he did not. And when Stacy went back to work at the end of her maternity leave, earning $80,000 a year as a senior associate at a prestigious Indianapolis law firm, Erin became the full-time caregiver. They yearned to switch roles, but that was hard to do. Stacy reduced her schedule to only three days a week, but then, under pressure from her firm, she agreed to four days, which spilled over into five. "I try not to work on Fridays," she told me, "but I am always checking in and answering calls."

A year later, Kyle was nineteen months old, chubby, active, and sociable. Erin had proven to be a first-rate caregiver. But as Erin and Stacy brought me up to date on their lives, there was an urgency and anxiety in the tale that spilled out of them, as if I were a counselor who might help them get back on track. Erin admitted to a reluctance to search for a job. He described the opportunity that had arisen to take over a plumbing business in Bloomington, ninety miles south of Indianapolis, where Stacy's mother, father, and stepfather lived, along with other relatives. Erin had backed away from the opportunity, which Stacy's family had helped to arrange. He would have to depend on the goodwill of a licensed partner while he waited the required two years to qualify for his plumber's license, he explained. That was too risky, he said; the partner could walk out on him before the two years were up. Stacy, listening quietly to her husband tell me this tale, observed that for all his optimistic talk about running his own business, he balked at each opportunity to do so.

By then he had been out of work for sixteen months. The entrepreneurial career that he had expected to slip easily into after losing his job at United had not materialized; their plans for him to be the breadwinner and she the caregiver were on hold. They were proud that their nonspending ways would allow them to live on one income: his—assuming he had any income at all. That was now becoming a concern. "Erin is really very strong at pushing other people to take risks," Stacy said, "but when you ask him to take a risk, like, okay, let's open a business, he's very fearful. And I think it is a real disconnect that he doesn't quite see." She was just beginning to realize herself that Erin's aversion to risk was not inborn, but an emotionally driven response to the layoff, a fear of throwing himself into another endeavor and failing again.

Her workload meant that Erin spent many hours caring for Kyle and that became an excuse not to hunt for a job. Stacy would ask her husband if he had found time during the day to look for work. She did not do that often, but the pressure was there and he finally applied for two openings that he found on the Internet. They were jobs for engineers. He landed one of the two jobs, at SAIC, a military contractor, but rejected the offer: the starting pay was only $37,000 a year, which Erin ruled out as too little even for his and Stacy's skimpy budget.

The other job, as an engineer at a nearby Rolls-Royce plant, paid enough—more than $45,000, including overtime—but Erin did not get it, and came away soured that the interviewer, a bureaucrat in Erin's eyes, had failed to recognize his potential value to the company, including the proficiency he had acquired, on his own, as a machinist, although he had no formal experience and no certification as one. "I had 95 percent of what they wanted on paper and they weren't willing to make a good faith leap on the remaining 5 percent," Erin said. He was angry that Rolls-Royce would not spring for the small cost of training him, if that turned out to be necessary. "They do not want to make an investment in people," he declared. "They think people are a necessary evil." To which Stacy added, speaking gently, standing behind her seated husband, her hand on his shoulder: "These couple of forays that he has tried back into the corporate world have only given him more fuel for his beliefs that that is not the way to go."

His efforts as a real estate entrepreneur had stopped. No rundown home in the neighborhood had been purchased for renovation and resale or rental. The carriage house in the backyard had not been touched for months, and the remodeling of their own home was also far behind schedule. The many hours spent caring for Kyle, Erin explained, had not left him with enough free time to make any progress on the carriage house or the remodeling. "The daily routine here is pretty all-encompassing," he said. Only the bathroom, on the second floor at the head of the stairs, had been finished, and Erin had done an elegant job; glistening white tiles, meticulously laid, covered all four walls to the ceiling. Here was the handiwork of an artisan, but also evidence, in Stacy's view, of Erin's irresolution. The wood molding had not been installed. Even in this undertaking, the completion of a bathroom that his own family needed, Erin did not plunge fully back into the world of achievement, and for Stacy that was a signal that she could not leave her job until her husband was once again on more solid emotional ground. "I suspect one of his biggest concerns, holding him back, is that he feels he will have great trouble supporting our family, at least in the style that I can," Stacy later told me.

They did not offer me dinner on this visit, or sit down themselves to eat. Stacy soon disappeared upstairs to bathe Kyle and put him to bed, and Erin and I sat talking at the dining room table, purchased second-hand like much of the furniture in this once elegant, high-ceilinged house. He was taking a class two nights a week in heating and air-conditioning repair, his thought being that he could work as a repairman in his free time, earning $13 or $14 an hour. He seemed to be trying to get back into work with as little emotional commitment as possible, not wanting to suffer again the rebuff that he had experienced at United. "When I met him," Stacy later told me in an e-mail, "he really loved his job there and had a ton of energy and enthusiasm for life."

As we talked, Erin explained what would force him back to work. Stacy's growing concerns worried him. If their situation made her miserable, he said, then he would simply take a job, any job, despite his reluctance, so that she could quit and stay home. And then he mentioned an option that, like heating and air-conditioning repair, would protect him from a rekindling of career aspirations. If she stayed home, he would sort freight part-time at Federal Express for $10 an hour, a lifeline that other mechanics had grabbed. That would give the family health insurance coverage in place of the insurance that Stacy's firm now provided, and he would make ends meet by drawing on his and Stacy's considerable savings to supplement the insufficient pay. "I would work on the house, finish the renovation, while working their ten p.m. to two a.m. shift, or something like that," Erin said.

In his unhappiness, he was sending himself backward, erasing each year of his advancement at United Airlines until he was back, mentally at least, at that first job, as a baggage handler for United in Denver. Baggage handling is roughly the equivalent of sorting air-freight packages for FedEx. "You throw boxes for a while, you get your benefits paid, and you know you have the potential if something comes up because they are growing the facility here in Indy," he said, trying to inject opportunity into his surrender. "You know, if a mechanic's slot comes up, you bid it."

CHAPTER FIVE

The Shock, Part 2

Until she lost her own job, Virginia Gibbs had nurtured employees. That was the nature of personnel work when she joined Macy's in 1965, soon after graduation from Simmons College in Boston. The whole idea was to help people manage their careers without leaving Macy's. "Someone could start out as a salesperson in the glove department and be promoted until they were furniture salespeople on straight commissions earning a lot of money," Gibbs said, remembering what for her was a better era. The emphasis was on retention and advancement, if not through promotion then through rising incomes. Millions of retail salespeople in those days thought of themselves as career employees, and that was still the case at Macy's in 1987 when Gibbs, having risen to vice president of employee relations for the New York division, decided to change companies, and industries, in midcareer.

She was in her early forties, married and childless, an articulate, energetic, and self-confident woman with short, thick black hair who favored, when I met her later, brightly colored scarves that she draped over her shoulders, enlivening the knitted suits and sweater sets that she often wore. She had tired of retailing and she had persuaded herself that if she did not make a career change soon to a different industry, the opportunity would be lost forever. "I had to decide whether I wanted to stay in retailing for the rest of my life, which I really did not," she said.

Looking around, she soon attracted Citibank's attention, and she landed there as an executive in human resources at a six-figure salary, arriving just as the transfer of back-office operations to lower-wage cities was gathering steam. Not long after Gibbs made her move, Federated Department Stores acquired the Macy's chain and layoffs ensued, as usual to help pay the costs of the acquisition. Later Gibbs's former colleagues told her that she had been so smart to see what was coming. But Gibbs had not foreseen what was coming, or that for the rest of her career she would be going against the grain.

At Citibank, she soon found herself nurturing the victims of the back-office outsourcing, applying the standards she had developed at Macy's. Most of the back-office workers processed checks or were operators in Citibank's customer-call centers, then mostly in New York City. They weren't simply laid off. Gibbs would arrange transfers within the company for those who were displaced or, if that was not possible, she would try to get them work elsewhere in New York. "We talked to our HR counterparts at other companies, who maybe were still growing and hiring," Gibbs said, "and we put together books of résumés and sent them out."

This was not subversive activity. Citibank's management encouraged her endeavors. The old concerns for steady employment that had been built into the American system still governed behavior, although less so each year. They were certainly bred into Gibbs, who soon found herself in the strange position of ministering to the displaced New York City workers while overseeing the recruitment of new people in Buffalo, New York, and Tampa, Florida, to staff the operations that were being shifted to those cities.

As a matter of policy, Citibank offered transfers to the soon-to-be-unemployed workers, on the assumption that not more than 30 percent would accept the offers, and those who did would help train the new local hires. The cost would be manageable, even allowing the transferees to retain their New York salaries. That had been the case for the first transfers, to Nebraska, where Citibank had been a pioneer in setting up a call center for credit card customers, and it was the case for Buffalo—but not Tampa. Living in Florida, near the beach, had an appeal, and rather than 30 percent, nearly 50 percent of the 350 employees whose jobs migrated from New York to Tampa raised their hands to go, too. Citibank stipulated, as it always did, that their wages would be frozen, and the employees agreed, but they soon asked for raises anyway, and in general set themselves apart from the people hired in Tampa at lower wages. Or, as Gibbs put it, "Two wage scales, two cultures, two everything, which becomes problematic over time."

The Tampa experience stiffened Citibank and its parent, Citicorp.

They continued to shift back-office clerical work and call-center opera-tions to lower-wage American cities—and also to Dublin, Ireland, a proj-ect that Gibbs herself directed. But the bank ceased offering transfers to the New York employees whose jobs left town. Still, Gibbs in the late eighties and early nineties worked at redeploying these workers within the bank. "We did not have a central hiring area, but a good, seasoned HR person could get on the phone and find out where in the company they were hiring," she said.

She even organized in-house training centers to prepare employees for different jobs within the bank—employees who without her efforts would very probably have been laid off. She drew praise for her work, and she came to think of herself as valuable to Citibank. Her efforts, she argued much later to me, lessened the damage to Citicorp's reputation as an employer. "You didn't want them talking about what a terrible place Citicorp was to work," she said, "and so, to the best of your ability, even if you had to separate an employee, you wanted to send them out, maybe not agreeing with what's happened to them—I was not that Pollyanna—but at least understanding what had happened and why, and in the case of layoffs, knowing that HR did everything it possibly could to help them."

That did not last. The openings at other companies for Citibank's displaced workers soon disappeared. Too many other firms, particularly in financial services, were mimicking Citibank's outsourcing practices. "The options for placement, whether it was internally or externally, kept shrinking because everybody in New York was now doing the same thing, sending the jobs away," Gibbs said. Her work nevertheless earned her a slot in 1997 in an elite group of HR executives whose job it was to range across Citicorp, helping HR managers in line jobs solve particularly thorny problems. In doing so, they set common standards for all the line managers. Gibbs was at the top of her game, age fifty-four, earning in the six figures. And then it was over.

A year into Gibbs's new assignment, Travelers Group acquired Citi-corp, creating the largest banking organization in the United States, and soon Gibbs realized that she had become as disposable as the back-office workers she had often helped. Sanford I. Weill, the new chairman of the merged giant, which was renamed Citigroup, and his top executives, saw no useful role for a corporate-level human resources team trying, as Gibbs put it, "to bring structure or similarity or common things." The separate line operations could handle personnel; that was enough. And the money saved would improve Citigroup's profitability, helping to justify, and pay for, the $73 billion spent on the merger.

Robert Lipp delivered the message that canceled the elite HR team to which Gibbs belonged. Lipp, a former vice chairman of Chemical Bank, a bank later merged out of existence, had joined Weill in 1986 when Weill was just beginning to build his corporate empire through acquisitions. Along the way, Lipp had stood out as the cost-cutting lieutenant who made the acquisitions more profitable, and he outlined the plans for the new Citigroup in an interview for an article in the January 1999 issue of *Fortune* magazine. The old Citicorp had too many people doing unnecessary things, Lipp told the writer. "We want to have more people selling instead of watching people sell and fewer human resources people watching—God only knows what they watch."

The Lipp pronouncement altered Virginia Gibbs's life as if she were a planet struck by a meteor. The profession she practiced no longer existed, not at the company that employed her. "You have to understand," Gibbs told me, "that from an HR professional's point of view, whose whole profession is about helping companies attract and retain and motivate the best possible people and make it the best possible work experience for the individual, what Lipp did essentially says, Everything you think is important and do for your life's work, isn't. To have someone senior in the company say that so bluntly in public is terrible."

Gibbs, who was fifty-six then, did not leave right away. After the *Fortune* article, she remained for more than two years, hanging on while her team of elite HR executives gradually disappeared. "They didn't think the team had any function, even in trying to prevent people from bringing lawsuits and discrimination claims," she said. Now that Gibbs's work was gone, Citigroup put an early retirement package on the table, as if she were a doomed prisoner offered a pistol to execute herself. And she took it, not even trying to maneuver herself into some other job, assuming that would have been possible. "The last thing I ever wanted to do in any company would be to stay and become one of those sort of, you know, bitter, disgruntled people who is always talking about the way it used to be," she said.

The defeat that Gibbs experienced is not uncommon among workers her age, who entered the workforce in the sixties and seventies when long-term employment was still a given. Younger people were not immune either to this sense of defeat, not if they had performed well for an employer and thought they were valued. But by the early nineties, most of those who still saw themselves this way were white-collar employees with some years at the jobs. Layoffs were just making inroads in their ranks after decimating blue-collar workers for more than a decade. In addition, white-collar employees were more likely than blue-collar workers to see their corporate performance as a personal achievement, and that often intensified the shock of layoffs. Gibbs thought that way. "The work that I did was no less a profession than doctor or lawyer," she insisted. The abrupt cancellation unraveled her professional life. Like many others, she scrambled to fill the void with new forms of importance, but none restored her old sense of herself. The forced separation from Citigroup sent her into a diaspora occupied today by tens of millions of Americans who, whatever the form of their particular layoff, rarely shake off the effects. Despite their efforts to repair the damage, the experience is incorporated into their outlook.

I ran into that over and over. My conversations with men and women who had been laid off often lasted for two hours or more, until we tired. Their layoff experiences remained unresolved in their minds, and perhaps cannot be. Several psychiatrists I asked to explain the syndrome gave explanations similar to that of Dr. Theodore Jacobs, the psychoanalyst and professor of psychiatry in New York. A small number of people, he said, have the capacity to blame their layoffs on forces outside themselves and beyond their control. Most people, however, blame themselves, and that is reinforced by the social thinking of the day, which insists that people are responsible for their own employability. Self-blame flourishes in such a petri dish, feeding on personality traits embedded since childhood. "People who, growing up, experience some sense of personal rejection, or throughout their lives feel they have not lived up to their own standards or the standards of others, and those who by nature tend to be self-blaming, they are at risk," Dr. Jacobs said.

Logic suggests that Gibbs should have no scars. Money was not a problem. She has more than enough in savings and pension to live com-

fortably, she assured me. Her husband, in addition, still earned a living in
the export-import business. They rented a comfortable Manhattan apartment and owned a summer home in the Hamptons. No one meeting
Gibbs on the street or talking casually with her over lunch in a restaurant
would have guessed that she had been laid off and had suffered as a result.

Even the statistics camouflaged her experience. She showed up in
the "worker displacement" surveys of the Bureau of Labor Statistics as
voluntarily retired, not laid off, which helps to explain why federal data
undercount layoffs and, in doing so, help to hide the damage. Lipp's dec-
laration, however, was unmistakably a layoff—a cancellation of Gibbs's
services and professional skills—and she dwelt on what he had done to
her every time we spoke. "Maybe what he said was correct from a business
point of view," Gibbs said, trying to sound reasonable. "But a lot of people like me don't want to work in an environment where what you do isn't
viewed as valuable."

The early retirement package included, as balm, a fully paid stay at
Right Management Consultants, the nation's largest outplacement company, with more than 150 offices in cities across the country. Big corporations like Citigroup hire outplacement firms to help their laid-off
executives and middle managers get work again. In doing so, they
lessen the likelihood of legal action and place the responsibility for reemployment on the victims, who are told, in effect, that here are the tools
to get another job: use them.

Gibbs enrolled at Right's Manhattan office, which occupies the four-
teenth floor of a modern midtown skyscraper. The location was new. In
place of the warren of enclosed offices and cubicles, where the downsized
of a few years back kept to themselves in their furtive pursuit of jobs, the
new space was well-lit with open areas for people to gather, and cubicles
and conference rooms whose glass partitions put the occupants on display
to anyone walking along the hallways. Layoffs are out of the closet, the
interior design declared. You deal with them openly and collegially in
Right's pleasant, carpeted, pastel surroundings. That was the interior
design talking. The inmates sent a different message. They were still
furtive. Passing them in the halls or walking by the office cubicles with
their big display windows, I tried to make eye contact and rarely could.
Eyes were averted. What struck me was how quiet these dispossessed

were, and with good reason. They had six months in most cases, as much as a year for a few, to land a job before their time at Right ended and they lost even this semblance of their old office life.

Most of the discussions in the conference rooms were bland exchanges of information about various job-hunting techniques, particularly networking, which means endlessly calling friends or friends of friends or anyone you ever met or whose name you could get who might offer you a job or steer you to someone who might be hiring. Once in a while in these discussions someone spoke angrily and bitterly about his or her situation. When I mentioned these outbursts to Andrea G. Eisenberg, then the manager of Right's Manhattan operation, she would explain that the people involved were newcomers, their layoffs recent and still raw. Right's services include individual job counseling, and one of the tasks of the counselors is to restrain people from going out on job interviews until their anger no longer shows in their demeanor. "An optimistic front is essential," Eisenberg said.

Gibbs was beyond anger or optimism. She did not want corporate employment again. She was not alone in making this decision. A noticeable number coming through Right balked at going back, unwilling to expose themselves to the risk of another demeaning layoff. Most were in their fifties and could afford to balk. They had accumulated at least $1.5 million in savings and were receiving or would soon receive from their former employers pensions of $50,000 to $100,000 a year, enough to get them through old age, they said, if they lived carefully. That put Eisenberg on the spot. She did not want to lose payments from their former employers for outplacement service. So she organized what she called the "portfolio group," eight or nine participants who met every other Monday and, sitting around a conference table, spent ninety minutes jointly exploring what they really wanted to do with the rest of their lives: what they would include in their "personal portfolios."

I met Gibbs at one of these sessions, and also Kenneth Halajian, an ex–publishing company executive who had been battered by mergers and new technologies and now focused resolutely on peace of mind: fly-fishing for trout, singing in his church choir, becoming a vestryman engaged in balancing the church's budget, participating in a book club, helping an old woman in his neighborhood sell her home, volunteering for "stream maintenance" at Rockefeller State Park, not far from his home. "I go to the movies, I read books (mostly paperback novels checked out of the library), I hike, I go to the symphony, the opera, museums," he said.

Halajian's wife, Jean, told me that it took her a year to get used to having her husband at home. Among other things, he managed people at the office, and he had to learn not to manage his family's daily routines. His two sons, still in high school, were "stunned and silent," Halajian said, when he announced during dinner one evening in June 2000 that he was no longer going to hold a job. They liked to mention to schoolmates that their father was an executive at an important company; the father's importance gave them status. But Halajian felt compelled not to work, and he forced the adjustment on his family, even agreeing to cook dinner during the week while his wife prepared the weekend meals, reversing the practice that had prevailed through Halajian's working years.

The numerous activities he now engaged in were all substitutes for the satisfactions that had been drained from his work. The company that employed him was going through constant change and consolidation. His own job would soon disappear. He had become certain of that. He hated waiting for it to happen. So he provoked his own layoff at the age of fifty-three and withdrew, giving up a salary of $160,000 and getting a year at Right Management as a departure present, although he postponed actually using the various services until Eisenberg, whom he knew socially, invited him to join the portfolio group.

Halajian is a lawyer, a couple of inches short of six feet tall and overweight, with a neatly trimmed dark beard. He was casually dressed in yard clothes at each of our meetings, even in Manhattan. The family lived in what once was a farmhouse and is now an old clapboard home, painted white, sitting on a broad piece of property and surrounded by much newer homes in Briarcliff Manor, New York, a suburb north of Manhattan. Halajian had spent his career in legal publishing, all of it at Matthew Bender & Company, once a family firm headquartered in New York but owned by the Times Mirror Company when Halajian joined in 1974, just out of Boston College Law School.

Bender produces and publishes articles that interpret the constantly changing law. Bender's publications on admiralty law or on bankruptcy, for example, were well-known reference books. Over the years, Halajian rose to editor in chief and also to a vice presidency that straddled marketing and editorial content. Technology brought on the upheaval that eventually ended in Halajian's departure. It forced Bender to switch its delivery system from books to CDs and electronic databases—and management, in response, initiated a reorganization, starting in 1992, that eliminated eight hundred of the two thousand employees. Halajian supervised the layoffs and six months into the process found himself in a hospital suffering from angina, which his doctors treated with angioplasty. He blamed stress for the heart trouble. "They had done nothing wrong in their jobs," he said of the employees he had laid off, "but we needed computer people and technicians, and to make room for them, we had to let the others go."

Feeling vulnerable himself, and guilty, Halajian made an extra effort to build up his savings, in case he had to leave early, too, and when that finally happened in 2000, he had put away just over $2 million, an amount that soon fell to $1.8 million as the stock market dropped. Once the severance payment ran out, Halajian and his wife found themselves drawing down $100,000 a year from their savings to pay for their sons' college educations as well as health insurance, which in 2005 cost $1,400 a month, and daily living expenses. At sixty-five, he would qualify for a $75,000 pension from the Times Mirror Company, in addition to Social Security and Medicare. He refused to consider that his savings might not last that long. He would become a public school teacher if necessary, he said, to get the health insurance. That rising cost worried him.

For all his stated pleasure in his new life, Halajian did one day acknowledge that he would probably still be a Bender executive if only Times Mirror had remained the owner of the company. Instead, Reed Elsevier, a British-Dutch publishing giant, acquired Matthew Bender in 1998. Reed Elsevier already owned LexisNexis, a vastly larger legal research database. That meant consolidation to eliminate duplication, and Halajian became involved in the process of folding Bender into the LexisNexis Group. As the consolidation proceeded, his own job became hard to justify. His duties could be transferred to someone else, he realized, or that person's to him. It was a crapshoot. "If I could see that the position that I held was not necessary to the efficient running of the company," Halajian said, "then someone else would see it too." He told his bosses before they could tell him. They agreed and he asked for a severance package. They wanted him to stay, but in an assignment away from New York. Halajian did not want to move. "My wife and I talked and we felt we had enough money saved to make it," he said.

So he left, and at meetings of the portfolio group he described the pleasures of his liberated life. Phyllis E. Tama, a senior vice president at Right Management, who chaired the portfolio group sessions, listened impassively to such talk. "If someone came to him with the right job," she told me, "he'd take it in a millisecond. But he does not want to admit that to himself. So he convinces himself that he is happy."

Virginia Gibbs is more up-front. Set loose from Citigroup, she had gotten into volunteer work, although less compulsively than Halajian, and she, too, went regularly to museums and the theater. But she also landed several consulting jobs, mostly at not-for-profit organizations in need of HR help. "I missed using my professional ability; I just missed that," Gibbs told me. As a girl, she had studied tap dancing and had aspired for a while to dance on Broadway. The portfolio group, hearing this, encouraged her to join a tap dancing class, to make that part of her personal portfolio, just as Halajian had been encouraged to take up fly-fishing. And Gibbs did, going once a week to the Broadway Dance Center. She justified the classes in her own mind as healthy exercise. But her classmates included a few younger, semiprofessional dancers, and that lifted the experience above mere exercise. "When we get our steps, we're all tapping in unison, I can close my eyes and think, I'm in the chorus of *42nd Street*," she said. "It's great."

For six months after she left Citigroup, Gibbs, closing her eyes, could also imagine that the skills she had first developed in the sixties and seventies, particularly the techniques for maintaining employee morale and loyalty, were still valued at Citigroup. They would ask her for help in a crisis, she told herself. And then immediately after September 11, 2001, when the attack on the World Trade Center endangered a number of Citigroup employees, she surrendered that last illusion. "Our old HR group would have been kind of at the center of things in terms of giving advice on policy decisions relating to employees," she said. She thought that surely former colleagues would call her "for my input," tapping her expertise in dealing with the crisis. No one called. "For the first time," Gibbs said, "I realized that I missed being needed in that organization. I really had not missed it; I had enjoyed the extended vacation too much. And suddenly it dawned on me that I really did miss it."

•   •   •

Stephen A. Holthausen is a different kind of exile. He still cannot believe that his success as a bank loan officer, and his standing in his community, failed to protect him from the layoff that took him by surprise on Monday morning, August 13, 1990. What happened to him was the age of layoffs at its cruelest, theatrically cruel. Here was a vice president for business lending at the New England Savings Bank in New London, Connecticut, the co-chairman of the board of trustees of the Congregational church in nearby Westbrook, his hometown, the vice chairman of the police advisory board, a past president of the Junior Chamber of Commerce, just forty-six years old, who got swept away in a staff reduction to save money.

The ax fell on his first day back from a two-week family vacation in Maine. His immediate boss wanted him gone that very Monday morning, but a higher officer granted Holthausen's request for a two-week reprieve so that he could respond to the mail that had piled up during the vacation and clean up pending matters with customers. He was told that his position as vice president for business lending was eliminated, and he was too. But toward the end of the two weeks, he met the twenty-two-year-old who had taken over his duties, and who was earning less than Holthausen. "I was costing them $50,000 plus health insurance plus group life insurance plus stock options; I had all that stuff," he said. "I was not terminated for failure, or putting my hand in the cookie jar. They just took the most expensive people and tossed them out. I was on the wrong end of the numbers."

It was a classic downsizing in which the victim, Holthausen, after twenty-two years in banking, sporting a résumé that chronicled successes, was told in effect that his cost outstripped his value, and he had to go. Never mind that New England Savings profited from Holthausen's lending activity. The $15 million in loans he had negotiated that were then on the books earned enough interest income for the bank to cover his salary, benefits, and bonus and also earn a profit, even allowing for defaults, Holthausen contended. "It's a dumb strategy not to look at income stream; there are other ways to positively affect the bottom line other than the elimination of salary and personnel," he argued to me more than once, making his case, to himself and to me, that he was the victim of false economy, not lack of value.

Virginia Gibbs got roughly the same message, but while she shunned another round of employment, Holthausen did not. For one thing, he needed income; his savings were insufficient. In addition, his sense of himself was too intertwined with his job. He did eventually get steady work again, as a full-time employee of the State of Connecticut's Office of Tourism. He even managed to view his new job as requiring the same "reaching out" to people that in his view had made him a successful banker. That former career remained his standard. He couldn't seem to exorcise the shock of losing it so arbitrarily. "My job and my hobby were banking, and that was a mistake," Holthausen said, trying to explain why the loss had affected him so much. "I would go to a wake and pass out business cards."

As a banker, he had survived two mergers, and the cost-cutting that inevitably followed. He attributed his survival to the strengths that he brought to his work. These were a combination of salesmanship and civic involvement, including the many shallow relationships that good salesmen cultivate. "I have the gift of gab," Holthausen explained, obviously pleased to possess that talent. His civic activities brought him borrowers from his community, and his status in banking gave him standing in Westbrook, a small southern Connecticut town of mostly middle-income families like the Holthausens. He thought he had survived the third merger, in October 1988. That merger made New England Savings the owner of his employer, First Federal Savings. But banks everywhere in the country were in trouble, in many cases in danger of folding. They had made too many bad loans in the eighties, and the nation soon tipped into recession, compounding the pressure on them. New England Savings, in response, continued to cut costs, and when Holthausen lost his job, the stature that he had acquired from his mixture of banking and civic activity collapsed. But not right away.

He had thought that he could take his customers with him to another bank; their regard for him would keep them loyal. "They did not care what bank's name was on the loan documents or on their deposit slips as long as I was their banker," he said. The recession and the banking crisis blocked that strategy before he could test it; he could not get another job in banking. After his severance ran out, he did work for a while as a consultant to the Saybrook Bank and Trust Company, giving advice on how to deal with loans in default, but Saybrook failed in December 1991. At home, his already shaky marriage collapsed, brought down finally by the layoff. To this day, Holthausen remains critical of his ex-wife, Diane, for failing to provide emotional support and faith in her husband's skills, just as he is forever critical of New England Savings for failing to value his earning power as a loan officer.

Feeling panicky, Diane Holthausen solicited food packages from the Westbrook Congregational Church, although her husband was then co-chairman of the board of trustees, and compounded this humiliation by asking the minister and several parishioners for money, telling them the family was destitute. Years later, their daughter, Gretchen, by then out of college and working as a research assistant at Yale University's School of Medicine, in the psychiatry department, offered a more nuanced explanation of that devastating period in which neither parent gave comfort to the other. "My father's job and income and health benefits were so much a part of our lives that we did not recognize where they came from until they ended," she told me. "My mother was so shocked by the layoff and she blamed my father because she did not know anyone else to blame. She could not be angry at the bank because it was not part of our lives any longer. She was frustrated with herself because she had no other source of income, and she blamed him because he was putting the family through so much hardship."

Diane Holthausen did in fact qualify for food stamps and the church did make donations. She and the couple's two teenage children stayed in the house while Holthausen himself moved to the upstairs apartment of a two-family house owned by his brother, who gave him a discount on the rent. Tapping his scant savings and borrowing against his 401(k), Holthausen managed to keep up the mortgage payments on the family home, and he also helped to pay for utilities. His mother provided money, too, and she later set up college funds for Gretchen's education and that of her brother, Christian. (Gretchen graduated from Bryn Mawr, Christian from Vassar.) But their father slid steadily down the economic ladder. He pumped gas for a while at a station owned by a former bank customer, drove a car for a salesman who had lost his license for drunken driving, got paid to be a guinea pig in the testing of a prescription drug, and did odd jobs as a handyman until a ladder fell while he was trimming trees and he broke his arm. For a while, he was treated at a Veterans Administration hospital for depression.

In the year after his layoff, Holthausen gradually resigned from his various civic posts, each time receiving a letter expressing regret, letters that he collected and showed to me. He had put together a feel-good portfolio, archeological evidence of a better life now destroyed. One letter in particular reflected Holthausen's own sense of himself, the person he wanted to be again. The writer was Lisa M. Jernberg, vice president of marketing for New England Savings. She had been a colleague at work and a fellow participant in Westbrook's civic life. "His involvement is never limited to showing up for one or two meetings," she wrote, addressing her letter "To Whom It May Concern" and dating it just ten days after her employer, New England Savings, fired Holthausen. "This highly respected member of the community can be found moving furniture at Dream Auctions for retarded children, passing out balloons or candy at local parades, participating in phonathons for local hospitals. He will always help if asked. On a personal note, Steve has guided me through some difficult personal times. Similarly, he has been a mentor and a friend to many other people throughout his career. Although he may sometimes mask his caring behind an entertaining sense of humor, you can always count on the fact that he will be there when you need him."

I met Holthausen in the fall of 1995, first through telephone interviews and then in person on a rainy November afternoon at the tourist information center along Interstate 95 in North Stonington, just over the Rhode Island line. He is a balding, chubby man of medium height, dressed that day in nondescript slacks and a loose-fitting woolen sweater with a crew neck. He was seated behind a horseshoe-shaped reception counter stocked with tourist brochures. By then, layoffs were rising in the United States more quickly among white-collar than blue-collar workers. Holthausen was an early white-collar victim, and his story illustrated the growing reality that jobs could be lost and lives forever changed no matter what the jobholder's skill or his value to a company or his middle-class credentials.

Holthausen had finally converted part-time work at the tourist center into a full-time state job, although eight years would pass before his salary climbed back to the $50,000 he had earned in his last year at New England Savings. Like so many others of his generation who ran head-on into layoffs they never anticipated, he nevertheless learned to live with his misfortune, and so did his family. His children, who had shunned him at first, in time reestablished relations, in part because parents of school friends were also laid off and the experience became familiar. Holthausen's wife, Diane, took a job as a special education teacher in a public school, ministering to autistic children, and her income was enough for her to take over the mortgage payments. "My mother really struggled with redefining herself," Gretchen told me, "and she feels good about herself now."

Holthausen grew particularly close to his daughter, an honor student in high school and then at Bryn Mawr. He reveled in her achievements. Her success and her willingness to share it with her father pleased him and took some of the edge off his own downfall. So did his new career in tourism, which had finally ended the downward income slide. He thought of himself as a particularly friendly greeter and pitchman for Connecticut's tourist attractions, and he rose over the years to supervisor of the busy North Stonington center, a first stop in Connecticut for travelers coming south from Canada and the rest of New England.

It was a modest post, but he added an embellishment to his job that mimicked his banker's life, stretching his importance. Two or three times a month he changed into a dark business suit—his banker's clothes, he told me—and attended an evening reception at a hotel, museum, or restaurant. These gatherings were invariably to promote the latest wrinkle in the state's tourist attractions. There Holthausen rubbed shoulders with mayors, sometimes the governor, many businesspeople, and occasionally former customers from his banking days whom he now greeted once again. Sometimes he brought his girlfriend, a woman he had known in banking, who was still a bank officer. He was reaching out at these gatherings, a necessary task in tourism, he said: "I need to be seen to do my work."

He also felt the need to insulate himself from another humiliating layoff. In his new state job, he had almost been caught in a cost-cutting campaign and it frightened him. "Every Friday he would open his mailbox and wonder if a pink slip would be in there; he was just so anxious," Gretchen told me. Instead of Holthausen losing his job, however, his chief assistant at the North Stonington center lost hers. She had less seniority. Her last day was in mid-January 2003, and Holthausen eulogized her—and himself—in an e-mail that he sent to a dozen people in his tourism network. "Losing a person who you have worked with the better part of six years is similar to a death," he wrote. "We all have a personal family, but where do we spend most of our days? With our professional family. When one of our family is abruptly taken away from us, there is certainly a reason for us to be in shock. This should not sound like a eulogy, but rather the writings of a grateful supervisor who has been able to excel in this industry. I have been able to outreach and attend tourism functions because I knew that Nicole was handling issues of the welcome center, including scheduling of full-time and seasonal staff, brochure inventory and ordering supplies."

Two months later, Holthausen qualified for retirement. At fifty-eight, he was three years past the state's minimum retirement age, and he had finally managed to accumulate the necessary ten years of tenure: eight years actually worked and two years of credit for army service in the 1960s, a credit he spent countless hours negotiating. If the ax threatened again, he would invoke retirement before the ax actually fell, and walk away with a retiree's health insurance in his pocket, paid by the state for the rest of his life; his pension and savings would be enough to somehow get by until Social Security kicked in. Not that he wanted to retire. He could not really afford to stop working, not on a pension of about $700 a month and only $135,000 in savings, a big chunk of it recently inherited from an uncle. Nor did he want to give up a post that simulated his former banker's life. If he retired he would still look for a new job and hope that, with his health insurance paid by the state, he would be attractive to an employer eager to dodge that expense. But whether he worked again or not, he had passed in his own mind beyond the reach of arbitrary, humiliating dismissal. "They can no longer penalize me," he said. "I am all set."

He wasn't all set. Gretchen made that clear to me. She is tall and blond, with pale, delicate skin, like her father's, and was dressed casually in khaki pants and a gray shirt when we first met in the spring of 2003. She was living with a young man who would soon become her husband. Her work at Yale involved her in the treatment of women suffering from various emotional ailments and she was taking the necessary courses at night to get licensed as a school psychologist, a profession she considered relatively safe from layoff.

She had decided while at Bryn Mawr that if she did not take the lead, she and her father would drift apart. Not wanting that to happen, she made the effort, and the two now saw a lot of each other. They had gone over in great detail the terrible period in the family's life after he was laid off. In their conversations, he had dwelt on the fatal day itself, August 13, 1990, and, listening to her father, Gretchen absorbed the humiliation he felt. The humiliation, it became clear, stemmed as much from the manner in which Holthausen was replaced as it did from the layoff itself. In naming a twenty-two-year-old to take over his duties, the bank's management had nullified Holthausen's experience and skills, and his numerous community contacts and business relationships. "He still can recall exactly how he felt that day," Gretchen said, "and exactly what he was wearing that day, and the age of the kid who replaced him. I mean a person my age basically replaced my father. I mean, I think it's disgusting, I think it's disgusting."

She stopped, to get control of her emotions. We were in a nearly empty coffee shop and, lost in her thoughts, she unconsciously began to fold the paper placemat into pleats, which she ironed absently with the flat of her hand. I asked her to tell me what she was thinking, and she replied: "Just the whole process of getting laid off, all of it, my father working at a gas station. Did that affect my sense of pride? No. It didn't affect me. It affected me because it affected my father so much. Just to see that happen and watch his pain, and to know—and it's still right there under the surface. You can tap it. And even though he has gone on and, like, done very well for himself and established himself in, like, a new field, and he enjoys his job and people respect him there, and he has a lot of friends and he's close with his family and he's got a good relationship with his partner, he still has that anger in him. Has he worked through it? Yeah. I don't think he is directing it inappropriately anywhere, but it's still there. And I don't know if you can ever ask him to dispel that. Like, oh, Steve, let it go. I don't think he ever could. I think it is unfair to ask people to let that go. . . . There's no closure for my father, so there's no closure for me."

•   •   •

Elizabeth Nash had worked for Procter & Gamble for twenty-five years, joining the giant consumer products company right out of St. Lawrence University in upstate New York, working in sales in Rochester and Boston and then transferring to headquarters in Cincinnati in 1980. Over the next twenty years, P&G shifted from a no-layoff, we-take-good-care-of-our-own policy—*all* of our own—to one in which there were too many employees and the excess had to go. "We built up tons of extra capacity," said Richard Pease, a vice president for human resources, "and that included people capacity unfortunately."

One way to deal with the problem was to think of the company as having a core and a periphery. The core employees were engaged in what Procter considered its flagship operations, the operations that produced the profits. These were its legendary prowess in developing new soaps, detergents, paper diapers, toothpaste, skin creams, and lotions, and then popularizing them. The people who did this work—particularly the popularizing through compelling commercials and other novel marketing devices—were declared to be Procter's most valuable employees, while those in the peripheral functions became secondary and expendable. Many companies bent on cutting labor costs have adopted this corporate dichotomy, taking advantage of the growing acceptability of layoffs to peel off the outer layers.

Nash unfortunately found herself in an expendable function. She had done well at Procter. She had risen to associate director of human resources for information technology, and while she was in that job, information technology became a peripheral function. Like any big corporation, Procter had developed a complex computer network, but it no longer saw the need to manage or operate a system that was not in itself a source of profits. The computer network would soon be outsourced, and partly in preparation, partly to simply cut labor costs, Procter offered buyout packages, aiming many of them at IT employees. In the spring of

2001, management signaled to Nash that it wanted her to accept a package, which she did, taking early retirement from a company famous for early retirements, although not as early as age forty-seven.

Procter made more of an effort than most companies at dressing up a forced retirement as a mutual decision and Nash, as a result, did not feel the shock of separation—the loss of control—until she was going out the door. That was not all trickery on Procter's part. Few companies in America came into the age of layoffs with a sturdier reputation for loyalty to employees. There were no staff reductions until 1993 and then the instinct was to shrink the payroll through voluntary departures. "We had allowed the concept of inseparability to really become a sort of understanding that there would be lifetime employment," Pease said.

Constrained by this culture, the company tried to make the forced departures seem like voluntary decisions for early retirement. Procter's pension plan was ideal for this ruse. It consisted of annual bonuses in Procter stock, each bonus a percentage of an employee's salary. The stock did well and many employees had pension savings of $1 million or more by the time they were in their mid-fifties. Standard retirement in the prelayoff age began at fifty-five and very few Procter employees elected to stay beyond sixty-two. What Procter did now was to sweeten the retirement package for people like Nash and apply a little pressure, although not enough to rob her of the illusion that it was her decision to leave.

Nash is attractive and athletic-looking. Thick dark red hair frames and softens her long and narrow face. She was intense and cautious as she outlined her story, grim about what had happened, but taking pains to speak well of Procter, to separate the good years from the awkward departure. Occasionally she smiled at something that was said. The smile was a surprise. It was friendly and warm, and it came more often as we got to know each other. "I don't want to sound bitter, and indeed, I hope I am not bitter," she said. "Maybe this whole discussion brings back thoughts that say I'm still not finished letting go of this transition."

Nash resisted the notion that she was laid off at Procter & Gamble. "We knew they no longer valued us," she told me. That festered in her. But unlike Holthausen and Gibbs, she would not use the word "layoff" or allow herself to think of her experience in such raw terms. Whenever I referred to her separation from P&G as a layoff, she objected, her voice sharp with annoyance. Her departure was voluntary, she insisted. "I did not choose to stop working," she said. "I chose to stop working for Procter & Gamble. That is a very different scenario."

Procter & Gamble has shed more than twenty thousand employees since 1993, but very few were formally laid off. Whatever the disguise, the former Procter employees I have talked with over the past half-dozen years suffered from the same inability as Nash to put behind them the transition, with one or two exceptions. Richard Kiley was one, a short, stocky, ebullient man who was fifty-four, nearly old enough for respectable retirement in the Procter culture, when the company put several enriched departure packages on the table. None was aimed at Kiley, he assured me, but they were available to him, and he took one. Procter, in response, asked him to stay for one more year, continuing in his post as the manager of a venture capital fund that Procter had set up to invest in promising and potentially profitable outside companies. He stayed the extra year. He made a big point of that. That Procter wanted him to stay was evidence of his value, and it set him apart from the not-so-voluntary experience that Nash endured. His was truly voluntary, he said, and that gave him closure.

Actually, Procter would have liked him to stay beyond the one year, he said, but that he would not do. Staying meant risking being told, midway through the extension, that it was over. "I did not want to face being at a company thirty-three years and then being told I was of no value and would I please leave," Kiley said. "I wanted to leave when everyone thought I was doing a good job and they wanted me to stay. I wanted to feel good about the thirty-three years. So I left at age fifty-five. I was always going to retire at fifty-five but I might have stayed longer if I was not at risk of ending on a sour note."

Elizabeth Nash had originally planned to retire in her late fifties, a decade later than her actual departure. But with Procter offering a rich severance package to encourage early retirement, she managed to persuade herself that this was not such a bad moment to leave after all, for two reasons. Her pension savings, then valued at $1.2 million, nearly all of it in Procter stock, would benefit from her departure, she reasoned. In retirement, she would be free to hire a financial adviser and diversify her portfolio in pursuit of a higher return. As an employee, she was restricted mostly to Procter stock. "They were offering me a chance to get my hands on my retirement account and move it out of P&G stock into investments that I could control," she said. The diversified portfolio did eventually grow, although not more quickly than the undiversified one would have grown if she had remained a P&G employee.

Nash described her choice as a "mutual divorce." There was even alimony: a year's salary as severance and fully paid health insurance for the rest of her life, the sort of perks that other big companies—Verizon, for example, and Federal Express—have used in recent years to get tens of thousands of employees to accept voluntary early retirement, camouflaging layoffs. "They say people recover faster from a divorce if it is a mutual decision or they initiate the process themselves," Nash explained. "It's a control thing. You have the illusion of control."

Nash thought that once on the street, she would soon land a job in her specialty—information technology and staff training—at a salary not much different than her final pay at Procter: $150,000 a year. A counselor at an outplacement service, hired by Procter to help Nash make her decision, had been just vague enough to give her the impression that there were jobs in Cincinnati in her specialty at a comparable six-figure salary. There weren't, she realized, once she was out on the street. "I'm sort of mad at Procter for withholding in the predecision counseling the real information that I needed," she told me. The counseling contract had gone to the Right Management office in Cincinnati. "We are not told to encourage this one to go and this one to stay," Peter Hainline, who headed the Cincinnati office, insisted. But Kiley thought otherwise. "Their job," he said of Right, "is to help people decide to leave."

Nash was vulnerable. She wanted to believe that she could land a good job. That belief was central to her notion that she had chosen to leave, that the choice had been hers, not Procter & Gamble's. Her alternative was to stay at Procter, which meant taking a chance that she would qualify at her salary level for a vacant slot in another department. Her performance rating played a role; she wasn't a "consistently exceeds expectations," the highest level, or a "consistently below average," the lowest, but somewhere in the middle—"a solid performer," Kiley said. She had worked for him in the past. If transfer to another department failed, she would have to take her chances on outsourcing—becoming an employee, at some unknown wage, of whatever company took over the information technology function and then contracted this service back to Procter. Early retirement seemed to her the safer choice, and the handsome settlement package would not be on the table for long, or so the company said. "Looking at all the pros and cons," she said, "I decided to take the retirement offer and embark on a new adventure."

The new adventure—and Nash's sense of having acted voluntarily—began to come apart almost as soon as she committed herself in writing to leave. There was a retirement party, but neither of her bosses showed up. Nor did either send a letter to be read at the party, letters that might have praised her contribution to the company over twenty-five years and wished her well. The silence of Richard Antoine, Procter's senior vice president for human resources, was especially painful. She had worked with him on projects in the past, and just eight months earlier she was dining at a downtown restaurant and he walked over to her table to say hello. She clung to the memory of that encounter, describing it to me as recognition of her value. "Even if he didn't send me a personalized letter, any letter would have been better than complete silence," Nash said.

She speculated later that Antoine had probably distanced himself from everyone who elected early retirement, not wanting to risk being told that the departures were not so voluntary. "He would like to believe they were," she explained to me. But that explanation did not occur to her the night of the retirement party. The "lack of acknowledgment," as she put it, "had felt like a door hitting me in the back on my way out." She had been declared inessential and disposable, shunted into a diaspora that, three years later, she had not yet found a way out of. If she had known what would happen, she told me later, she might not have left so willingly.

Nash's search for another job dragged on for eighteen months. She did not want to leave Cincinnati in pursuit of good pay in some more promising city. Her aging parents lived near her and she saw to their needs. An expert horsewoman, she kept three horses on a seventeen-acre farm and she did not want to give that up, although she lived in the three-bedroom farmhouse alone now, having been divorced from her husband, also a horseman, seven years earlier, ending a ten-year, childless marriage. So she hunted for work in Cincinnati, and in January 2003 she finally landed a job as an executive at a publishing company, F+W Publications, at $82,000 a year—just 55 percent of her old pay. She worked in a modern glass and pastel office park on the outskirts of Cincinnati. It was a rural outpost compared to Procter's fortresslike headquarters downtown, where Nash had worked for years in a complex of concrete buildings forming a V-shaped wedge overlooking the Ohio River.

To live within her reduced income and not draw on savings, she sold two of the three horses. They were horses she had trained and ridden in steeplechase events. She traded in her aging car for a secondhand SUV instead of a new one, and caulked the leaky picture windows in her living room rather than replace them with watertight ones. She was not exactly falling out of the middle class, not with more than $1 million in savings and a seventeen-acre spread. But the accumulation of wealth that had marked her years at Procter was over and the descent had begun.

Nash had joined a downward mobility now widespread in the United States, euphemistically known in academic studies as "income volatility." It is most common among the less educated who lose a well-paying factory or office job and end up in lower-paid work, but the rate of increase has been more rapid in the last decade among the college-educated.

Downward mobility got considerable public attention when it first became noticeable as layoffs multiplied in the 1980s. In recent years, however, the link between layoffs and falling living standards has been much less discussed, although millions of people share Nash's experience. "The downwardly mobile are in a transitional state, a psychological no-man's-land," Katherine S. Newman, a sociologist at Princeton University, wrote in *Falling from Grace,* published in 1988 when downward mobility precipitated by layoffs was still a novelty. "They straddle an 'old' identity as members of the middle class and a 'new' identity as . . . unemployed. They are in suspended animation. The chaotic feeling of displacement creates confusion that can only be resolved through reintegration in a new capacity. Yet the downwardly mobile are unable to find a 'new place' that satisfies their expectations. Hence, they are left hanging, with one foot in the world of the professions, the corporate empire, the realm of the economically secure, and another in the troubled world of the . . . dispossessed."

Nash thought that in her new job she would return from the dispossessed. A former Procter executive, Stephen Kent, then the CEO at F+W

Publications, hired Nash, even creating a title and position for her: director of strategic planning and organizational development. F+W, which publishes special-interest books and magazines like *Deer & Deer Hunting* and *The Artist's Magazine,* had grown rapidly through acquisitions and Kent wanted Nash to take charge of integrating personnel in the various acquired divisions, fostering a common culture. As part of the endeavor, Nash would set up an intranet to facilitate communications and design training programs for the staff that would standardize practices, "making people feel a part of this organization," as Nash put it.

She achieved very little. As she tells the story, she never got the sort of guidance and support that Procter would have furnished through frequent meetings of leadership teams in which she was included. At F+W there were no such meetings, and Nash floundered. "One of my strengths is that I am pretty tenacious," she said, "but my confidence had been shaken and I did not know the people at F+W as well as I had the people at P&G." In the end, Kent took a different route. He integrated some peripheral operations—purchasing paper in bulk for all the divisions, for example—but he let most of the acquired companies function independently as stand-alone operations. That was the very opposite of what Nash had been hired to achieve.

By mid-June 2003, six months into her new job, she realized that it was not going to last. She had not yet printed up business cards, a sign of the fatalism that the exile from Procter had bred into her. She wondered whether she should have allowed herself "to be stampeded" out of Procter. The handsome retirement package that she thought would soon be taken off the table was still on the table, still luring people into early retirement. The few former colleagues who had resisted the pressure to retire early had not been laid off. They had gambled successfully so far. And the IT operation in which Nash worked had not yet been outsourced, although it would be on August 1. Hewlett-Packard, the outsourcing company, had agreed to employ two thousand of Procter's people at their same wages and benefits for two years. That would probably have been Nash's fate if she had stayed—a two-year stay of execution, so to speak.

The ax fell for her at F+W Publications on October 28. Kent walked into her small corner office, its bay windows overlooking an asphalt parking lot, and told her that unfortunately her salary had not been funded in the 2004 budget. "He said they were going to have to reorganize the human resources area and cut some money," Nash told me. Her departure this time was clearly involuntary. She had been bluntly laid off, again declared of no corporate value. The verdict delivered by Procter still preyed on her mind, but not the one rendered in this afterlife. "Having gone through the Procter & Gamble experience, you never again feel secure," Nash said. "My counselor at Right Management told me that. He also said you shouldn't feel secure."

Her severance pay from F+W ran out in late February and that month she sold $16,500 worth of Procter stock, cutting into savings to support herself while she hunted for work, this time without any illusion that the next job would last. Burned twice, she sought an insider position, one that her next employer considered part of the firm's "core competency" and thus relatively immune to layoffs. "You can't decide not to play, but you don't allow yourself the same enthusiasm and adventure," she said.

The next job did not come soon. There were interviews, much interest expressed, but no offers. She was "getting rejected a lot," as she put it. Like so many others in her situation, Nash fell back on networking. She mingled with consultants and with others like herself trying to make a living as consultants in the absence of steady employment. In her efforts to network, she gave presentations at several business conferences and exchanged calling cards with the executives in attendance, "hopefully people who might need my services," Nash said. She also agreed to help organize a knowledge management association composed of consultants whose expertise was similar to Nash's. They would help companies construct security systems for proprietary information, for example, or upgrade other aspects of a company's electronic data. "It is undefined," Nash said when we spoke in June 2004, "but I am going to give it a little time and energy for the next few months."

And then Procter & Gamble called. Her old employer, it turned out, was shorthanded. In the outsourcing of information technology, too many people had been turned over to the outsourcer or had taken early retirement packages. Specifically, an internal Web site had been set up to help boost the morale of IT people still on staff. It furnished some career guidance and also information useful to IT workers. But the young staffer assigned to run the Web site was inexperienced, Nash told me, and his boss could not get an experienced person to transfer in from another department. "No one wanted the job for fear the Web site would be outsourced, too," Nash said. Her name came up in a discussion of the problem and she was approached. Would she come back, not as an employee but as a consultant to help the young staffer?

She asked for $200 an hour, or somewhere in that ballpark, but settled for $75 and only three to five hours of work a week. Out of pride, she told Procter that given the small fee and the minimal hours, she considered the arrangement short-term, that she was interviewing for jobs and she explicitly reserved the right to drop the consulting work on a day's notice if a job came through. She wondered whether she would in fact land a lasting job. "You become aware, when you realize what has happened to you, that it can happen again and again," she said.

She did not communicate that uncertainty to Procter, however. She was pleased to be back on even skimpy terms. That her former employer wanted her services at all lifted her self-esteem. And the work itself made her feel almost as if she were a seasoned Procter executive again. Part of the young man's job was to interview high-level people and put the information they furnished onto the Web site. "I went with him on one of these interviews," Nash said, "and when he was blown away a bit—he was a little starstruck—I picked up the questioning. I knew this vice president from before and I got the interview back on track."

She would not have made this comparison herself, but to me the consulting contract put her, in her own mind, almost on a par with Richard Kiley, who had retired from Procter while it still wanted him to stay. On a much more tenuous basis, Procter now wanted her services, too. "It is sort of vindicating," she said. "It vindicates that I have value." She turned fifty at the time and on a Wednesday she impulsively invited fifty friends to a birthday party at her home that Saturday night. They all came, she reported in an e-mail, pleased that so many people she knew, out of regard for her, would come on such short notice. "Life is good," she said, "and may still get better!"

CHAPTER SIX

Dismantling Job Security, 1977 to 1997

There was one more stab at mandating full employment before the nation slid into the age of layoffs. The circumstances seemed to require drastic action. The worst recession since the Great Depression engulfed the country in the mid-1970s. The unemployment rate reached 9 percent in May 1975, nearly double what it had been only twelve months earlier. Stock prices plunged, wiping out a decade's gains, and the economy contracted for two straight years despite a 36 percent increase in government spending to prevent just that from happening. Out of this turmoil came a bill that would guarantee a return to full employment by making the federal government the employer of last resort—resurrecting a solution that Congress had rejected in 1946.

Barely thirty years ago, Congress was debating a proposition that seems strikingly radical and utopian today: whether government should provide a job at decent pay for every American who is able to work and wants to do so. The original bill even included the right to sue if the promised job was not forthcoming. The arguments dragged on for three years. By then, the recession had ended, prosperity had returned, and a rising inflation rate overshadowed full employment as a national issue.

The moment was lost, and the law that President Jimmy Carter finally signed—the Full Employment and Balanced Growth Act of 1978, better known as the Humphrey-Hawkins Act—turned out to be as toothless as its forebear, the Employment Act of 1946. It was "stripped of its original provisions calling for government [to create] 'last resort' jobs for the unemployed," the *Congressional Quarterly* reported at the time. The bill's principal author, Representative Augustus F. Hawkins, an African American Democrat representing the Watts area of Los Angeles, a ghetto bereft of jobs, had argued that full employment would pay for itself. It "will increase the nation's output and quality of life," he insisted, in effect summarizing an axiom in economics known as Okun's law, which holds that for every percentage-point drop in the unemployment rate, the overall economy grows by 3 percent. (Senator Hubert H. Humphrey, Democrat of Minnesota, sponsored the bill in the Senate.) Hawkins's argument failed to sway his congressional colleagues and a huge potential support for job security—for a respectable job at decent pay if the private sector did not furnish enough—was pushed aside.

True, the Humphrey-Hawkins Act, in its final form, spoke grandly of full employment. It directed the administration and the Federal Reserve to reduce the unemployment rate to 4 percent by 1983 and keep it there. But it did not say how this should be done. The act also spoke grandly about inflation, directing the administration and the Fed to reduce the inflation rate to zero by 1988 from the current level of 9 percent in 1978. This the Fed under Paul Volcker and Alan Greenspan diligently tried to do through the manipulation of interest rates, and soon full employment became a casualty of their strategy to control inflation. If too many people had work, Volcker and Greenspan argued, they would demand raises and that would force employers to raise prices. Inflation would accelerate. So each time the unemployment rate fell below 5.5 to 6 percent, or threatened to do so, the Fed raised interest rates, which inhibited economic growth and hiring. Not surprisingly, the unemployment rate climbed over the next twenty years to its highest levels since the Depression, enlarging the pool of people seeking work. There were more candidates to choose from, and that reduced the pressure on employers to avoid layoffs and hold on to their workers.

Tight labor markets are a barrier to layoffs and that barrier came down. So did other barriers, one after another from the late 1970s to the late 1990s, until we finally incorporated layoffs into our expectations and, in doing so, gave up on the sort of collective solution that Augustus Hawkins had proposed. Each layoff became the victim's problem, not society's, or the victim's fault, and once people shifted to this view, their employers were free to incorporate layoffs into their tactics and operations. They could ignore what Richard Layard, a British economist, describes as the self-esteem and identity that a stable workplace—a communal setting—confers on its employees. Mergers, outsourcing, constant corporate reorganizations in obsessive pursuit of short-term profits, the frequent migration of factories and offices to lower-wage cities and countries, wage stagnation, plant closings, the shrinking or abandonment of entire industries—all these require an acquiescence to layoffs. In hindsight, after Augustus Hawkins lost his battle, the resistance to layoffs gradually disintegrated and acquiescence arrived.

Hawkins believed that job security was beyond any individual's control, and society therefore should maintain it, doing so mainly through government. Furthermore, when layoffs did have to occur, society should take some of the stigma and suffering out of them by recognizing an obligation to keep people employed. He had incentive for this belief, given the plight of his ghetto constituents. He was convinced that the private sector, on its own, could not generate enough work to achieve full employment at decent pay. As the first African American elected to Congress from California, having taken his seat in 1963 at age fifty-six, he felt that the mid-1970s recession, with its painfully high unemployment, offered the right backdrop for action. Government must step in more directly, he said, outlining key provisions of his proposed legislation. It should do so through the creation of a Standby Job Corps, for example, "in which qualified job seekers could be temporarily placed if no suitable (private sector) jobs are available." Or men and women seeking work could join "local reservoirs of public and private employment projects." That meant community job creation and public projects, funded by the federal government, in hundreds of towns and cities. Through such programs, Congress would finally do what it had failed to do in 1946. "We must not replay the drama of events which led to the watering down and lessening" of the 1946 act, Hawkins warned.

Senator Humphrey endorsed several of the early drafts and sponsored the bill in the Senate. But Humphrey was more in the mainstream than Hawkins. He had been Lyndon Johnson's vice president and he ran for president himself in 1968. He listened more to the criticisms. For one thing, the Hawkins approach went against the prevailing wisdom, born in the 1960s and 1970s, that the unemployed lacked the necessary skills or education to land a job and had themselves to blame for their lack of initiative and accomplishment. Hawkins insisted on taking people as they were, giving them jobs first at decent pay and training them on the job if that was necessary. Government would "respond directly to the needs of millions of Americans who have heretofore been excluded from consideration and attention," he said.

Employers of low-wage workers protested. They would be squeezed intolerably by rising wages, they insisted, if the government came in as a competitor offering good jobs to all comers. Partly in response, the open-ended guarantee was scaled back; there would be federally funded jobs for everyone, but only until the unemployment rate fell to 4 percent, a national average that included a 6 to 8 percent unemployment rate for African Americans and other vulnerable minority groups. In addition, the government would be careful not to compete with the private sector for workers.

The inflation argument also registered with Humphrey, although the Senate heard plenty of testimony that the rising Consumer Price Index in those years was mainly a result of higher prices for fuel oil, housing, and food, and not pressure from wage increases. After 1973 wages no longer rose fast enough for most workers to keep up with inflation. Still, despite this willingness to give ground, Humphrey thought of making Hawkins's full-employment proposals, or some of them, central to his platform in a run for the presidency in 1976. He saw that as good politics. The unemployment rate was still high that election year, although the numbers were beginning to fall as the nation recovered from the recession.

Humphrey did not run; cancer ruled that out. And Jimmy Carter, the Democratic candidate, turned out to be lukewarm to Humphrey-Hawkins, hardly mentioning the bill in his campaign. Carter saw inflation as the overriding concern, and public opinion polls seemed to confirm that view. Once he was elected, the watered-down version that Hawkins feared became inevitable, and there was insufficient public pressure to change that outcome. "You needed much higher unemployment, massive unemployment, to bring out a strong coalition for full employment," Stanley Moses, an economist at Hunter College in New York, told me years later. Moses had helped to draft early versions of Humphrey-Hawkins, and he wrote speeches for Humphrey in the seventies.

A strong coalition had brought the nation civil rights legislation in the sixties and similar public pressure ended the Vietnam War in the early seventies. By the late seventies, however, Americans were moving, or being pushed, in a different direction when it came to jobs. Humphrey-Hawkins turned out to be a last, futile salute to full employment through collective action. Thereafter, the headwinds were too strong to muster significant support. The oil price shocks, the loss of faith in government after Vietnam, the unsettling phenomenon in the seventies of a rising inflation rate even in a recession, the stiff competition from Japanese and Western European multinationals, a growing budget deficit that inhibited public spending, increasingly ineffective unions, the rise of income inequality separating the rich from the poor much more than in the past—all these soured Americans and eroded communal action, either on the streets or through government. Wage stagnation for the bottom 70 percent of the workforce only added to what Carter described in his famous malaise speech in 1979 as a "crisis of the American spirit."

The Depression had taught the value of a collective response during an earlier crisis of the American spirit, and the prosperity after World War II reinforced that lesson. The good times had bred in Americans a sense of inclusiveness and equality, and a respect for using government to lift everyone's lot. It was an outlook that prompted Congress to regularly raise the minimum wage, legislate working conditions, impose environmental standards, increase Social Security pensions, enact Medicare and Medicaid, subsidize universities, expand public health services—a collective effort to generate opportunity and a reasonable standard of living for as many people as possible.

Individualism was kept in check, but as prosperity deteriorated so did respect for collective behavior and for its corollary, Keynesian theory, the reigning view in economics and in public policy from the mid-thirties until the mid-seventies. John Maynard Keynes had civilized neoclassical economic theory, with its emphasis on individualism and its trust in self-regulating markets, by demonstrating that prosperity and full employment could often be achieved only when government and the private sector complemented each other. Keynes's influence now declined. Too much had gone wrong for America to keep faith in the communal responses that Keynes had advocated and that had worked so well.

Neoclassical economics came back to life in the new atmosphere, and a crude individualism reasserted itself; that is, the largely mythical, nostalgic, and debilitating view that in America, people pulled themselves up by their own endeavors, acting heroically and alone, as Jay Gatsby had in F. Scott Fitzgerald's 1925 novel *The Great Gatsby* or as Howard Roark did in Ayn Rand's 1943 novel *The Fountainhead*. Both books enjoyed renewed popularity in the eighties and nineties. Taxes and regulations only got in the way, as did unions and job security. Neoclassical economics celebrated this individualism. So did Wall Street and Silicon Valley, which recruited well-educated, self-absorbed men and women who saw themselves as very much in control of their lives and who took as a given that a nation once free of government constraints, or at least constraints on what they wanted to do, would prosper from the unfettered endeavors of millions of energetic, self-sufficient, masterly individuals like themselves.

In his best-selling book *The Culture of Narcissism*, published in 1979, the historian Christopher Lasch argued that Americans were increasingly fixated on their own grandiosity and their personal goals, forgetting in the process the collective achievements so prominent in the past. "To live for the moment is the prevailing passion—to live for yourself, not for your predecessors or posterity," Lasch wrote. Or for your neighbors, he might have added. He caught the trend early.

Infectious individualism helped immeasurably to put Ronald Reagan into office in 1981. But Jimmy Carter, his Democratic predecessor, pushed it along, too. Carter initiated the deregulation, inherent in individualism, that accelerated in the Republican Reagan years. It was a neoclassical economist, Alfred Kahn of Cornell University, who, as chairman of the Civil Aeronautics Board, became Carter's chief salesman for airline deregulation, explaining to the public in his articulate, often humorous fashion how unrestricted competition would bring down passenger fares, multiply services, and make airlines more responsive to passengers. He was right in a way. On the day that Carter signed the Airline Deregulation Act of 1978, a line of people representing airline ventures formed at CAB headquarters. Once the bill became law, two thousand dormant airline routes were doled out on a first-come, first-served basis.

What Kahn did not anticipate was the extent of the layoffs to come. In the unregulated, freewheeling competition that he helped bring to life, tens of thousands of airline employees lost their jobs, year after year, as giant carriers like Eastern, Pan American, and Braniff merged with other airlines or went out of business; new carriers like People Express came and went, or, like Southwest and JetBlue, came and stayed. Their success as discount airlines forced the survivors, particularly American Airlines, United, Northwest, and Delta, to try to remake themselves as lower-cost carriers. But that only perpetuated the layoffs and the pressure on employees to agree to wage concessions, and nearly thirty years after airline deregulation the upheavals and layoffs have not begun to subside. Regulation had created a set of airlines with steady earnings, predictable operations, and supervised growth, all of which was conducive to job security if not to more flights and rapidly falling fares, although fares had fallen during regulation, too. Deregulation in airlines and soon after in trucking, banking, telephones, railroads, and utilities exposed to layoffs the nearly 13 percent of the national workforce employed in these once safe industries.

Thirteen years later, long gone from government, Kahn had acquired more respect for the destructiveness that came with deregulation. He told me that, caught up in the late 1970s in the promise of unregulated competition, he could not then "appreciate the way in which the forces [of deregulation] began to take on a momentum of their own." He had not anticipated the predatory pricing that occurred, in which big airlines with considerable resources underpriced the small upstarts, like People Express, until most of the People Expresses went under, eliminating the competition and many jobs. Nor had he understood the determination of the big airlines to re-create the market control that regulation had made possible—through the hub airport system, through airline mergers, and through "yield management." In yield management, computers constantly revised fares in advance of each flight, lowering them as necessary to fill more seats. While discount fares got the publicity, yield management in fact maximized the sale of as many seats as possible at stubbornly high prices.

Only in the fall of 1978, on the eve of deregulation, Kahn said, did he begin to sense the potential for airlines to use acquisitions and predatory pricing to eliminate overcapacity and competition, as well as thousands of jobs. Traveling in Europe with his wife, celebrating their thirty-fifth wedding anniversary, he sat down in Venice and drafted a memo outlining his last-minute concerns. But soon after he returned to Washington, President Carter pulled him off the Civil Aeronautics Board, which would be dismantled over the next few years, and put him in charge of fighting inflation as chairman of the Council on Wage and Price Stability, an innocuous job. If he had remained at the CAB, he insisted to me when we met in 1991, he would have initiated antitrust actions to curb mergers and predatory pricing.

"I never was able to follow up," Kahn said, a little wistfully. Still, he had no regrets about the role he had played. Regulation had become associated in his mind with too many ills that the nation had suffered. "I felt that government regulation was so ridiculous that the most important thing was to wipe away its encrustations," Kahn said, "and in the process, I may have been overly enthusiastic about the benefits of free markets."

As regulation gave way, so did another source of resistance to layoffs. Tightly knit communities had formed around the factories and mills that dominated employment in dozens of towns and cities. When plants were shut, some of these communities tried to take them over and preserve the jobs on which the communities depended. By the mid-nineties, however, most of this resistance had failed and so had the will to keep trying as the people in the communities lost their incomes, their cohesiveness, and their optimism.

The steel industry produced the first mass layoffs to rivet national attention and the first notable attempt at community ownership to preserve jobs. Campbell, Ohio, figured prominently in this endeavor. It is an incorporated city next to Youngstown, whose men were employed at the Campbell Works, a steel mill owned by the Youngstown Sheet & Tube Company. On September 17, 1977, Youngstown Sheet & Tube announced that the Campbell Works would close and all five thousand workers would lose their jobs, a big layoff by seventies' standards.

The workers in Campbell and in other nearby towns and cities were in most cases the third generation employed in steelmaking. Their grandfathers had emigrated from Ireland, Italy, and Poland. They had taken jobs melting, pouring, and shaping steel in the blast furnaces and mills that were located along a twenty-five-mile stretch of the Mahoning River just west of the Pennsylvania border—an area known during World War II as America's Ruhr Valley, home in its heyday to forty thousand steelworkers. They lived in close-knit communities. People were linked to one another through unions, churches, bowling leagues, theatrical groups, marriages, and lifelong friendships born in public and parochial schools and extended through years of working together in the same mills and blast furnaces. They were homeowners and gardeners. High school basketball and football games were big social events, and graduation day was a festive occasion as the next generation entered the mills.

Eight days after the shutdown announcement, at a packed gathering in the city council chambers in Campbell, Phil Creno, a school board member, got up and said, "Why don't we all put up five thousand bucks and buy the place." The purchase plan that finally emerged was more complex, but Creno's suggestion and the follow-up efforts of Gerald Dickey, recording secretary of one of the union locals, soon produced a coalition of ousted steelworkers and other community members intent on acquiring the plant. Few such community coalitions went as far toward actual purchase as the one Creno launched that night. But theirs was a not uncommon response in the late seventies and early eighties to the mass layoffs that threatened to pull down entire communities.

"Community-employee ownership," as the Campbell campaign was called, drew national attention. By late October, the newly organized Youngstown Religious Coalition, representing nearly a dozen faiths, joined in the effort to take over the steelworks. A Catholic bishop and an Episcopal bishop lent their support, giving the campaign to acquire the Campbell Works added prestige, and various national organizations became involved. Their argument was that America's aging steel mills did not have to succumb to high-quality, less expensive imported steel. The mills could be modernized. The Campbell Works still used open hearth furnaces, which required nine to ten hours to make a batch of steel from iron, limestone, and other ingredients. Oxygen technology, in contrast—standard procedure in newer foreign mills along with even more efficient electric furnaces—produced the same batch in forty-five minutes, and with less labor. The steel industry promised modernization, but it never seemed to happen at the Campbell Works. Youngstown Sheet & Tube had pledged in 1974 to install an oxygen furnace, but two years later the company postponed the $90 million investment, blaming the just ended recession for a shortfall in investment capital.

That was not exactly true. As of 1969, Youngstown Sheet & Tube had ceased to exist simply to make steel. In the sort of deal that would become almost a weekly event in the eighties, Youngstown was acquired by Lykes Brothers, Inc., a conglomerate controlled by a Florida family whose principal businesses were agriculture, ocean shipping, and real estate. A boom in the domestic steel industry in the late sixties had attracted Lykes, which added the profits then flowing from Youngstown Sheet & Tube to its own cash flow. Instead of using the money to invest in steel modernization, however, Lykes over the next five years purchased businesses that seemed to promise higher immediate returns than steel—an insurance company, for example, and half ownership in a steamship company. And then when the mid-seventies recession and foreign competition produced a downturn in the demand for steel, Lykes closed the Campbell Works and concentrated what little investment it did make in steel on Youngstown Sheet & Tube's more viable Indiana Harbor Works, near Chicago.

That pattern of using mergers and acquisitions to chase higher and higher profits while closing or shrinking or selling less promising operations spread widely in corporate America, and layoffs greased the way. There was no greater practitioner of this strategy than Jack Welch, who became chairman of General Electric in 1981, and his successes encouraged other chief executives to emulate him. Chasing ever higher profits pushed up stock prices, raining wealth on shareholders and making them cheerleaders for the deal-making that promised still higher stock prices, a promise that the bull market of the eighties and nineties, if not the deals themselves, often fulfilled. The winners of the future, Welch said in his first presentation to Wall Street analysts as GE's chairman, will be companies that "search out and participate in the real growth industries."

Welch had an odd definition of growth industries. He purchased RCA in 1986, for example, mainly to get at NBC, which he saw as a pocket of demand and profitability. Two years later, he sold RCA's television manufacturing operation to the French company Thomson, getting out of an industry with too much global supply relative to demand, and he acquired from Thomson that company's medical equipment business, another pocket of demand, in Welch's view. All this buying and shedding became intertwined with layoffs. In GE's case that turned out to be one out of every four employees between 1980 and 1985, a total of 118,000 people. For a while the media nicknamed Welch "Neutron Jack," picking up the epithet from a 1982 *Newsweek* article, the image being, as Welch himself later described it, that he left the buildings standing but wiped out the people. The nickname soon faded. By the mid-eighties, layoffs in the Welch style had become commonplace.

While Welch set the pace, there was plenty of wind in everyone's sails for this way of doing business. If Welch had not appeared, someone else like him almost certainly would have. Unable to make the same profits from straightforward production, American companies took this easier path, shuffling assets to make the balance sheet look good. How could they resist? The postwar hegemony had diminished and with it the profit-enhancing economies of scale that came with America's unchallenged access to mass markets. While European governments pitched in with subsidies and other forms of support for their corporations, the United States government held back, except in military spending and in special cases, like the federal loan guarantees for the Chrysler Corporation, whose imminent failure in the early 1980s would have been too disruptive. There simply wasn't a constituency for what *Business Week* had dismissively referred to as "industrial policy."

The nation's financial markets, on the other hand, were more powerful than ever, and they offered a mechanism for making money through the sort of acquisitions and reorganizations that Jack Welch exemplified. The Welch way, however, diverted the wages of tens of millions of laid-off workers into corporate cash flow and profits, or into repayment of the loans that were floated to pay for all the maneuvering, or into the bloated incomes of the deal-makers. In the pursuit of success, other spin-off strategies developed that incorporated layoffs. Department stores or tire manufacturers or telephone companies merged, for example, to get rid of excess capacity and overlapping manpower. Or companies like GE and Wal-Mart forced suppliers to cut prices for the merchandise and services they furnished, and if that required the suppliers to relocate to a lower-wage state or overseas, well, so be it. Sometimes relocating became a condition of continuing to do business with the supplier.

Pension fund managers egged on the process. Huge sums had accumulated after World War II in the pension funds of companies, unions, and state governments. By the 1980s, so much of this money had been invested in stocks that it accounted for 20.9 percent of the value of all shares traded on the various exchanges, up from 13.3 percent in 1977. The managers and traders who moved this tidal wave about in the stock market acquired great leverage, which they used to pressure companies to book constantly greater quarterly profits—that being the quickest route, in this way of thinking, to higher stock prices and, in turn, even richer pension funds. Even the unions allowed their pension funds to flow into the market, although that same money invested in new technologies for manufacturing machinery and steelmaking, for example, could have saved industries and jobs. In the tail-chasing that actually took place with everyone's accumulated pension savings, the damage was rationalized. "There had always been the issue of balancing corporate profitability with protections for employees and communities," Peter Cappelli, the business historian, explained. "The shareholder value movement altered that balance."

For a while, however, community groups or coalitions like the one that formed in Campbell, Ohio, tried to preserve the balance and, in doing so, to hinder layoffs. The Campbell coalition proposed modernizing the steelmaking process at the shut-down mill in that community, and President Carter promised to help, even though his own priorities had perversely contributed to the closing of steel mills and of many other marginal manufacturing operations, particularly in the Midwest "rust belt."

Carter insisted that the United States, as the world's consumer of last resort, had an obligation to absorb the imports of Japan, Western Europe, and other noncommunist nations to help lift their economies in the wake of the mid-1970s recession. That included steel imports, although foreign steelmakers enjoyed much more support from their governments than their American counterparts. The Carter administration also saw in the influx of lower-priced imported steel a means of forcing domestic steelmakers to keep price increases in check, thus suppressing the inflation rate for the country as a whole, given that steel was so important an ingredient in American production. But for all his concern about inflation and America's role as the consumer of last resort, the president also wanted to grant some relief to blue-collar cities like Youngstown, a Democratic Party stronghold, and the Campbell Works was an opportunity.

Basing his decision on a study of the mill paid for by the Department of Housing and Urban Development, Carter in 1978 pledged $300 million in federal loan guarantees toward a $525-million modernization, with the understanding that the reopened Campbell Works would be owned by the community and the plant's employees, not by Youngstown Sheet & Tube. Contributions would also have to come from state government and from outside shareholders, who would have six seats on the board of Community Steel, as the proposed operation had been dubbed. Employees would elect six of the remaining nine directors, and a community corporation the last three. But soon after the November 1978 election, Carter withdrew the loan guarantee, counseled to do so by members of his own administration, who saw the project as unrealistic. Pressure also came from various steel company executives, who opposed competition from a reopened Campbell Works. And, surprisingly, the national leadership of the United Steelworkers of America came out against the plan to reopen the mill.

The opposition came from Lloyd McBride, the union's international president. McBride had his office at the union's headquarters in Pittsburgh, only seventy-five miles from Youngstown, yet he waited until six months after the Campbell Works shut before visiting his five thousand out-of-work members, and he refused to endorse community-employee ownership, even walking out of a meeting at which this was discussed. The reason he offered—reasoning that Lynn R. Williams, who succeeded McBride as president in 1983, described to me twenty-five years later—helps to explain why organized labor gradually let jobs disappear.

"Lloyd was much more of a mind from the beginning that we were into a different circumstance in steel," Williams said. Economic growth had slowed across the world, partly from the shock of rising oil prices, and suddenly the worldwide capacity to make steel exceeded demand by 200 million tons. "I was still arguing that it has always been a cyclical industry and that this was maybe a bigger and tougher cycle but demand will come back," Williams continued. "And Lloyd said, 'No, no, no, you've got that wrong. This is really different.' And he was right. The world had changed. And he said, 'The last thing we need to do to these people is have them start investing their money in a lost cause.'"

From then on, the steelworkers union went another route. The union pushed continuously and often fruitlessly for tariffs and quotas, to keep down imports. It encouraged the formation of employee stock ownership plans (ESOPs), which in the eighties and early nineties turned employees into shareholders of nearly twenty steel companies, most of which failed, costing the worker-owners their jobs and in many cases their investments, an outcome that McBride had ironically held up as a reason for opposing community-worker ownership of the Campbell Works. Concerned about falling membership, the steelworkers negotiated job security clauses that sought to protect current jobholders from layoff, but not to safeguard the jobs themselves. The latter disappeared as bankruptcies, early retirement, attrition, and the rise of superefficient mini-mills thinned the ranks, so that by 1995 only 180,000 steelworkers remained of the 600,000 employed in the United States in 1973—a ceaseless bloodletting that after a while no longer drew national headlines or handwringing concern, except in the towns where the jobs disappeared.

For Youngstown, the shutdown of the Campbell Works, never to reopen, was the first destructive blow, but within two years 5,000 more workers lost their jobs as two other mills closed in the city. The second shutdown announcement came on Thanksgiving Day 1979. The United States Steel Corporation said it would close fourteen plants across the country, eliminating 13,000 jobs, including the 3,500 at its Youngstown Works. Protests and rallies greeted that breathtaking decision, and on January 28 steelworkers occupied U.S. Steel's administration building in Youngstown, staging a sit-in that lasted through the afternoon and into the evening, the goal being to force the company to either reopen the mill or sell it to a community-employee coalition.

Neither happened. Three days later, after a gathering of steel industry executives in Washington, a reporter for the CBS television affiliate in Youngstown asked David Roderick, U.S. Steel's chairman, what he thought about the community-employee buyout proposal. "We obviously would not be interested in selling the plants to a group of people that can only be successful if they were massively subsidized by the federal government," Roderick replied. "We are not, in other words, interested in creating subsidized competition for ourselves."

But the protest left its mark. From then on, U.S. Steel softened its layoff tactics, and so did other steel companies. Instead of the traumatic plant closings, U.S. Steel got into the practice of shutting down a plant department by department, eliminating a few hundred workers in each action, spreading the process over months, and other industries adopted the technique. Those still employed after each incremental downsizing often stayed silent, hoping they would somehow survive. "Everyone is against a shutdown at first," Staughton Lynd, a lawyer and labor historian, said, "and then you have these divisions in the workforce, and in a relatively short time, people say, I'd better cut the best deal I can for myself."

The retreat from job security was drawn out in other ways. During the Reagan years public alarm over layoffs was sufficient for the administration to insist on import quotas for Japanese cars, and for the Japanese to accept the quotas while they set up auto assembly plants in the United States, generating relatively well-paying factory jobs for men and women who might otherwise have been unemployed or consigned to the low-wage service sector. Carefully, the Japanese automakers placed their plants in as many states as possible, the goal being to pacify senators and representatives from those states in an era of rising anti-Japanese sentiment and potential backlash.

But Japanese auto companies generated fewer than 25,000 jobs in the United States, less than one-tenth of the employment at the Big Three American manufacturers. Anxiety about layoffs remained great enough for Congress in 1988 to pass the Worker Adjustment and Retraining Notification Act, or WARN. That act required an employer of one hundred or more workers to give sixty days' advance notice of a plant or office closing, or of a layoff that involved at least five hundred workers. The hope was that with advance warning, workers consigned to layoff would have time to prepare for their ordeal, and some companies might even be discouraged from engaging in large layoffs.

Although he disagreed with the bill, Reagan signed it, relieving some of the pressure on his vice president, George H. W. Bush, to oppose layoffs in his campaign for president against Michael Dukakis. WARN has stayed on the books, but numerous exemptions were incorporated into the original legislation, and political pressure to apply it declined, so that by the 1996 presidential election it was no longer a campaign issue. "In most cases, companies either slip through the law's large loopholes or simply violate the law," Susan N. Houseman, a labor economist at the W. E. Upjohn Institute for Employment Research, found in a 1994 study.

Other quotas marked the Reagan years—on steel, textiles, apparel, motorcycles, and semiconductors, for example, each with the stated goal of giving American companies time to upgrade their facilities and regain sales. Modernization did occur. The inefficiencies that plagued many industries in the eighties were often resolved by the nineties. But given the worldwide oversupply of high-quality, competitively priced merchandise, there were not enough customers to go around. So the new efficiencies translated into roughly the same output with fewer and fewer workers, rather than more output with either the same number of workers or, better yet, an expanding workforce. As if insufficient demand were not enough of a problem, an overvalued dollar in the early 1980s also suppressed production, by making American exports very expensive in foreign currencies and imports relatively inexpensive—until exchange rates were finally adjusted starting in 1985.

By then, the United States had ceded the field in many industries or soon would do so. Rather than try to outstrip foreign competitors in innovation, a costly and risky process, we gave up in product after product. We stopped making subway cars in the United States and various types of high-tech machinery, to cite two examples, and we never produced flat-screen computer monitors within the country, or many of the numerous components inside the ubiquitous desktop computer. The result of all this was inescapable. Starting in 1979 the manufacturing labor force steadily declined, mainly through layoffs, from a peak of 19.4 million in 1979 to 17.6 million in 1998 and then precipitously to 14.3 million in 2005, as more and more efficiencies kicked in and more and more merchandise once made in America came from abroad.

America's entrepreneurial energy focused not on production but on the financial maneuvering and the chasing of profits through acquisition that Jack Welch had done so much to promote. Raising shareholder value became the great justification for merger and acquisition activity, and out of this breeding ground came a new creature, the corporate raider, who multiplied the acquisitions and reorganizations—and the accompanying layoffs. Corporate raiders were the "buccaneers who prowled Wall Street in the 1980s, taking and gutting companies for sport and profit," as *Fortune* magazine described them. The stars in this cast included T. Boone Pickens, a Texas oilman turned financier and speculator, Carl C. Icahn, Irwin Jacobs, and Saul P. Steinberg, financiers and speculators from the start. The raiders were doing God's work, they and their public relations representatives argued. They were forcing complacent managers of over-staffed companies to cut costs through layoffs and to close down or sell off underperforming divisions. True, mayhem often resulted but the alternative was bankruptcy, or so the argument went. Better to save sixty jobs out of a hundred if that could be done by laying off forty employees and thus ensure survival in the new global market.

For all the headlines these raids produced, the story line each time, like the story line in movie westerns, was monotonously predictable. The raiders would quietly acquire a small stake in a company, say 5 percent of the outstanding shares, and then announce a takeover attempt, offering to buy up a majority of the stock, almost always using borrowed money, the collateral being the target company's own assets. Through layoffs and wage concessions forced on employees, or outright sale of a division, cash would be raised to pay down the debt. Whatever the tactic, the price of the stock shot up after the raider's takeover announcement. In response, the target company would buy out the raider at a handsome profit, a vic-tim of "greenmail," or it would sell itself to a friendly "white knight" com-pany on better terms, or it would purchase hundreds of thousands of its own shares at premium prices to please shareholders and keep them away from the raider.

Phillips Petroleum picked from the selection of predictable alterna-tives in fending off Boone Pickens, and so did Walt Disney Productions to stave off Saul Steinberg. Pickens agreed in December 1984 to sell his stake back to Phillips at a profit of nearly $500 million, and the company laid out nearly $4 billion more to please shareholders by buying some of their holdings at a premium price. Steinberg got $325 million from Walt Disney in June 1984 to give up his stake and go away. Occasionally a raider would take control of a company, as Carl Icahn did at Trans World Airlines in 1985. Whatever the solution, it meant going into debt to finance the raid. To raise cash to pay down that debt, costs were cut, prin-cipally through layoffs. "What companies gradually discovered was there was no adverse reaction from the stock market and from consumers to the layoffs," Thomas Kochan, a professor of labor and management at MIT's Sloan School of Management, explained.

Leveraged buyouts were a variation of the corporate raid. In these cases, top executives raided their own company, hoping like ordinary raiders to profit handsomely. In the most talked about deal of the eighties, for example—the battle for RJR Nabisco in 1988—F. Ross Johnson, the chief executive and the raider in this drama, departed with a $53 million package, big stuff in those days. Johnson, who was fifty-seven, had concluded that if he did not try for ownership of RJR Nabisco, someone else would. The stock price had fallen relative to profits, making the company a bargain, an undervalued pocket of demand in the Welch way of thinking, and thus a target for raiders.

So Johnson and a small group of confederates offered $18 billion. They raised most of the money through high-risk junk bonds. The junk bond market itself was a creation of the eighties, brought into existence to finance the numerous, often ill-conceived takeovers. In the bidding war that Johnson ignited, Henry R. Kravis, the Wall Street deal-maker, came in as a self-appointed white knight—a competing raider, really—and won out at $25 billion, most of it also borrowed money. At the time, that was the most expensive acquisition ever, and to help pay the $3 billion in annual debt installments, Kravis raised money by selling off various corporate divisions and by shrinking the staff from 116,881, just before he took control, to 66,500 by 1993.

What made RJR Nabisco such a compelling national saga was the revelations it produced about Johnson's sumptuous CEO lifestyle, largely at company expense, and Kravis's intense determination to be the winner, seeing in this giant acquisition confirmation of his own status as a legendary financier. What got lost—taken for granted, really—were the layoffs and the hardship they produced. The men and women pushed out were not folk heroes. No *Grapes of Wrath* came out of the 1980s. The new heroes were more likely to be Gordon Gekko, the handsome, greedy deal-maker portrayed by Michael Douglas in the 1987 movie *Wall Street*, or Larry the Liquidator, the crudely drawn, caustic corporate raider in *Other People's Money*, a 1989 off-Broadway morality play and also a popular movie starring Danny DeVito. Their insolent behavior came across as romantic, smooth, enviable, despite the mayhem it entailed. Faced with such salutes, even the American bishops of the Roman Catholic Church eventually fell silent, although in pastoral letters in 1984 and 1986, they had bluntly petitioned the Reagan administration to subsidize employment, to strengthen unions, and to be skeptical of the ability of free markets to meet the nation's social needs, as neoclassical economics would have people believe they could. The bishops deplored "the constant seeking for self-gratification and the exaggerated individualism of our age" and, echoing Augustus Hawkins, they called on the government to sponsor "direct job creation programs."

Organized labor tried to raise its voice. But the long decline in union membership that started in the sixties had removed labor as a significant obstacle. So had union corruption and overreaching in wage negotiations in the seventies, which undermined public support. And then the air traffic controllers' strike in 1981 took the country a big step closer to the acceptability of layoffs. By firing the 11,400 striking controllers and replacing them en masse, barring them from ever being federal employees again, President Reagan served notice to private employers that they were now free, even encouraged, to bring in replacement workers during a strike and keep them on the job once the strike ended. In effect he was laying off the strikers and successfully undermining the collective behavior, the allegiance to a shared endeavor, that successful strikes require. Hiring permanent replacement workers had been legal since the 1930s, but no corporate employer of any significance had used them until Reagan gave the go-ahead.

Almost on cue, strike activity and union organizing, already in decline, fell more sharply, and with it union leverage in bargaining for job security. The public could have forced a different outcome. That happened in the late sixties when Cesar Chavez appealed to consumers not to purchase table grapes grown in California until the grape growers recognized the United Farm Workers Organizing Committee as the rightful bargaining agent for field workers. While that boycott worked, there was not a similar refusal in 1981 to forgo air travel until President Reagan backed down. No union leader even tried to organize a boycott. What reaction there was from the public came out mostly as annoyance at disrupted flight schedules. And as layoffs piled up, so did the pool of people, some of them former union members, willing to work as replacement workers—scabs—which further encouraged managers to lay off strikers.

With labor in disarray, other changes also undermined job security. The fixed monthly pension, funded mainly by the employer, with its built-in incentive to stay with one employer for many years to qualify for a large pension, gave way to the 401(k) and similar plans based on a worker's own savings. The shift relieved employers of huge fixed-pension obligations, and removed an incentive for employees to stay put and resist being laid off. On another front, managers rated employee performance much more than in the past, particularly white-collar performance, and the ratings became a tool in the layoff process. "Ranking and spanking," it is sometimes called, or the "hell curve," the hell part being the rear, downward slope of a bell curve.

The upper 20 percent in these ratings schemes got higher pay in exchange for their perceived value and also for tolerating the risk of layoff if their value declined in the eyes of their managers. The rest of the staff, particularly those who performed in the lowest 10 percent—a Jack Welch invention—became not only dispensable, but a drag on corporate profitability. Divided in this way, deprived of a collective response, more and more workers strove to be the survivors of layoffs, and in doing so acquiesced in the departure of those who did not make the cut. At some operations the bottom 2 or 3 percent were laid off annually, and those ranked just above them became the bottom 2 or 3 percent, vulnerable in the next layoff.

A core-periphery system also developed, as at Procter & Gamble. The core workers were those who performed the essential, profit-making functions—design and engineering at an aircraft manufacturer, for example—while the peripheral employees did support functions: human resources, accounting, clerical work, customer service, computer programming. They were disposable. Their work could be outsourced, and often was, or turned over to temps, whose numbers grew to more than 3 percent of the total workforce in the nineties from nearly zero in the mid-seventies. Temporary workers are rented by companies from temp agencies to work in offices and on assembly lines, and when the demand for their services slackens, they are sent away. Their departures, even after several years at the same company, are not recorded in government statistics as layoffs, a classification reserved for permanent employees who lose their jobs. But that is what they are.

Compounding the job insecurity, Congress let the minimum wage deteriorate after the seventies so that by 2004 more than 36 million workers, nearly 30 percent of the workforce, earned $10 an hour or less. The $10 was roughly double the minimum wage but so close to impoverishment that in most cases neither the employer nor the employee values the job. Until the eighties, these bottom-rung jobs were more valuable. Regular increases in the minimum wage kept pushing up pay for workers whose wages were several rungs above the minimum—and employers, forced to value their low-end workers, offered them training and advancement. All three attributes are missing today, which makes quitting such jobs hard to distinguish from being laid off. Telephone call centers, fast-food restaurants, and health care facilities are populated by these devalued workers, and employee turnover, as a result, is frequently 100 percent a year or more. Almost no one, in other words, stays a year. Far more than in the past, America lives with a chronically floating, low-wage workforce, one that would not exist if the deterioration in pay and in training, and the acquiescence to layoffs, had not made deep inroads into the dignity of work.

Still, both labor and management tried from time to time to salvage that dignity. No attempt was bolder than the Saturn project, which began in the early eighties as a response to the popularity of the gasoline-efficient, nearly maintenance-free small cars that the Japanese were selling in the United States by the tens of thousands. Saturn, a small car designed in America, was offered as an alternative. General Motors and the United Auto Workers conceived and jointly managed the manufacturing operation at a plant dedicated to Saturn cars, in Spring Hill, Tennessee. The hope was that with labor participating in management, a motivated workforce, enjoying good wages and job security, would produce a high-quality, reasonably priced vehicle.

Saturns did sell, but not in large enough numbers to lift GM's profits, and in some years, the Saturn operation lost money. The innovative attempt to make organized labor a full partner in corporate management eventually failed, just as it had failed in Roosevelt's first New Deal. Starting in the late nineties, General Motors gradually integrated the Saturn project into its overall operations, ending the UAW's role as a co-manager. And the unionized workers at the Saturn plant, rather than protest, acquiesced to the lost job security. By a vote of 2,886 to 305 in December 2003, the members of UAW Local 1853 endorsed a new labor agreement that eliminated a long-standing no-layoff clause. "We are in a position that either we adapt or die," said Michael Herron, the local's chairman. Adapting meant giving GM's managers a freer hand to achieve greater profitability through cost-cutting.

Other constraints on layoffs also dissipated. The collapse of the Soviet Union in 1991, ending the Cold War, relieved the pressure on companies to preserve job security. Or as Richard Freeman, a labor economist at Harvard, put it: "You had a different attitude toward your employees when you thought that Communism was still out there as an alternative." IBM, an icon of job security, resorted to layoffs for the first time in 1994, announcing that attrition was no longer sufficient to offset rising costs. Not that many of the people who lost their jobs weren't needed. One-fifth soon came back as consultants on contract, a practice that spread in the nineties to other companies and to other laid-off workers, undermining their resistance to layoffs. Adding insult to injury, companies like IBM concluded that efficiency and productivity did not necessarily require that employees feel secure in their jobs. Fear of layoff could get adequate results, which helps to explain why General Electric, which plays tough, is nevertheless successful, Paul Osterman, a professor at MIT's Sloan School of Management, argues.

From another quarter, the surge in immigration undercut job security by providing a ready supply of workers, particularly at the low end of the wage scale, to replace employees inclined to challenge their bosses or resist layoffs or value their labor at more than $8 or $10 an hour. Older people also contributed to this ready supply. Starting in the 1980s, they held jobs beyond normal retirement age in greater numbers, or they worked because Social Security and diminishing company pensions were insufficient to make ends meet. Perhaps most important, women piled into the labor force, adding to the pool of available workers and making it easier for a family to struggle through the layoff of a husband, now that so many wives brought home second incomes. That extra paycheck became a means of accommodating layoffs.

The women's movement came out of the 1960s. So did the antiwar protests and disillusionment with government. That, too, undermined job security. The young people formed in that decade turned out to be more inured to layoffs than their predecessors, partly because of the pummeling they took in their formative years as students. The shift in attitudes shows up in a comparison of the layoff experiences of the classes of 1958 and 1968 at Harvard.

Layoffs wormed their way into the ranks of Harvard's alumni in the early 1990s, and members of the class of 1958, alarmed by the inroad, went public with this unexpected disruption in their lives. They chose their thirty-fifth reunion, in 1993, to do so. Several members of the class of '58 who had been separated from their jobs formed a "job network," and they asked the reunion organizers to put their plea for help on the program. The organizers agreed, and a circular went out to all class members inviting them to a breakfast during the three-day reunion. The mailed invitation targeted two groups: class members who had been laid off and those classmates "in a position to offer employment directly or through quality referrals." Twenty-five people showed up for the breakfast, filling the headmaster's private dining room at Lowell House.

Layoffs had devastated blue-collar and clerical workers, and now they were spreading into the upper reaches of the white-collar world, touching workers with the most elite educations. What was happening to Harvard men clearly constituted another milestone in the layoff saga, another barrier breached.

Erich Segal, the novelist, was a member of the class of '58. He based his book *The Class*, published in 1985, on the lives of his classmates from graduation day to their twenty-fifth reunion. In that quarter century, they endured divorces, loneliness, alienated children, thwarted ambition. There were some suicides. But nowhere in the 592 pages of *The Class* is anyone out of work, or pressed for cash. "It was not merely that you were going to make your way, but as a Harvard man the way was prepared for you," Segal told me. "We were brought up to believe that we were immune from that kind of circumstance."

The autobiographical sketches collected ten years later for the thirty-fifth reunion book added layoffs to the list of experiences that Segal had written about—not a lot of layoffs, but enough. Most of them were straightforward dismissals. Others in the class were forced into early retirement, the alternative being outright layoff. Several had taken over family businesses and these had gone under, unable in some cases to compete against giant discount wholesalers and retailers that did not exist a generation earlier. One victim, Thomas A. Stalker, the proprietor of a family hardwood-flooring business, was wiped out and went through a divorce at roughly the same time. He came to the reunion with food stamps in his pocket, he told me.

Segal had not attended the reunion, but the distress over layoffs was on his mind. "By curious coincidence," he faxed me afterward, "I was snowbound two weeks ago, picked up a copy of the thirty-fifth anniversary report and for the first time read it cover to cover. Unlike the twenty-fifth anniversary edition, it did not radiate with expressions of success and optimism. Quite the contrary, it seemed like a litany of loss and disillusion. . . . Not only was there a striking amount of unemployment, but for people in their early to middle fifties there seemed quite a large number of retirees. Another way of viewing them would be as dropouts from the system. Their dominant emotion seemed to be relief. Thank God that's over."

The victims included Lynn D. Sprankle, who had lost a good corporate job and could not land another, although he had sent out thousands of résumés, "made thousands of phone calls, and contacted virtually everyone I've ever known," he told his classmates in his autobiographical sketch. "I even targeted five hundred Harvard alumni—some of whom are listed in this very book—whose names I found in major business directories. But the response from these people was also zero—no phone calls, no leads, no interviews, and of course no offers. So much for the camaraderie of the 'ten thousand men of Harvard.' " The sketch ended with this bitter observation about a Harvard education: "I no longer look upon it with the pride I once did; and I have come to view my graduate degree [an MBA from the University of Pennsylvania] the same way. In fact, they may even have been detrimental—in that they caused me to set higher personal expectation levels than I was ever able to attain."

The thirty-fifth reunion of the class of 1968—this time the "Harvard and Radcliffe Class of 1968"—offered a different face. Pain and novelty were not on display. The reunion book had layoffs sprinkled through the autobiographical sketches, although no angry outbursts like Sprankle's. Rather than joining companies, a number of class members were doctors or academics or researchers or they engaged in not-for-profit work and public service. These endeavors reflected the idealism characteristic of the class of 1968, with the added bonus that the work was relatively immune to layoffs. A striking number of class members had shifted careers in middle age, getting into fields they considered more socially uplifting than the careers they initially chose. Or they were planning to make the switch. Frederick Alan Connell, associate dean of the University of Washington School of Public Health, wrote that he and his wife were contemplating the next stage in their lives, "the next adventure, which will probably be overseas: pounding nails, teaching, distributing food or doing something that we hope will be useful." He regretted that "I (and my generation), who had so much promise, privilege, opportunity, and idealism, have not left our country, the world, or the earth in better shape."

At the reunion itself, layoffs were not on the agenda at any of the scheduled gatherings and panels. I interviewed a woman who was laid off from a software company and before that from a bank, a chemist who took a buyout to avoid a layoff, and several class members who as owners and bosses initiated layoffs. They said they were comfortable doing so. One was an architect, William F. Wilson, principal partner in William Wilson Associated Architects, in Boston, who used layoffs to trim staff and considered the process healthy. "You're really talking about who's good for the firm," he said. "That speaks to the idea that you don't want to have people who are kind of—not misfits, but sort of in the backwaters of an organization."

For those who lost jobs, fear, humiliation, hardship, and damage to self-esteem were all present in their stories, as they were for those who had lost their jobs in the class of 1958. And yet the framework was different. The surprise at losing a job was gone. The job security that the class of 1958 had taken for granted was not an expectation of the class of 1968. In their experience, America had let them down. The dismantling of job security was part of the disappointment.

The members of the class of 1968 were freshmen when Vietnam was not yet much of an issue, the civil rights movement was at its peak, and the women's movement was just getting started. An apparently progressive nation ushered them into Harvard. By the time they graduated, that same nation seemed to be coming apart and many in the class were caught up in protests against what was happening. Martin Luther King

Jr. was assassinated in April of their senior year and Robert F. Kennedy within days of their graduation. The Tet offensive gave the lie to the Johnson administration's claims that the war was being won, exacerbating the distrust in government that the war had produced. Johnson himself announced in the class's senior year that he would not run for reelection because of Vietnam. But he left the men in the class facing the draft to fight a war that many considered immoral.

Bill Clinton graduated from Georgetown University in 1968 and in his memoir, *My Life,* published thirty-six years later, he wrote that the tumult of that era shattered the Democratic Party's traditional policies, and in the process "conservative populism replaced progressive populism" as the dominant political force. "The deeply embedded nightmares of 1968 formed the arena in which I and all other progressive politicians had to struggle over our entire careers," Clinton wrote. "Perhaps if Martin Luther King Jr. and Robert Kennedy had lived, things would have been different."

Several explanations offered at the class of '68 reunion linked layoffs and the 1960s experience. Some were elaborate and fanciful, but they boiled down to the view that the irrational events of the mid-sixties radicalized and disillusioned students who had entered college as mainstream Americans and then found themselves isolated and attacked for participating in the protest movement. Richard A. Licht, a senior partner in a Providence, Rhode Island, law firm, explained the transition more succinctly. His firm had merged with another and he had gotten the task of whittling down the enlarged staff through layoffs. "What the sixties did," he said, "was set us up to deal with the notion that institutions can let us down." What the sixties did was produce a generation of liberals who became cynical about institutions and that made it easier for Licht and others in his position to carry out the layoffs that the more traditional generation of the fifties resisted, expecting more from institutions.

Self-reliance helped to fill the void, and self-absorption. Lasch described the process in *The Culture of Narcissism.* The self-absorption displaced collective behavior, which in turn was connected to stable institutions, such as long-term employment, and these institutions were anchored in a common past—a past now being discarded. "Americans," Lasch wrote in 1979, "seem to wish to forget not only the sixties, the riots, the new left, the disruptions on college campuses, Vietnam, Watergate and the Nixon presidency, but their entire collective past, even in the antiseptic form in which it was celebrated during the Bicentennial."

Bill Clinton fits this mold. As much as anyone, he disconnected the Democratic Party from its past, specifically its New Deal concern for job security and full employment. They became casualties of his ad hoc, centrist policies with their veneer of concern for people's well-being. On the one hand, his administration pushed idealistically for universal, federally subsidized health insurance and the Family and Medical Leave Act, both supportive of workers' needs—although the former was stillborn and the latter amounted to time off without pay. On the other hand, with Republican support, he prodded Congress to ratify NAFTA, the North American Free Trade Agreement, in 1993 and GATT, the General Agreement on Tariffs and Trade, in 1995, out of which came the World Trade Organization. All were milestones in the acceptance by Americans of layoffs. Whatever the long-term benefits of free trade might turn out to be—and Clinton insisted there would be long-term benefits—for a decade or more NAFTA, GATT, and the WTO have facilitated the movement of production and jobs to lower-wage countries.

There was political resistance to Clinton's achievement in undermining job security: Pat Buchanan's surprising popularity in the 1996 primaries, for example, and the Seattle demonstrations in the winter of 2000 against the World Trade Organization, a protest that disrupted a WTO meeting while the president himself was in attendance. By then, however, the Clinton administration—forgetting the past, never mentioning Augustus F. Hawkins, massaging the present—had brought down what was left of government barriers to layoffs.

CHAPTER SEVEN

A Green Light from Clinton

Allan Sloan is a sixtyish, slightly overweight, good-natured, dedicated journalist who in 1996 wrote an essay for *Newsweek* that denounced as a "mark of shame" the way in which chief executives who earned millions laid off their employees by the tens of thousands. His essay stuck in my mind as a powerful outcry against layoffs, but when we met seven years later, at an awards dinner for business journalists, Sloan explained that it was not the layoffs themselves that had prompted him to write his famous condemning essay. It was the way they were carried out that drove him to skewer nine very prominent chief executives. As a columnist, Sloan has often held up executive misbehavior to scrutiny and public ridicule, and this was misbehavior in the extreme.* The memory still angers him.

Sloan's 2,300-word essay appeared in the February 26, 1996, issue of *Newsweek,* and perhaps more than any other single article, it reflected the rising public anguish over what was happening. It also reflected the pressure on corporate executives to tone down their behavior and the pressure on President Clinton to make layoffs politically acceptable. Both would happen. But in the late winter and early spring of 1996, damage control was the order of the day. Too many voters were losing their jobs. Layoffs had spread from blue-collar to white-collar workers and increasingly up the wage and prestige ladder, invading once-sacrosanct upper-end occupations.

---

*Sloan's columns have appeared in *Newsweek* since 1995. He is the magazine's Wall Street editor. His columns also appear in the *Washington Post,* more frequently there in recent years than in *Newsweek.*

Patrick Buchanan's early success in the New Hampshire primary, championing protectionist save-the-jobs policies, had made layoffs a front-burner campaign issue. Ignoring the anger and discontent that Buchanan had tapped into, many chief executives made matters worse by going out of their way to publicize layoffs, their goal being to push up their companies' stock prices with a public demonstration of toughness and resolve in cutting labor costs. "Chainsaw" Al Dunlap, chief executive of the Scott Paper Company, who threw workers away right and left, had become an emblem, almost a caricature, of this cruel behavior; he had not yet been discredited. The chest thumping and disregard angered Sloan, who had joined *Newsweek* a year earlier as Wall Street editor, and it angered Sloan's boss, Hank Gilman, the editor in charge of the magazine's business coverage.

Over lunch at a favorite restaurant near the *Newsweek* building, the two men cooked up the essay, which Sloan went back to the office and wrote in two days, on deadline. In the bluntest language, he zeroed in on chief executives for arrogant, greedy, boastful behavior—those are Sloan's words even now—in staging layoffs in the early and middle nineties. *Newsweek*'s editors, sensing the readership appeal of Sloan's denunciation, elevated the essay to cover story. Gilman had pushed them to do so, Sloan recalled. And the layout they devised multiplied the outrage. "Corporate Killers" was the cover headline in red block letters; inside, over the story itself was the headline "The Hit Men." For illustration, there were mug shots of the nine well-known chief executives, each with a police-style caption: name, corporate rank, company, fat annual salary, date of crime, and the crime itself, a five-figure job cut.

But even for Sloan, a prizewinning critic of unacceptable executive behavior, laying off workers had by 1996 become a legitimate corporate tactic. The layoffs themselves could not be avoided, he wrote, making a distinction in the text of his essay—although not in the headlines and captions—between the "in-your-face capitalism" that too many executives indulged in and layoffs properly motivated and carried out. "Companies like IBM and Sears and GM had to downsize or die," he declared. And in the second paragraph of his essay, he offered a model of how to do this, praising United Technologies, the manufacturer of helicopters, aircraft engines, air conditioners, and elevators, not for avoiding layoffs—

it certainly had not—but for "a nifty program to help UT workers re-educate themselves for their next jobs." Such good behavior went unnoticed on Wall Street, Sloan wrote.

Robert Allen, the chief executive of AT&T, in particular, had angered him, and Buchanan had laid into Allen, too, accusing him of collecting a huge salary—$16 million in 1995, including the current value of stock options—while announcing the layoffs of tens of thousands of workers. His latest downsizing announcement, the elimination of forty thousand jobs, had come right in the midst of the New Hampshire primary campaign. Sloan, who was fifty-one then, felt particularly touched by it. AT&T had its corporate headquarters and several major operations, including Bell Labs, in northeastern New Jersey, not far from Sloan's suburban home. He lived among AT&T employees, and he considered himself a kindred spirit, a salaried worker himself. He had grown up in Brooklyn, the son of a fund-raiser for Jewish organizations, and had broken into journalism in Detroit as a business reporter for the *Free Press* in the 1970s, just as the auto industry was coming under fire from Japanese competition. "I am labor, for God's sake," Sloan said to me, "not in the union sense, but in the labor sense. . . . I am a worker, not an owner. This is where it [the anger] all came from."

He interviewed Allen after the announcement that AT&T would eliminate those jobs and found him emotionally shut off from his employees. "He said these amazing things," Sloan recalled, "like, 'What do you want me to do, go on television and cry?' I'm asking the question in different ways and he dug himself in deeper. I verified the quotes with AT&T; you want to be fair. These were amazingly damaging quotes. Bob Allen is a human being. He has a family. He has children. He is not an evil man. I believe he was stunned by the article I wrote and being on the cover of *Newsweek*. He never called me again."

Two ingredients of Sloan's scathing essay, bloated CEO pay and numerous layoffs, are still very much in place. But the corporate arrogance has disappeared. Damaged by the public anger that Sloan's essay represented, the nation's chief executives softened their behavior in the spring and summer of 1996. Bell Atlantic and Nynex, to take just one example, announced that they would merge and in doing so eliminate three thousand "overlapped" jobs. But rather than boast, Ivan G. Seidenberg, who would become chairman of the two merged Baby Bells, declared reassuringly: "We think we will create enough new jobs to redeploy most of those 3,000 people." Redeployment happened infrequently, but the shift in rhetoric worked, and by the November presidential election, which gave Clinton a second term, the corporate killers whom Sloan had pilloried for their outrageous layoff practices were well on their way to becoming historical curiosities. Or, as Sloan put it, "the ethos moved on."

The Clinton administration pitched in vigorously to move the ethos on. The president had signaled soon after he took office that layoffs would be allowed. He did this by pushing in his first year for enactment of the North American Free Trade Agreement, and with NAFTA in place, manufacturers in particular stepped up their migration to Mexico, laying off American workers as they closed factories in the United States and reopened them across the border. Clinton did appoint a blue ribbon commission on labor law reform, but when the commission submitted its report in 1995, he ignored recommendations that would have inhibited layoffs. He also abandoned a campaign promise to stop corporations from hiring permanent replacements for workers on strike, so they could lay off the strikers. Not surprisingly, when the uproar developed in 1996 over the arrogant layoff practices of the nation's chief executives, Clinton pushed a formula intended to neutralize layoffs as a political issue—without curtailing them. In doing so, he avoided having to criticize chief executives for their layoff practices, a confrontation that would have risked class warfare during an election year, as the president's campaign strategists put it.

The strengthening economy made the neutralization process possible. The nation was just entering the very robust expansion that would last through Clinton's second term. During his last five years in office, the workforce grew by 12 million jobs, or nearly 10 percent. The president, harnessing this windfall, made job creation the solution for layoffs. He argued in effect that layoffs were acceptable, a civilized form of behavior, as long as the companies doing the layoffs observed the amenities and as long as there was support for the victims, through retraining and education, so they could qualify for the next job. There were plenty of those next jobs out there, the president boasted, crediting his economic policies for the abundant hiring.

Selling this message took some artful doing, however. When the *New York Times* found, in a seven-part, fifty-thousand-word series—published a week after Sloan's essay—that Americans were caught in "the most acute job insecurity since the Great Depression," the White House responded with a white paper, "Job Creation and Employment Opportunities." There was insecurity across the country, the white paper acknowledged, but the number of layoffs was now falling, and rapid job creation was putting the laid-off back to work in jobs that paid well. Both claims stretched and twisted the truth.

The twelve-page white paper, drafted by the president's Council of Economic Advisers, asserted, for example, that while "worker displacement" rates rose in the eighties and early nineties, particularly for older, better educated workers, layoffs had diminished in the last couple of years. It was a bogus claim, one that took advantage of a temporary blind spot in the displacement data collected by the Bureau of Labor Statistics. The bureau had not yet tabulated the layoff numbers for 1994 and 1995, so the council used instead the number of people who had recently begun to collect unemployment pay. That number showed a decline, but it represented only some of those counted as laid-off workers. Once the broader worker-displacement survey was brought up to date four months later, with the release in August of the counts for 1994 and 1995, layoffs turned out to have occurred at a higher rate in the first half of the nineties than in the first half of the eighties.

These were comparable years of recovery from recessions. The layoff rate was higher, in fact, in almost every year of the nineties expansion than in the nearly as long eighties expansion—a signal that layoffs were spreading even in good times. By August, however, corporate America's layoff announcements had become more tactful, public anger had subsided, and, in this calmer atmosphere, the updated layoff numbers got very little media attention. The ethos had indeed moved on and the administration had every incentive to encourage amnesia. "We did not want to confront the idea that job insecurity had increased during Clinton's first term," recalled Michael Ash, a young labor economist on the staff of the Council of Economic Advisers in 1995 and 1996. "That would be bad election-year strategy."

With this goal in mind, the council relegated the entire subject of layoffs to the tenth page of the twelve-page document. The focus instead was on the good news. The workforce had grown by 8.5 million jobs during Clinton's first term, the white paper noted. That was true, but the sequel was questionable. The paper argued that two-thirds of the new jobs paid well—that is, above the median wage of $480 a week for the workforce as a whole. Maybe they did and maybe not. No one knew the actual pay of the new jobs. Wage data collected by the Bureau of Labor Statistics is not detailed enough to provide this information. All it can do is pinpoint the industries and occupations where job creation or job loss takes place and the range of wages for those occupations, but not the pay of the specific jobs created within each range. The wages for the specific new jobs could just as easily be at the low end of an occupational range as at the high end—a shortcoming the white paper did not mention. It also ignored a disturbing trend in the wage ranges themselves. Some were lower in 1996 than they were when Clinton took office, and the median itself, $480 a week, amounted to a very modest $12 an hour for a full-time worker. "Although there is still much left to be done," the white paper declared, "recent trends show that the labor market is on the right track."

That was the verdict in the white paper as published. The first draft, however, written by the Council of Economic Advisers and sent to the Labor Department for its consideration, did not mention layoffs at all, not even on page 10. "We in the Labor Department went ballistic at that omission," Lisa Lynch, then the Labor Department's chief economist, told me years later. The drafts went back and forth between the council and the Labor Department, with the council pushing for positive findings and the Labor Department insisting that caveats must be included. Although Joseph E. Stiglitz was then the council's chairman, Martin N. Baily, a member and later the chairman, supervised the preparation of the white paper. "You guys were really laying it on with a trowel," Baily told me much later, referring to the media coverage, particularly the *Times* series and articles like Sloan's. "We were trying in a sense to counteract the view that the labor market was falling apart." This was, after all, the Clinton administration. "And so we were saying let's look at some of the positive things."

At the insistence of Lynch and her boss, Labor Secretary Robert B. Reich, the final version acknowledged that the president's "dynamic economy" had some unpleasant aspects, chief among them a finding that

people who got jobs again after having been laid off earned less on average at the new jobs. "The average real wage loss due to displacement was
significant and persistent; we must reduce these adjustment costs," the
white paper said, incorporating language that Reich and Lynch had
insisted upon. It was language that challenged the white paper's main
thesis that the economic expansion was generating new jobs that paid
well. That was happening. But subsequent research showed that it was
also generating just as many low-paying jobs. And the laid-off, in any
event, took pay cuts in most cases, if they got work at all.

"We negotiated as hard as we could [for stronger language], but we
had no real negotiating power," Reich recalled. "After the spring of 1995,
when Dick Morris came to the White House, the word was we could not
be sour on the economy. We couldn't be sounding doom and gloom. We
all had to be upbeat. That struck me as potentially dangerous. . . . I
thought that it was important for the Democratic base to know that the
administration was sensitive to what was going on . . . and was taking
steps to try to deal with the problem."

A follow-up to the white paper came a month later. Clinton invited a
hundred business executives, most of them CEOs, to a White House
conference in mid-May to discuss corporate responsibility toward workers. The daylong event at Georgetown University, Clinton's alma mater,
showcased companies with enlightened labor policies such as on-site
child care, flexible work hours, paternity leave, and health insurance for
part-timers. Nothing was said about curtailing layoffs. "Everyone—the
audience, the administration—is assuming that layoffs are inevitable,"
said Donald F. Hastings, CEO of Lincoln Electric Company in Cleveland, nearly the only company at the conference with a no-layoff policy.
They *were* inevitable, in the eyes of the other executives. "We must start
with the reality that corporations cannot guarantee anyone a lifetime job
any more than corporations have a guarantee of immortality," John Snow,
then chairman of the CSX Corporation and later secretary of the treasury
for George W. Bush, told the gathering.

The emphasis instead was on the obligation of socially responsible companies—the ones with on-site child care, flexible work hours, and
the like—to treat the laid-off and those who might soon be laid off
humanely. The way to do this was to help pay for tuition and training so

that employees could acquire skills useful not only in their present jobs but in their next jobs, too, after the layoff. The Clinton administration would pitch in, the president declared, with more subsidies for education and training and with "portability" for health insurance and pension benefits, so that a laid-off worker could transfer those items from the lost job to the next one, or qualify for benefits more easily in the next job. And Clinton did eventually make it easier to move pensions and health insurance from one employer to the next. "There are some things we have to do to help people become more employable, even if they don't have specific job security," the president said.

The twelve-page white paper and the follow-up White House conference on corporate responsibility constituted, in hindsight, a milestone in the effort to make layoffs disappear as a political issue. For the first time, a Democratic administration gave its explicit consent to the practice, distancing itself from support for job security through government intervention and strong unions that the party had for so long represented. Demand for workers in a tight labor market became a substitute for job security, and as job creation multiplied, driving down the unemployment rate to below 5 percent, the president and his advisers asserted the view that skill and education would pay off in higher incomes as companies vied for the best workers.

There was one other leg to this new political stool: monetary policy. If the vying for workers got out of hand, the Federal Reserve was there to raise interest rates and, in doing so, to reduce economic growth as well as hiring and wage pressure. The Fed, in fact, spent most of the Clinton years holding down interest rates to maintain the stimulus and the hiring. It counted on layoffs and job insecurity to suppress wage pressure so that companies would not have to offset rising labor costs by raising prices. Wages did rise in the tight labor markets of the late nineties, but at an annual rate, adjusted for inflation, of only 1.4 percent, which was not enough to force employers to resort to inflationary price increases. They resorted instead to labor-saving technologies and, above all, to layoffs or the threat of them. Workers were too uncertain of their jobs and too unorganized to resurrect the belligerent demands that had characterized the seventies. Alan Greenspan, the Fed's chairman, recognized and welcomed the dampening effect of layoffs and even worried in 1997—unnecessarily, as it turned out—that "the force of [job] insecurity may be fading." So Clinton had low interest rates going for him and these in turn generated plenty of hiring simultaneously with layoffs. As Gene Sperling, who advised Clinton on economic policy through both terms, put it much later: "I don't think there is any question that we represented a break with past Democratic administrations in that our focus was far more on . . . finding private sector jobs [for the laid-off] than in relying on government as a source of support and employment."

In *My Life*, Clinton fails to discuss in any detail the historic transition from the Democratic Party's old ways. The same is true of Clinton's Wall Street–oriented treasury secretary, Robert E. Rubin, whose memoir, *In an Uncertain World*, was, like Clinton's, the autobiography of a man who grew up during the heyday of the old Democratic Party, and then changed the party.

Clinton's memoir refers in generalities to his key role as a founder of the Democratic Leadership Council, the intraparty movement that shifted the Democrats toward "a dynamic but centrist progressive movement of new ideas rooted in traditional American values." Almost nothing is said in the 957-page book about the uproar over layoffs that erupted in 1996 or the white paper or the conference on corporate responsibility at Georgetown. Rubin's account is equally sparse and unspecific on the vital issue of job security. In its 406 pages, layoffs are not mentioned. There are numerous abstract references to education, job training, unemployment, and various aspects of the social safety net, but all of them are subordinate to deficit reduction, the "threshold act" that ushered in "the sustained, robust recovery of the 1990s." Reich, who was leery of too much deficit reduction, is described as an able cabinet officer, but one who wanted to move the administration "in a much more populist direction," a strategy that Rubin rejected as counterproductive and likely to anger the corporate hierarchy, whose goodwill and confidence Rubin considered essential.

These were still Rubin's views when I went to see him in February 2003 at the Citigroup building in midtown Manhattan. He had joined Citigroup as a sort of consigliere in the office of the chairman, and he occupied a spacious corner office in the elegant, richly carpeted executive suite. His name was not yet connected with John F. Kerry's in the jockeying for the Democratic presidential nomination, although by the time of the election twenty months later, Rubin would be Kerry's flagship adviser on economic policy and Clintonomics would be the flag, with its emphasis on education and training to recycle laid-off workers back into jobs.

In the sitting area, a bronze bust of Dwight Eisenhower sat prominently on a narrow table behind the sofa on which Rubin was seated. Eisenhower seemed to be looking over Rubin's shoulder. I did not ask why Eisenhower instead of Franklin Roosevelt, but the answer seemed obvious. Eisenhower, who was president when Rubin entered Harvard as a freshman in 1956, was closer to Rubin's centrist approach to economics, with its combination of deference to markets and a limited role for government in areas that markets got glaringly wrong. Government, for example, sees a clean environment as a public trust. The private sector, on the other hand, resists the cost, which cuts into profits. Rubin favored government in this case. Government protects people, too, through unemployment insurance and other components of the safety net, but only after markets have chewed them up, often in the form of layoffs. Rubin was all for the safety net, but not for policies that inhibited layoffs and thus limited corporate "flexibility," undermining American capitalism's competitive advantage.

Layoffs were not a subject that concerned him. He did not remember the white paper in the spring of 1996, although it was an act of capitulation to layoffs. Nor did he remember the administration's occasional attempts in Clinton's first term to preserve job security or at least hamper layoffs. "I'm trying to think back; there may have been some idea about sixty-day notices for plant closings," he said, referring to a law on the books since Reagan's second term, an often ignored law that some Clinton officials wanted to enforce more actively. For Rubin, enforcing a law that gave soon-to-be-laid-off workers extra time to hunt for new jobs while still on the payroll was all well and good, but a detail.

The desirable chain of events in his head started with robust economic growth. That required efficient companies with lean cost structures and enough profits to prompt investment in new technologies and in expansion. All this, in turn, required low interest rates to encourage the borrowing that greased the expansion, and interest rates fell in the Clinton years. Certainly job insecurity played a role in the Fed's tolerance of low interest rates. For Rubin, however, the falling rates were mainly a response to the administration's focus on deficit reduction. And Rubin's thinking, widely shared on Wall Street, prevailed. The chain of events in his mind was a disappearing deficit resulting in low interest rates resulting in robust economic expansion. The expansion, once under way, also required flexible labor markets, in Rubin's view. Flexibility in hiring and firing resulted in plenty of hiring if the economy grew strongly enough, but in plenty of layoffs in a weakening economy—or in a strong one, for that matter, if new efficiencies required fewer workers or if labor costs could be cut by shifting operations to lower-wage communities either within the United States or abroad. "Maybe there is a way to accomplish the cost-saving without laying off people," Rubin told me, "but I have not seen it. Basically, well, I just don't know how you do it."

Neither for that matter did Reich or Stiglitz, who as chairman of the Council of Economic Advisers in 1996 signed the white paper along with Reich. They were easily the two most politically liberal members of the White House economics team. Largely because of their views, they left the administration early in the second term and became critics of Clinton policies. Stiglitz decried such things as too much deregulation in banking and telecommunications, distorting markets, and Reich lamented that deficit reduction starved necessary social programs. But neither challenged the layoff, retrain, and reemploy formula that was a central tenet of Clintonomics. That surprised me in Stiglitz's case. He shared a Nobel Prize in economics for research that brought him to the conclusion that government intervention is essential to offset a market system's numerous imperfections. "I could always find, in my modeling, a particular [government] intervention that made everyone better off," Stiglitz once explained to me.

But that finding did not apply when it came to layoffs. Too much had changed. Interventions that preserved jobs triggered other results that Stiglitz considered unacceptable. Everyone did not end up better off. Take the auto industry, he said to me, by way of an example. "The point is that American car companies cannot compete against Japanese car companies. In this situation, should we guarantee jobs for American car workers? Our [the Clinton administration's] view was that if you're going to guarantee jobs for American car workers, you have to guarantee output

for American car makers, and that meant you have to have trade protection. You go down that line of reasoning and you say, that is not
acceptable. So you don't go down that line of reasoning. What do you do?
You make it easier for people to move—more education, job training,
portability of pensions and health insurance."

Reich took this view a step further. Like Stiglitz, and many other academics, he accepted the findings of empirical research concerning education. In virtually all of this research, people with a college education
earned more than workers with only a high school diploma. That was
particularly the case in the eighties. By the end of that decade, men and
women with bachelor's degrees earned nearly 40 percent more than those
with high school diplomas, or almost double the percentage in 1980, and
through most of the nineties the college wage premium continued to rise,
although much more slowly than in the eighties. Given the gap, when five
engineers are competing for a single opening and their competition drives
down the offered wage, that wage rarely falls as low as the pay of a store
clerk, a restaurant worker, or a taxi driver. The educated and skilled also
qualify for a greater array of jobs than the uneducated and unskilled. An
engineer might find himself driving a taxi because no job opening exists
for engineers, but when one appears he can apply while the taxi driver
who lacks an engineering degree cannot.

An educated workforce also makes possible feats of technology
and production, and these feats generate economic expansion and jobs.
College-educated workers were critical, for example, to the success of the
space program that President Eisenhower initiated in 1957 in response to
the Soviet Union's Sputnik and that President Kennedy intensified with
his goal of manned space flight. Supply and demand interacted and out
of that interaction came jobs, income, and wealth. When the demand is
not there, however, the payoff from schooling declines, a setback that
Reich minimized. In a leap of faith, he argued that the existence of an
educated worker generated a demand for his or her services. Build
the field and the players will come, as in the fantasy movie *Field of
Dreams*. The engineer driving a taxi won't be doing so for long. A job
will find him. His skills alone give birth to a demand for his services.
Many mainstream economists and policy makers share this leap of faith,
which is expressed as Say's law: Supply generates its own demand. The

French economist Jean-Baptiste Say, whose life overlapped that of Adam Smith, coined this oversimplification of the master's teachings—and, after decades of oblivion during the Depression and the immediate post–World War II decades, it became gospel again.

Reich came up with an unusual formulation of the concept, and it caught the attention of his old friend Bill Clinton, whom he had known since they were Rhodes scholars together in the 1960s. Reich laid out his case in *The Work of Nations*, published in 1991, just months before he joined Clinton in the latter's quest for the presidency. Clinton even carried a copy of the book with him, one with passages underlined and notes in the margins. *The Work of Nations* noted that Americans increasingly must participate in an international labor market regardless of the home country of their employer. Standard job classifications do not apply in this new market, Reich explained. The new division is between workers who do their jobs in a routine, repetitive fashion and those who apply to their work imagination and originality as well as conceptual and analytic thinking. The first category of work is vulnerable to outsourcing; people in other countries can perform routine, repetitive work as well as Americans, and at lower wages. That goes not just for factory and clerical tasks, but for many higher occupations. Law, accounting, medical technology, computer programming, electronics, and engineering all have among their practitioners those who perform their jobs in routine, repetitive fashion, and they, too, are sinking in the world economy.

Workers in the second classification are not sinking, Reich maintained. College-educated "symbolic analysts" stand at the pinnacle of this innovative second group. They are researchers and scientists, marketers and financiers, design engineers, architects and biotechnology experts, film producers and public relations specialists. The best of them are in demand everywhere in the world, and that demand bestows on them the highest form of job security. But any worker, college-educated or not, can be a symbolic analyst, to one degree or another, Reich argued. That is because symbolic analysts are in essence problem solvers, and even assembly-line and clerical employees can engage in problem solving. When they do so, they increase the likelihood that their jobs will stay put as a reward for the productivity that results from their problem solving.

"Consider, for example, the checkout clerk, whose computer enables her to control inventory and decide when to reorder items from the factory," Reich wrote. "Instead of replacing her, the computer empowers her to assume more responsibility and thus add greater value to the enterprise. The number of such technologically empowered jobs is limited only by the ability of [workers] to learn on the job. This means that a far greater number of Americans would need a solid grounding in mathematics, basic science, and reading and communications skills."

The government's role in this process, Reich argued, is to subsidize education and training for vast numbers of people so they can acquire the necessary problem-solving skills. He estimated that 60 to 70 percent of the population had the potential to become problem-solving symbolic analysts using complex computer software. The remaining 30 to 40 percent would have job security through a different route, in jobs that cannot leave the United States because they are site-specific and require personal attention—bus drivers, for example, hospital attendants, caregivers, and restaurant workers. Being in less demand than the symbolic analysts, these site-specific workers need support from government in the form of a rising minimum wage, a more generous Earned Income Tax Credit, health insurance, and greater access to unions and their bargaining power. This was the thesis that Clinton, the candidate, and Reich, his chief economic adviser in those early days, incorporated into Clinton's push for the presidency. "Comfortably integrating the American workforce into the new world economy," Reich wrote, "turns out to rest heavily on education and training, as well as nutrition and health care sufficient to allow such learning to occur."

That was still Reich's thinking when I visited him in February 2003 at his rambling, Victorian-era home in a quiet Cambridge neighborhood. While Reich's faith in education and training as the principal solution was unshaken, he did not believe they were the entire solution. More than anyone else in Clinton's cabinet, he favored public investment to help generate demand for workers. But even for Reich this was secondary. Education and training were at the heart of the matter. "They are extremely important," he said. "Without them, you cannot possibly get to higher levels of productivity and wages." Clinton shared this view, but in the end the president did not push Congress for anywhere near enough money to tap the nation's human potential and thus give rise to the demand for workers that, in Reich's view, materializes in response to a growing supply of properly trained and educated men and women.

The opposite was true. Reich's four years as secretary of labor had made him acutely aware, he said, that the great majority of the nation's jobholders were distinctly disposable in the eyes of their employers, very often despite their education and skills. They were the "anxious class," a phrase he memorably coined in a Labor Day speech in 1994. For all his faith that the demand for educated and trained workers is self-generating, assuring job security, Reich had wanted the White House and the media to pressure companies "to lay off people only if necessary." He had also wanted the administration to require companies to help government with the cost of training and education to make their workers more valuable. That would inhibit layoffs; an employer would think twice about shedding a valuable worker in whom the employer had invested. If there were layoffs anyway, then the education and training would make it easier, Reich said, "for someone to move from job to job [reducing] the psychic and economic cost of losing a job."

These ideas were incorporated into a proposal for a training tax that Clinton and Al Gore, Clinton's running mate, featured in their 1992 campaign platform, published as *Putting People First*. In three sections of the platform, the two candidates reiterated their intention "to require every employer to spend 1.5 percent of payroll for continued education and training, and make them [the employers] provide the training to all workers, not just executives." If the training outlay fell short of the 1.5 percent, then the unspent portion would go automatically to the government. There is evidence that employees trained in-house do advance to more skilled jobs, and unemployed workers benefit, too, if their training is linked to specific job openings and the companies with those openings agree in advance to fill them, at specified wages, with qualified graduates of publicly funded training programs. The point is that training works when employers are directly involved. The payroll tax spoke to that dynamic. Clinton, however, abandoned the proposal in the month before his inauguration, perhaps out of concern that the 1.5 percent for training would conflict with a payroll tax that his advisers had in mind to pay for government-funded health care.

Reich, in our interview at his home a decade later, criticized the "elite press" for having failed to hammer away at the layoff problem and the principal solution—namely, enough money to pay for massive education and training. "If the elite press stops paying attention to something, then whatever it is they were paying attention to ceases to be on a lot of people's minds," Reich insisted. When that happens, then astute politicians like Bill Clinton lose interest, too. But Reich was wrong. The elite press, and plenty of not-so-elite publications, had hammered away at the layoff phenomenon and its disastrous impact on incomes and family stability. Sloan's corporate killers essay in *Newsweek* and the *Times*'s downsizing series were two notable examples of the media outcry in the winter and spring of 1996. And the administration, in reply, stonewalled. Its answer was the white paper, which Reich endorsed, although he had agitated for stronger language. The white paper proclaimed that layoffs were diminishing, that a healthy economy had generated 8.5 million jobs in Clinton's first term, and that contrary to all the talk about wage stagnation, the new jobs paid well. As Gene Sperling put it, "We were pulling into better times, and that became the answer to layoffs."

None of the Clinton administration's eventual permissiveness toward layoffs was discernible in the 1992 election campaign that brought Clinton and Gore to office. Apart from the training tax, the candidates had spoken glowingly in *Putting People First* of lifetime learning, subsidized scholarships, tax credits to offset a family's outlays for college tuition, and school-to-work apprenticeship programs "to give kids who don't want to go to college the skills they need to find high-wage jobs." The emphasis was on preparing people to be Reich's symbolic analysts, secure in their jobs, or at least in the workplace, because of their skill and initiative. There was even a proposal for a national board that would set job standards for every industry and occupation and link the standards to training programs and to community college courses. "If job applicants did not meet the standards, you would not hire them," said Anthony Carnevale, an economist whom Clinton appointed as chairman of the new National Commission for Employment Policy.

The standards board never materialized, the school-to-work apprenticeship program was eventually reduced to experimental status, and the subsidies for education and training turned out to be a fraction of what *Putting People First* seemed to envision. Public spending also fizzled as a solution. Clinton had been elected in November promising to spend $50 billion on public works, mainly as a means of generating jobs for the unemployed, many of them laid-off workers. That shrank to $16 billion by the time the proposal got to Congress, where it was voted down by a combination of Republicans and conservative Democrats. And Clinton did not try again.

By inauguration day his interest in a big outlay for public investment had all but disappeared as job creation finally picked up steam, ending many months of a "jobless recovery," during which the workforce had continued to shrink, although the 1990–91 recession was long over. The renewed hiring and the emphasis on deficit reduction doomed the public spending proposal. Even Reich signed on to the demise, doing so before Congress killed the program anyway. "If, come January, employment is substantially on the rebound, then obviously there's less need—there may be no need—to take immediate action," Reich told journalists a month after the election, while he was still chief of Clinton's economic transition team, the custodian of the president's economic policies. Come January, Lloyd Bentsen came aboard as the first treasury secretary and Rubin as the first director of the National Economic Council. In their hands, deficit reduction became the priority, not public works or sumptuous outlays for education and training or a payroll tax that would inhibit layoffs.

There was other backsliding. During the 1992 election campaign, Clinton had signaled that while education and training were high on his agenda, resistance to layoffs had a place, too. The candidate promised, for example, to push for a law that would prohibit employers from hiring replacement workers during a strike and then keep them after the strike while laying off the strikers. When Caterpillar threatened in April 1992 to break a five-month strike by hiring permanent replacements, Clinton showed up in Peoria, Illinois, Caterpillar's home city, mingled with the strikers, and reiterated his opposition to striker replacement. He was cheered, of course, but Caterpillar's announcement that it would replace the strikers, who were represented by the United Auto Workers, soon ended the walkout. More than half of those on strike were within six years of retirement and many feared they would lose their pensions. Once in office, Clinton made good on his pledge, endorsing a bill already before Congress that would outlaw permanent striker replacement. The House passed such a bill, but in the Senate, the Democrats, although they were in the majority, fell seven votes short of the sixty needed to stop a Republican filibuster in the summer of 1994. Five months later, the Republican victory in the midterm election closed off congressional action.

So the administration tried a different route. Vice President Gore, speaking at the AFL-CIO's annual convention in Bal Harbour, Florida, on February 20, 1995, announced that the president would issue an executive order banning striker replacement. The federal government would no longer purchase goods and services from companies that permanently replaced strikers. It was a bombshell announcement, satisfying a major political goal of organized labor, whose support Clinton needed in his bid for reelection. Private companies take in billions of dollars through federal contracts and the executive order, energetically enforced, would endanger some of that corporate revenue while strengthening the bargaining power of unionized workers. The Bridgestone Tire and Rubber Company, for example, had recently begun to hire permanent replacements for striking workers, and it sold tires to federal agencies.

The executive order, however, came with some significant exceptions not spelled out in the announcement. It would not apply to companies that hired replacement workers before the order became effective. Bridgestone would be exempt and the exemption would continue as long as it sold tires to the government under existing contracts. In addition, the chiefs of federal agencies purchasing goods and services from the private sector were given leeway to ignore the order, although the Labor Department could bar offending companies from future federal contracts.

Even so, Clinton's executive order did not survive. The United States Court of Appeals for the District of Columbia soon ruled that it constituted an improper end run around the National Labor Relations Act. The ruling came in the early months of the 1996 election campaign, just when the administration was courting corporate support and extolling companies that voluntarily behaved responsibly. Rather than fight on, Reich announced, in the final weeks of the election campaign, that the administration would not appeal the court's ruling. "Further litigation on the validity of the executive order is not productive," Reich said in a statement at the time. And the subject did not come up again in the Clinton presidency, although companies continued to hire replacement workers and lay off strikers.

Years later, Sperling introduced me to a nuance about striker replacement that had escaped me—and the public—during Clinton's presidency. "For President Clinton, striker replacement was not really about preventing layoffs," Sperling said. "The president did not believe in substituting his judgment for a private employer's about layoffs. He was interested, however, in taking steps where he thought employer behavior was out of bounds." That preference for civilized layoffs explains other attempts during Clinton's first term to reform the practice. But each attempt ran up against concern at the White House that the nation's corporate executives would be angered at the intrusion on their autonomy and, in retaliation, would inflict political damage. So the administration backed off, just as it had over the issue of striker replacement.

Late in the first term, for example, Reich pushed for a change in corporate income taxes, one that would lower taxes for companies that invested in job training while refraining as much as possible from layoffs. Tax revenue would be lost, but that loss would be more than offset, Reich argued, by the reduction in federal outlays for unemployment benefits and to retrain dislocated workers. What he now proposed was a watered-down version of the pledge, enshrined in *Putting People First,* to require companies to spend an amount equal to 1.5 percent of their payrolls on their workers. This watered-down version, however, went nowhere at the White House; Rubin and others vetoed the idea, concerned that it smacked of economic populism and would be politically dangerous.

If a change in the tax law was out of the question, then maybe the goal of inhibiting layoffs could be achieved by enforcing existing rules governing corporate premiums for unemployment insurance. Reich's Labor Department attempted to do that in 1995. The idea was to restore "experience ratings" to the premiums that companies pay to help support unemployment benefits. Most of the money for unemployment insurance comes from a uniform payroll tax mandated by Congress, but in addition companies pay an insurance premium, a form of taxation, that is supposed to be higher for employers who send more workers into unemployment than for those who send very few or none. Each state administers this system of "experience ratings" for companies in its jurisdiction. Let the offenders bear a disproportionate share of the cost, the message is, and they may think twice about shedding workers.

In the late eighties and the early nineties, however, many states, particularly those with Republican governors, let experience ratings lapse. As a result, companies engaging in mass layoffs paid no more in premiums than companies that sent very few workers into unemployment. The deterrent was gone and Reich wanted the federal government to intervene and restore it, particularly in the case of profitable companies that closed plants and moved them offshore or to another state. "It will discourage firms from laying off workers, and therefore provide more job security," Reich's chief economist at the time, Alan Krueger, stated in a memo.

Premiums would be reduced not only for companies that refrained from layoffs, but also for those that added workers. The result would be revenue neutrality, Krueger argued: the higher premiums for corporate offenders would be offset by what amounted to a tax break for companies that preserved job security. Reich took the proposal to the National Economic Council at the White House and Gene Sperling vetoed it. Others on the council were lukewarm, anyway. Krueger's assurance of revenue neutrality was not sufficient for them. "They were worried that in the coming election campaign Reich's initiative would be portrayed as a tax increase," Krueger said.

While corporate America increasingly cowed the Clinton administration, the AFL-CIO increasingly did not. Organized labor had supported Clinton in 1992, just as it had regularly supported Democratic presidential candidates for decades. In response, Clinton tried to meld labor's interests with those of management. That was the goal of a day-long conference in Chicago in late July 1993, barely seven months into the Clinton presidency. The sponsors of the suggestively titled Conference on the Future of the American Workplace were the Commerce Department and the Labor Department, management and labor symbolically joining hands. Only they didn't really. Ron Brown, the commerce secretary, and Reich were both there, and they tried to sell—to an audience of managers, workers, and union officials gathered in an amphitheater whose seats formed a semicircle overlooking a small lecture platform— the concept of "empowered" hourly workers who helped to run their companies. These were workers who, as Reich put it, would engage continuously in training that honed their skills. They would also help to set production levels, would keep production moving, and would worry about product quality. Rather than standard annual wages, incomes would rise as a result of profit sharing or "gain-sharing" bonuses that rewarded improvements in production. Or there would be raises pegged to a worker's skill and endeavor, a reward for participating in continuous training or in work teams that took responsibility for production, eliminating the need for a foreman.

Reich is a master teacher. His forum was not unlike a lecture hall at Harvard's Kennedy School of Government, where he taught before joining the Clinton administration. He laid out his case with enthusiasm and conviction. Not many American companies had achieved what Reich was describing, everyone agreed, but a few had, Reich insisted, and as evidence he called on Thomas J. Zidek, a line worker and union leader at the L-S Electro-Galvanizing Company in Cleveland. What did Zidek consider the most important component of the high-performance work organization that his company exemplified? "The opportunity to have input into determining our own pay system, and to set gain-sharing goals," Zidek replied.

President Clinton showed up in time to give the luncheon speech and chair an early afternoon discussion, during which an executive and an employee of US West, the telephone company, and a representative of the Communications Workers of America, the union representing the phone workers, described their cooperative efforts, including their efforts to cut costs and achieve efficiencies without excessive layoffs. "The most interesting thing that you said is that what turned out to be good for the company turned out to be good for the employees," Clinton said of the US West experience—not anticipating the layoffs to come at US West.

Thomas R. Donahue, the secretary-treasurer of the AFL-CIO, was not as sanguine. He argued that cooperation deteriorates into management getting its way at labor's expense, unless workers are represented by unions with sufficient bargaining power. To help achieve this goal, Donahue called for changes in existing labor law to make union organizing easier. Following up, John T. Joyce, president of the International Union of Bricklayers and Allied Craftsmen, called for tighter labor laws to limit "the option that companies have to escape collective bargaining." Neither Clinton nor Reich nor Brown responded to these proposals, but later when I asked Brown whether he endorsed Donahue's suggestion, Brown replied that changing the law to make union organizing easier "was not necessary" to the cooperative process, although such changes "can be an important part of the equation."

It was a nonanswer, very much in keeping with the Clinton administration's quixotic endeavor to argue, at media events such as the conference in Chicago, that job security—that is, minimizing layoffs—was intertwined with workplace efficiency and profitability. Unions had a role to play in the intertwining, but rather than strengthen them through labor law reform, self-interest would give labor and management the leverage each needed at the bargaining table. "We have spotlighted the best practices," Reich declared at the conference. "There are a lot of people out there who don't know they are embracing a new movement."

That myth got a protracted outing with the formation in March 1993 of the Commission on the Future of Worker-Management Relations. The AFL-CIO asked Clinton to create the commission in the hope that out of it would come recommendations to strengthen labor laws and thus protect jobs. For their part, many corporate executives in the early nineties sought to group their employees in teams that would take the initiative in meeting production goals and would even bargain with management over wages and working conditions. Such arrangements ran afoul of the National Labor Relations Act, which prohibited company-dominated unions, and management wanted the commission to come up with a recommendation to remove this obstacle. "The thought was that maybe there was a deal here that would help both sides," Ronald Blackwell, the AFL-CIO's chief economist, said.

Reflecting the dual goals, the commission's ten members were a mix of corporate executives, labor union leaders, and academics. John T. Dunlop, the chairman, seemed to lean toward labor. Lane Kirkland, then head of the AFL-CIO, had asked Clinton to name Dunlop, who was then seventy-eight and back at Harvard, where he had taught labor economics between his frequent forays into public life. He had served every president from Franklin Roosevelt through Gerald Ford, mainly as a savvy mediator, although in Ford's case he was secretary of labor for a while. The commission soon became known as the Dunlop Commission and its final report, issued in January 1995, tried to keep to a middle ground.

It declared that workers do indeed want to work more closely with managers, but to do so effectively, Congress should strengthen the bargaining power of workers. Otherwise the cooperative effort could end up dominated by management. Specifically, the law should be changed, the commission report said, so that the employees of a given company can more easily authorize a union to represent them. They should be allowed to do so through an election that takes place more quickly and with fewer obstacles than the current lengthy procedure, which gives managers considerable opportunity to defeat organizing efforts, sometimes by firing the organizers. Such dismissals should be stopped through changes in the law, the commission also concluded.

The recommendations sat well with organized labor but not with business, and they were shelved. "My interpretation is that the Dunlop Commission failed because business did not want to strengthen labor's organizing rights," Blackwell said, summarizing the view of the AFL-CIO leadership. "Business wanted the teams, but the teams were not valuable enough to get them in exchange for a stronger labor movement, and the business community let Clinton know this."

Clinton let the recommendations die. That was not hard to finesse. The commission's report was addressed to the secretaries of commerce and labor, not the president. The president did not have to respond and he didn't. "I don't think the administration appreciated the importance of trade unions in a modern, democratic economy," Richard Freeman, the Harvard labor economist and a commission member, told me. "They were more inclined to the view that workers in a high-tech economy have or should have so much skill they don't need unions." David E. Bonior, the Michigan Democrat, offered a more nuanced view, born of his dealings with the White House as House whip during much of the Clinton presidency. "I don't think Clinton was comfortable with or understood the historical struggles of the worker movement," Bonior told me. "He should have stepped out strongly in favor of union organizing drives, but he was raised in Arkansas, where union density is low. This is the home state of Wal-Mart and Tyson's, which are two of the most antiunion companies in America."

Early in the deliberations of the Dunlop Commission, Freeman lost hope that the commission's work would end up being very helpful to labor. Too much anti-labor pressure was coming from business. The pressure was directed mainly at Paul Allaire, chairman of Xerox and the most prominent representative of business on the commission. Allaire told the others about the pressure, and the AFL-CIO, in Freeman's view, failed to stir up the necessary public support to counter the opposition from business. "There had to be pressure from labor, and it did not exist," he said. He had in mind demonstrations, even strikes, all in support of strongly worded pro-labor recommendations that Clinton would feel compelled to implement. Freeman even conveyed that view, off the record, to the AFL-CIO leadership.

Stirring up strikes and demonstrations was not Kirkland's way of doing things. Nor was it Dunlop's. They were old-style labor figures accustomed to arranging compromises between two roughly equal parties—but in the mid-nineties, the parties were not equal. Business clearly had the upper hand. "It was the last gasp of a world that no longer existed," Lawrence Mishel, president of the labor-oriented Economic Policy Institute, told me. "They thought you could broker an agreement between labor and management and that was not possible."

Clinton understood this, and in the fight over the North American Free Trade Agreement in the fall of 1993—eight months after taking office—he sided openly with management. The president campaigned forcefully and successfully for congressional approval of NAFTA, doing so over the bitter opposition of the AFL-CIO, which feared the loss of union jobs. Clinton, a committed free-trader, found himself presiding over an economy increasingly dependent on imports and on inexpensive foreign labor. But trying to pacify the AFL-CIO, and workers in general, he argued that NAFTA would create jobs in the United States, not destroy them. Companies locating factories in Mexico would import machinery, materials, and components from the United States for their new Mexican operations and this would generate work in the United States. There would be job churning, of course. Companies would lay off workers when they moved factories to Mexico. But the victims would be retrained, at government expense, for the jobs that would be generated to supply the Mexican operations. Or they would be retrained to work at companies making the consumer products that the Mexicans would import from the United States, now that tariff barriers were gone. No one who submitted to the prescribed education-retraining would be left behind, and in the end, the net gain in jobs as a result of NAFTA would be 200,000 over the coming ten to fifteen years. Or so Clinton's experts projected.

A decade later, instead of a net gain, an estimated 425,000 to one million jobs had been lost. Most of them disappeared as companies shifted production to Mexico at a much faster pace than they stepped up production in this country to serve the Mexican market. The trade deficit with Mexico, a good indication of job loss, was too lopsided to leave any doubt about what NAFTA had wrought. NAFTA cost jobs, and the irony is that even if Clinton had been right—if NAFTA had resulted in net job growth—the money never materialized to retrain and reeducate all those caught in the job churning, or the millions of other dislocated workers whose layoffs were not connected to trade.

Reich managed to squeeze some extra money from Congress by arguing that the expanded training would pay for itself; the unemployed would get back to work sooner and, as a result, less would be spent on unemployment benefits. There was even a line in the budget showing the estimated savings. But apart from this sleight of hand, deficit reduction took precedence over education and training, despite the importance the Clinton administration attached to the education-training solution.

Opposition to additional allocations for education and training came from the AFL-CIO, too. Organized labor did not want layoffs in the first place. They were decimating union membership, and when the opportunity arose during the NAFTA fight to block funding, the AFL-CIO did just that—by opposing the administration's attempt to attach $3 billion in training funds to the NAFTA legislation. Republicans had agreed to the extra funding to help get NAFTA through Congress. For the AFL-CIO, however, training funds were a mockery. Training for what? So that workers could be laid off from jobs that should not be lost to Mexico in the first place? "We were not going to settle for a few coins to provide coverage for Democrats who wanted to pretend that NAFTA kept the interest of workers in mind," Blackwell said. He was directly involved in the NAFTA battle in the early 1990s as chief economist of the Amalgamated Clothing and Textile Workers Union, whose members would be hurt by the trade agreement.

The upshot was that instead of having $3 billion in training funds attached to NAFTA, only $100 million survived, and that angered Reich's Labor Department. "The only time there was ever any leverage [to get training funds] was during the NAFTA debate," Lawrence Katz, a Harvard professor then serving as the department's chief economist, told me, "and the unions blew it." More than the unions, the emphasis on deficit reduction and budget balancing blew it, and so did the futility of educating and training people for an insufficient number of skilled, well-paid jobs to replace the ones that were lost. Clinton gave the impression that he was moving forward on education and training, but the money was never there. During his presidency, federal outlays for education, training, and job placement services for all dislocated workers, whatever the reason they lost their jobs, rose to a total of $7.4 billion in 1995 from $6.7 billion in 1993. The outlays then fell back gradually to $6.77 billion in 2000—roughly the same amount in the year the president left office as in the year he arrived.

The president, however, billed the Workforce Investment Act of 1998 as a major advance in his training and education agenda. This was an illusion. WIA, as it was called, only replaced the similar Job Training Partnership Act (JTPA), which was passed in 1982 under Reagan. The funding for the Job Training Partnership Act became the funding for Workforce Investment, and the only change was in the responsibility for disbursing the money. This shifted much more from Washington to the state and county level, where the training and job-search assistance took place, often at centers attached to state unemployment offices.

Federally subsidized "rapid response teams" also came into use, so that when a company announced an impending layoff, a team would go in and get the employees started on training and job search before they collected their last paychecks. But that only accentuated the acquiescence to layoffs. "We accepted the fact of layoffs," Harry J. Holzer, the Labor Department's chief economist in 1999, explained, "and we went in and helped with the readjustment process."

Katz insisted that in time the public would have accepted layoffs, or at least tolerated them, if only there was enough government money to properly underwrite the other aspects of the equation: education and training to qualify for the next job, and subsidies for the job search to find it. The necessary financing would have materialized, he said, if the

Democrats had kept the White House in the 2000 election. The budget surpluses that accumulated in Clinton's second term would have been drawn down to expand worker training and education—not dissipated through tax cuts—and the stepped-up spending would have made the program successful as a solution for layoffs. "You could have imagined a third Clinton administration or a Gore administration that had a system of revenue and spending that valued education and training over tax cuts," Katz said. "We would have redefined the social insurance system in terms of employability."

But Gore did not win. George W. Bush did, and the budget surplus turned into a deficit. Bush continued the funding for education and training at the same level Clinton had, and the myth lived on in the minds of Clinton's followers that retraining and education would work—despite so much evidence to the contrary—if only the funding were sufficient.

CHAPTER EIGHT

The Consequences—Undoing Sanity

Hard as she tried, Stacy Brown could not rekindle in her husband, Erin, the passion for work that he lost when United Airlines laid him off as a mechanic at its giant aircraft maintenance center in Indianapolis. She loved Erin; that is, she loved the engaged and energetic young man she had married three years earlier. "He was just going a million miles a minute before this all happened," she said. She wanted that Erin back, and soon. Not for the income. If need be, she could support the family quite handsomely herself, as a litigator at a white-shoe Indianapolis law firm. But as we talked in late 2004, she was six months pregnant with their second child, and it was time to embrace the roles they had planned for themselves when they married: she as the mother and care-giver, he as the really skilled engineer, mechanic, and craftsman rising adventurously in the corporate world, or going out on his own as an entrepreneur. The layoff had destroyed all this and her distress was un-restrained.

"I think the layoff destroyed his self-esteem," Stacy said, her words coming rapidly and intensely. "I don't think he will ever admit that but I think it has. That is a hard thing to overcome and I don't know how you overcome it to get back into the working world, which is what I think he is going to have to do. When he fills out résumés and applies for jobs, you can see it is not with the extreme belief that he is going to get one. He waits until the last minute and gets the résumé in, but maybe doesn't get it in completely. I think that is because he is probably depressed."

Two years after Erin Brown lost his job at United Airlines, his wife was attempting, in a drastic, risky way, to jump-start her husband's self-confidence—to puncture his inertia and bring him quickly to the point that he would once again want to step into a career and take on the risks involved in pursuing uncertain goals. She had insisted on the purchase of a rundown three-bedroom house half a block from their own home in their once splendid Victorian-era neighborhood, which was now coming back as a downtown enclave for young professionals and executives. Erin had balked at the purchase, as he had balked at earlier opportunities to acquire and renovate rundown houses in the neighborhood, then flip them at a profit. Too risky, he insisted. This time, ignoring her husband's reluctance, Stacy put in a bid anyway, winning the house for a rock-bottom $95,000 at a mortgage foreclosure sale. She closed the deal by doing all the paperwork herself, moving forward decisively once Erin assured her that the eighty-four-year-old dwelling with its spacious front veranda was structurally sound.

They paid cash, drawing on their savings, and immediately put the house up for sale at $165,000, untouched. They were ready in their own minds, or at least Stacy was, to accept a counteroffer of $140,000 for this handyman special. Gentrification alone would bring them a sufficient profit, she reasoned, and that success would rebuild in Erin some of the self-esteem and energy that the layoff had destroyed. Or, faced with ownership—having been pushed by his wife into a gamble—Erin would renovate the house and they would then resell it for at least $195,000, an even greater success for him. Mainly, however, Stacy hoped for the quick resale. She doubted that Erin possessed the self-confidence to carry out the renovation. "He's going to want to start this and then he's not going to be able to finish it in a very timely manner," she said, "so we will end up hanging on to two houses, which is okay, but what it doesn't do is give him that sense of accomplishment and purpose and financial reward, which is what he needs to function effectively again."

In the cataloging of damage that results from layoffs, incapacitating emotional illness almost never appears on the lists that economists, politicians, sociologists, union leaders, business school professors, management consultants, and journalists compile. There is much discussion of income loss, downward mobility, a decrease in family cohesion, a rise in the divorce rate, the unwinding of communities, the impact on children, the impact on survivors who dodge a layoff but are left feeling insecure and guilty that they kept their jobs while colleagues did not. Extended periods of unemployment bring a cascade of damages, including depression, and these too are documented. One study, for example, found that for every percentage point change in the unemployment rate, up or down, the national suicide rate rose or fell in tandem, and so did the frequency of strokes, heart attacks, crime, and accidents.

The layoff, however, is seldom singled out as damaging in itself, quite apart from the unemployment that follows. But the trauma of dismissal—the "acuteness of the blow," as Dr. Theodore Jacobs, the New York psychoanalyst, put it—unwinds lives in its own right, damaging self-esteem, undoing normal adaptive mechanisms, and erecting the sort of emotional barriers that have prevented Erin Brown and thousands of others, perhaps millions of others, from returning energetically to the workforce in jobs that draw productively on their education and skills. "There are many people who do not want to face that trauma again and to some degree they lose a sense of reality," Dr. Jacobs said. "They give themselves a lot of conscious reasons why they cannot accept this job or that job, but deeper down they don't want to face the rigors and anxieties of work and the fears they won't be up to it and they will be dropped again."

I did not think in the early stages of the reporting for this book that I would be drawn so persistently into the psychiatric aspect of layoffs. But a surprisingly high number of the laid-off people with whom I talked described from every angle and over and over again what, in their minds, had been done to them, the mistakes they had made, their bad luck in being caught in the particular situation that cost them their jobs, the shortsightedness or outright evil of the bosses who failed to protect them or did not want to do so, how cut adrift they felt, or, hiding their loss and hurt in elaborate rationalizations, how comfortable they insisted they were in some new way of life, safely separated from challenging work.

The emotional damage was too palpable to ignore. Whenever I insisted that layoffs were a phenomenon in America beyond their control, they agreed perfunctorily and then went right back to describing their own devaluing experiences, and why it was somehow their fault or their particular bad luck. When I turned to psychiatrists and psychologists for an explanation of what I was finding, they offered similar observations of their own. "Chipping away at human capital," Dr. Jacobs called it. "Even when a person accurately realizes that he has done a good job, that the company is in a bad way, that it has to lay off a lot of people and it is not about me, there is always some sense of diminishment. Others at the company are not laid off, so why me? And that sense of having been judged and found wanting dovetails with older feelings of inadequacy about one's self that were acquired growing up."

Dr. Kim Cameron, an organizational psychologist at the University of Michigan's business school, focuses in his work on developing ways for corporate managers to carry out layoffs benignly, the goal being to limit the damage to the victims and in doing so soften the blow to morale among the survivors. In the same vein, management consultants and business school professors write endlessly about the various techniques for finessing layoffs. Dr. Cameron has concluded, however, that no matter how sophisticated the technique, there is not much balm: layoffs are destructive psychologically for the individuals who lose their jobs.

I told him Brown's story, including the conflicts with his manager at United Airlines over his inspection reports and the related setback in his application to advance to the engineering department at United's maintenance center, and Dr. Cameron replied that Brown seemed to be an example of a "fundamental in-the-bones blow to ego and self-worth.

"You can have all kinds of people like spouses and friends say you are terrific, you are wonderful, you are great," Dr. Cameron said, "but in the core you say, I am not, and I have big evidence that I am not. Layoffs diminish the ability to restart. They are the opposite of life giving; they literally deplete life." In Breen's case and in many others, Dr. Cameron said, the damage is hard to observe. "It is subversive in that it limits all kinds of other activities—for example, the ability to form emotional bonds with people, the ability to be energized and aggressive in pursuing a new job or position, and the ability to try new things. Trial-and-error learning is diminished. If I am feeling awful about myself, I don't want one more failure. If you try new things, the probability seems higher that you will fail, so you don't try them."

Psychiatrists and psychologists uncover these hidden linkages in therapy. Living with Erin, Stacy also gradually saw them, although her husband tried to hide what he was feeling from her, and from himself. The emotional damage from layoffs varies, of course, from case to case. Brown had to contend with his wife's success as a lawyer and her earning power. His parents' divorce when he was a boy may have also undermined his sense of himself as an effective worker. But who among us does not have contributing factors embedded in our lives waiting for a catalyst, like a layoff, to set them off? At age thirty, Erin was frozen, unable to act, not just in home renovation but in elbowing his way back into a job that would draw on his considerable skills. Denial and anger justified his inaction and hid its deeper causes.

A year after her husband's layoff, Stacy prodded him into applying for a job at a Rolls-Royce engine plant in Indianapolis. The opening was for a technical specialist in the engineering department, a job involving research on jet engines that Erin later said he wanted. But his description of his encounter with the human resources manager who interviewed him was laced with resentment and insult, and the manager must have noticed. "I was well-qualified and I went through a lot of effort to get that one," Erin said, "and it turns out the guy who was doing the hiring had not bothered to understand the nature of the job he was in charge of filling."

In Brown's view, the candidate finally selected was inferior to him in education and know-how. "He had no bachelor's degree in engineering and he lacked the analytical skill that the job required," Erin asserted, berating the interviewer for bureaucratically placing too much importance on a relatively insignificant aspect of the job description: shop-floor experience in machining. The winning candidate had that experience and that made the difference, Erin said, despite his plea to the interviewer that he could come up to speed as a machinist in two weeks. "I said to this guy, 'Hey, look, I have the training, I just don't have the experience in the field, but I'll do whatever you want me to do on my own time to get it.' No interest on his part. They want everything exactly according to the specifications. . . . And then, even if you are among the top applicants, they don't have the decency to get back to you and say, Thanks, but no thanks. I mean you have to call them and hound them to see what happened with the position."

His account of the purchase of the house down the street from their home differed alarmingly from his wife's subsequent explanation. He did not mention her decisive role in making the purchase or that she was trying to prod him out of what she described as a mild but incapacitating depression. Instead, he left the impression that he had taken the initiative in making the purchase. If the house did not resell quickly—and it was already on the market—then he would remodel the kitchen and add a garage to increase the resale value. None of Stacy's anguish came through in the optimistic plans that Erin described. Before doing any of the remodeling, he said, sounding sure of himself, he just might move his family into the new dwelling while he completed the long-drawn-out renovation of his own home. The Rolls-Royce debacle, he said, he had put behind him. He had made no further attempt to apply for challenging jobs in big corporations. Henceforth, he said, he would go the entrepreneurial route, relying on himself. As evidence of his determination and effectiveness, he declared that he had finally completed construction of the two-story carriage house behind his and Stacy's home. It was ready to be sold or rented as office space, he said.

This was the project that Erin had started while Stacy was on maternity leave in the winter and spring of 2003, shortly after he lost his job at United. Birth, layoff, and maternity leave melded. During Stacy's leave, Erin did 60 percent of the construction work and then, when she went back to her job, he stopped, not touching the carriage house again for more than a year; caring for Kyle took up too much of his time, he said. Now, after all those months of inactivity, Erin told me by phone that he had completed the project, the work carried out in what appeared to be a spurt of energy and activity despite the time consumed in child care. He e-mailed me a photo of the exterior, freshly painted green and white. But he had not finished the interior. Inside that cozy two-story house, wiring and electricity were yet to be installed and studs were still exposed.

Stacy set me straight on the status of the carriage house. Her husband had indeed completed the exterior, she said. "He did beautiful work." But he had acted because he had no choice: either he used the materials he had purchased or they would "sit there and rot." As for the interior, Erin found reasons to put off doing that essential work, and Stacy saw the postponements as a signal from her husband—a signal whose true meaning he suppressed—that he did not want to take the risk of actually finishing the carriage house and then somehow having that achievement, too, taken from him.

She had finally concluded that Erin's emotional damage had become a barrier to the family life they both seemed to want. "Our hope is that . . .

there will be a time for me to stay home with our children for a while," Stacy told me. "But at the same time, just this morning, we were talking that it was time to make elections next year for my work and my contributions to the medical savings account and things like that, and he says, 'What happens if you have to go back to work?' And I thought, What do you mean what happens if I have to go back to work? I thought the plan was that *you* were going to go to work. So I think at the same time he's just such an optimistic soul, but I think in the back of his mind, I think he is doubting. I mean, I think he is doubting his ability to get gainful employment and employment that supports our family. I mean, all along, even though he wanted to be laid off in the sense that he thought he was ready to leave United, I firmly believe the layoff impacted him very much. To think back to the person he was when I met him—he enjoyed his job, he really thought he had a career going. And to watch the person that he is today, so averse to employment and so averse to being a worker."

Stacy asked me for help. She had appealed to Erin's father, but father and son did not communicate easily, and Erin resisted taking advice from members of her family. "He talks to you," she said. So I waited a couple of weeks and called Erin. I said that he had misled me at times, without meaning to, and that Stacy and I were concerned about his inaction. I suggested that he see a therapist, that therapy might help him get through this crisis. He did not respond directly to my suggestion, nor did he veer from amiability. "What worries Stacy and you is that I am not really concerned about working to my potential," he replied.

That did worry us, but Erin would not be swayed. He had just completed a two-evening-a-week course in air-conditioner repair, learning very little that he did not already know, to get the necessary certification for a $13- or $14-an-hour dead-end job. Driving about in a panel truck making repairs to air-conditioning units would give him health insurance and some income for the family, once Stacy left her law firm, he explained to me. Most important, he would have a nondemanding, unthreatening platform from which to branch out and ample spare time for truly challenging work: renovating and reselling rundown homes, for example. "I know that I will be overqualified for the next position that I take," he said.

Not everyone has as much difficulty as Erin Brown in shaking off the emotional setback that layoffs produce. Some of those whose stories have been told earlier managed to move on to a next stage in their lives with their mental health more or less intact. But the majority did not. Psychiatrists and psychoanalysts view layoffs as catalysts for emotional damage. There is no mechanism, however, for collecting and disseminating what they know so that the consequences of corporate layoffs can be publicly flagged. The Centers for Disease Control and Prevention in Atlanta track the number of cases of flu, AIDS, measles, polio, Lyme disease, and other physical illnesses, and when the number spikes for one of these ailments, the center alerts us that an epidemic may be brewing, one that requires stepped-up medical treatment and a concerted public effort to shrink the number of cases. While doctors and hospitals funnel data about physical illness to the Centers for Disease Control, psychiatrists and psychologists do not similarly report the incidence among their patients of disabling neuroses connected to layoffs. Nor do the organizations that represent them adopt resolutions that declare layoffs to be a source of mental illness and therefore a menace to public health.

The American Psychiatric Association, whose 35,000 members are likely to treat mental illness related to layoffs, has never formally declared that the modern American layoff is hazardous to health. The president of the association, Dr. Steven S. Sharfstein, readily acknowledges the linkage as do other leaders of the organization. Divorce, however, also damages mental health, Dr. Sharfstein said. So does the death of a spouse or a parent, not to mention the trauma of war. For psychiatry to oppose these events on public health grounds would be futile, he argued, and in the case of layoffs very possibly counterproductive. "If a company refrains from a layoff and then, as a result, is forced out of business, everyone would end up laid off," he said. So the American Psychiatric Association acquiesces in the practice and pushes instead to expand treatment of the victims. It lobbies business, for example, to expand coverage for mental illness. "We do see there are major shortcomings with employer health insurance in terms of access to mental health care," Dr. Sharfstein said, "and that is how we go at this issue."

Only one group of psychiatrists that I could find had singled out the layoff, the act in which a worker is sent away, as damaging in itself to mental health. The alert had come from the three hundred members of the Group for the Advancement of Psychiatry, or more specifically from the dozen or so in the group's Committee on Psychiatry in Industry. These were psychiatrists whose practices focused on working with companies as consultants. Their client companies engaged in layoffs and they had first-hand knowledge of what people went through. In 1982, when the modern layoff was still a raw American experience, they published a monograph, *Job Loss—a Psychiatric Perspective,* in which they declared: "Our experience in industry and with patients suggests that those who lose their functional role as workers may behave as if their society no longer values them. Because they accept that as true, they suffer a consequent loss in the perception of their value in their families and to themselves."

They distributed that study, with its straightforward, unpleasant observation, and eight years later, three psychiatrists on the committee expanded their findings into a book, *The Psychosocial Impact of Job Loss.* Neither drew any attention. "Company managers were more interested in talking about the coping skills of those who remained on the job than they were about the damage to those they had laid off," Dr. Stephen Heidel, a consultant to businesses and a clinical professor of psychiatry at the University of California, San Diego, told me. I asked the doctors why, in their opinion, they had had so little success in publicizing the message in their monograph and book. Various possibilities were mentioned, but all seemed to agree with Dr. Heidel's observation that managers don't want to be told about damage to mental health that results from a layoff they initiated. "If a psychiatrist goes out and says, I am an expert in job loss, the manager does not want to hear that and the psychiatrist won't be consulted about other services he can provide to a corporation," Dr. Heidel said. "If you lead with that, the door will be shut. You need to put a positive spin on things."

While the nation's psychiatrists remain all but silent as a group, psychologists and sociologists in academic research seldom spot the sorts of debilitating neuroses that are evident in one-on-one therapy. Academics place much more faith in what they can document through empirical studies. They seek quantifiable evidence and shun the diagnostic judgment that is unavoidable in psychotherapy, whose raw material is narrative and free association. Their work, in consequence, relies heavily on surveys that blend together layoffs and unemployment and correlate the undifferentiated experience with measurable reactions: elevated blood pressure; an increased incidence of stomach problems, headaches, and insomnia; noticeably greater anxiety; a tendency to drink and smoke more; an increase in hospital admissions for ostensibly physical ailments. No survey of observable symptoms would pick up Brown's malady.

Psychoanalysts like Dr. Jacobs are also reluctant to single out layoffs publicly as damaging to mental health. By way of explanation, Dr. Jacobs said that people who seek psychoanalysis do so because of "long-standing character problems and in the course of analysis they mention a layoff, which has magnified what is already there or latently there." As a result, the layoff is not a central issue for the 2,500 members of the American Psychoanalytic Association. None of the numerous sessions at the association's four-day semiannual conferences have focused on layoffs and mental health. When I posted a request at the winter meeting in January 2005 to interview psychoanalysts concerned about the linkage, the only response came from Dr. Alexandra K. Rolde, a psychiatrist and psychoanalyst in private practice in Boston and a clinical instructor in psychiatry at Harvard Medical School. For some of her patients, layoffs were indeed a central theme.

Dr. Rolde, a Czech immigrant in her late sixties, lived through the German occupation of Prague during World War II, in "semihiding" with her mother, as she puts it, to escape deportation and death as Jews. It was an experience that familiarized her with trauma, which is now her specialty in psychiatry. After the war she moved to Canada with her mother and stepfather, and the parents thrived in the jewelry business, first in Montreal and then in Toronto. When they moved the business from one city to the other, acting out of concern that Quebec's separatist movement might isolate the province from the rest of Canada, all fifty of the employees moved, too. No one was laid off, Dr. Rolde said, proud of the loyalties that kept her parents and their workers together. She has treated roughly thirty patients over the past twenty years for layoff-related ailments, she said, and she considers the layoffs to have been life-changing for them. Like Dr. Jacobs, she sees children as well as adults, and they, too, are often damaged.

"It is a trauma to the entire family," she said. "You have a parent working at a prestigious full-time job. All of a sudden the parent sits at home and can't find a job and is depressed. And suddenly the child's role model sort of crumbles. Instead of feeling admiration for the parent, the child eventually begins to feel disrespect. Because the children identify with their parents, they begin to doubt that they can accomplish anything. They feel they won't be successful in life and their self-esteem plummets. This of course is a long-term thing. We call it transgenerational trauma; it is similar to what we used to see with Holocaust survivors and their children. The children feel as damaged as their parents, even though they did not experience the trauma directly themselves."

She told me about a woman she had treated for years after the woman was laid off from an executive job at General Electric. "She got back into the workforce quickly enough, but in a job she did not like, yet she clung to it anyway," Dr. Rolde said. "She was so traumatized by the layoff that she did not have the self-confidence to risk moving on to more suitable work."

Tim Dewey also got quickly back into the workforce after United Airlines laid him off as a mechanic in Indianapolis. Unlike Erin Brown and Dr. Rolde's patient, he was not frozen. Instead, he quieted the emotional blow by persuading himself, and trying to persuade others, that he was embarked on work that had a logic to it and a future. At first that took the form of a manic determination to be immune to layoffs in his next career. When the water taxi failed, he got himself trained and certified as a technician who could maintain computer networks, his assumption—his fantasy—being that his new specialty was in high demand and would remain so. If he continued to educate himself in the complexities of computer networks, he would in time be a success as a freelance technician contracted by small companies unable to afford their own employee with that much skill. "There is always going to be the middle-sized business that doesn't have the tech support in-house, but has twenty computers and calls in a systems administrator for help," Dewey explained.

En route to that independence, he detoured. With his unemployment insurance about to run out, Dewey had posted his résumé on Career-Builder, a Web site, and within twenty-four hours Bell Tech, which is headquartered in Indianapolis and has call centers in various American cities, hired him for Bell Tech.logix, a computer services company, to help staff the call center in its headquarters building, thirty minutes by car from

Dewey's home. Working in cubicles and seated at computers, Dewey and his colleagues provided technical support for people who called in asking for help to solve network problems—getting access to the Internet, for example, or installing an Ethernet line.

The job he had taken had all the earmarks of work hastily sought, easily offered, and just as easily terminated. But he convinced himself that he had landed once again in the structured existence that working for a successful corporation often bestows on its employees, and that United Airlines had once bestowed on Dewey, until that company's "total betrayal," as Dewey puts it. Nothing about Dewey's circumstances at Bell Tech suggested corporate opportunity or a set of circumstances that enhanced self-esteem, but that was the spin he gave his latest reentry into the workforce. "I feel appreciated here," he said in late December 2004, four months after he had started at Bell. "When someone looks at me they don't look at me like I am making $12 an hour," he said, referring to his meager wage. "They look at me like I am an important part of this company. I know I have only been here since August, but when I walk into this place I have a smile on my face."

His wage was less than he had ever earned in twenty years as an aircraft mechanic. Bell offered no pension plan other than whatever savings an employee could accumulate in a 401(k), and Dewey did not take the company's health insurance, remaining instead on his wife's less expensive policy at a Lowe's store, where she was a supervisor of cashiers. He was put on a four-day week, ten hours a day, plus an hour for lunch, unpaid. He fielded seventy calls a shift, or an average of 8.5 minutes per call, some of them requiring step-by-step explanations. There was no idling on this job.

Call center work is notoriously vulnerable to layoff and migration, most recently to English-speaking countries where people as skilled as Dewey but earning only a fraction of his $12 an hour are taught to speak like Americans, as if they were sitting next to him in Indianapolis, taking calls dialed into an 800 number. Yet Dewey managed to see in Bell Tech a savvy, principled resistance to outsourcing and a reluctance to lay off valued employees. "What Bell Tech is pioneering," Dewey said, "is the bringing back of work that has gone to India, Pakistan, South Africa. It is bringing back jobs because people are so outraged at the service they get from people in those countries. If you call America Online right now and talk to their tech service department, you are getting South Africa and it is a horrible experience."

For Bell to keep the work in America, Dewey explained, his salary could not go much above $12 an hour. He was wary of being burned again for the loyalty and commitment he now extended to Bell, as he had been burned at United, but he had convinced himself that Bell would help him advance, and not outrageously throw him away, as United had done. He needed to believe that. "It is hard to look in your son's eyes and explain to him that you are making only $12 an hour and know his high school friends are making that much on the side," Dewey said, adding that his seventeen-year-old son was a nearly all-A high school senior, earning those As in advanced placement courses. "And so I want to be able to explain to my son that I am working for something better. It is hard for me to explain that you have to make a choice of lesser to have more later."

Bell's president had his office on the same floor as the call center and Dewey walked in one day to introduce himself and thank the president for the opportunity to work at Bell. "I explained to him that I was an aircraft mechanic for nearly twenty years, and at United for twelve of them, and I was now on a new career path. He was very cordial and not a stuffed shirt at all." Dewey signed up for additional computer courses, to earn more certifications, and Bell paid the tuition. "Before I leave here I will be doing network administration," he said, explaining that network administrators see to it that a company's computers function in harmony, programmed to share several laser printers, for example. "The people just across the aisle from me are network administrators. We share a common area and I'm already volunteering. This company lets me do that. It treats people very well. . . . There are huge upside opportunities to grow with this company."

Dewey insisted that his new employer would be only one stage in his journey to independence as a freelance contractor. But he yearned for an anchor in a trustworthy company. As the sociologist Richard Sennett points out in *The Corrosion of Character,* people like Dewey are engaged in a basic human activity, the creation (in Dewey's case, the re-creation) of a life narrative. Career is essential to the narrative. "Not to make a career out of one's work, however modest its content or pay," Sennett wrote, is "to leave oneself prey to the sense of aimlessness which constitutes the deepest experience of inadequacy—one must, in modern slang, 'get a life.' " Careers, in turn, are an antidote to corrosion of character, "particularly those qualities of character which bind human beings to one another, [furnishing] each with a sense of sustainable self." Bell Tech seemed to offer Dewey a career and an opportunity to bind himself productively to others, or so he had convinced himself. "You are stuck on the money issue," he scolded me when I asked what his pay would be as a network administrator. "I could have gone back to work for $18 an hour as an aircraft mechanic," he said, not answering my question, "but then I would have had to contend with all the destructiveness of that industry."

Dewey did work again as an aircraft mechanic. Nine months into his new job, unable to get a raise, he quit Bell Tech and offered himself to a temp agency that was supplying mechanics to the AAR Corporation, the outsourcer that was now doing aircraft maintenance in three of the hangar bays at United's old center in Indianapolis. Dewey was back in the building where United had employed him, this time repairing aircraft at $18 an hour, roughly half his old wage, without benefits. But he did not bad-mouth Bell Tech. "They treated me well in every respect but pay," he said, explaining that he needed the extra money to help send his son to college. "If the kid had not been going to college, I might have stayed at Bell Tech." He considered the AAR work a temporary step en route to the sort of meaningful, career-oriented job that in his eyes Bell Tech had offered, but this time with respectable pay.

His sights were set on NetJets, Inc., a company that leased corporate jets or provided them on a time-share basis. The maintenance work for AAR qualified him to renew his mechanic's license, and with the renewal in hand, he was qualified to apply for a job at NetJets as a service coordinator, reviewing maintenance reports from the field for the company's hundreds of planes (the maintenance is outsourced) and ruling whether to put a plane back into service or insist on further work. A few months after he applied, NetJets hired Dewey and assigned him to its office in Columbus, Ohio, where he took a small apartment, commuting to Indianapolis on his days off. At NetJets, his starting salary was $50,000 a year—not yet the $60,000-plus that he had earned at United, but getting there, particularly with the extra pay for working the overnight shift.

Given the commute and the rigorous schedule, Dewey did not intend to stay at NetJets for more than a couple of years, but he did not think he needed more than that. "What I learn from this job is really going to be a transferable commodity," he said, embracing once again Sennett's life narrative. "I'll be in demand. NetJets has a real good name in the industry, so if people see I've worked in the return-to-service department, I can get a job with an airline or with a cargo outfit like FedEx."

What Sennett calls the corrosion of character other sociologists describe as the unwinding of "social capital," a hard-to-quantify form of collective behavior in the workplace that is, the evidence increasingly suggests, essential to corporate efficiency. Social capital in the workplace has several ingredients. Education and skill of course play a role. But so does the recognition by management of one's worth, through job security and the opportunity to advance within a company. Company-financed training is part of the package, the goal being to hone an employee's skills, or add to them, in either case benefiting the company, which has decided to keep and value its workers, rather than throw away those who lack a needed skill while hiring replacements who happen to have that skill. These ingredients feed into the relationships that workers build up with one another, the networks they form as part of these relationships to get the work done, and the respect they acquire for one another's work, a respect that contributes to trust and self-esteem. Trust is essential in this process and so is its offshoot, commitment; without them, organizations do not function effectively. "All this layoffs destroy," Arne Kalleberg, a sociologist at the University of North Carolina at Chapel Hill, argues.

Kalleberg is prominent in a small group of scholars, mostly sociologists, psychologists, and business school professors, who are trying to describe the components of social capital and pin down, if they can, its contribution to a company's productivity and success—to the very efficiencies, if you will, that should make layoffs unnecessary, and certainly counterproductive. They present research papers regularly at the annual meetings of the Allied Social Science Associations, but they are not yet a main event: their panels are shunted to satellite hotels, not given the central conference halls. Indeed, the prevailing wisdom in mainstream economics insists that America's flexible labor markets give us a competitive advantage over Europe and Japan, with their greater job security—a proposition that the importance of social capital undermines.

"Academics engaged in this research understand social capital as trust, communication, and value generated by people working together," Thomas Kochan, of MIT's Sloan School of Management, explained to me at one of these gatherings. He likens the mood that is generated to the spirit of the little engine that could in the children's tale. "But since no one is able to quantify in dollars the loss of these intangibles," he said, "the decision is to go with the visible savings from layoffs. You see this in staffing decisions all the time. You can easily calculate the direct dollar savings from fewer people on the payroll."

One recent attempt to place a value on social capital has come from Jody Hoffer Gittell, an assistant professor of management at Brandeis University's Heller School for Social Policy and Management, who wrote *The Southwest Airlines Way: Using the Power of Relationships to Achieve High Performance.* In her book, she argued that Southwest's singular success in the airline industry is mainly a result of social capital, and she detailed the various ways in which Southwest achieves social capital, including an outsize effort to train people not just in the skills required for their jobs, but in the skill of working together. As part of her argument, she noted that Southwest, which eschews layoffs, specializes in relatively short, frequent, and inexpensive flights. That strategy requires quick turnarounds to keep the planes in the air, maximizing the number of fare-paying passengers. The turnarounds are fast, Gittell maintains, because teams of people who know one another and work well together are able to quickly fuel, clean, and check a just-arrived airliner and rapidly debark one set of passengers while another is lined up to embark. "An airline without good relationships among its workers can't turn a plane in only twenty minutes as Southwest does," she said.

Michael Burawoy, a sociologist at the University of California at Berkeley, argues that such achievements are a source of self-esteem, which he describes in this context as the confidence that workers have—blue-collar and white-collar alike—in their aptitudes and skills and in the contribution they make to the enterprise that employs them. Layoffs undermine this corporate effectiveness, subtracting from the competitive edge the layoffs are intended to enhance. Kim Cameron makes this point rather bluntly. "Corporate downsizing remains the most pervasive yet unsuccessful organizational improvement strategy in the 1990s business world," he wrote in a 1997 paper.

Cutting staff may appear to be sensible, particularly when sales revenue is not keeping up with the costs of production. Getting rid of excess labor brings the two back into balance quickly, and that gets the attention of investors and shareholders. "There is this continuous-improvement mentality that employers have embraced because they can't raise prices," Jerry Jasinowski, president of the National Association of Manufacturers, told me. "It requires you to continually look at how you can make business processes less costly by whatever means, including reducing employment." The irony is in the unreported damage to social capital that layoffs inflict and the costs that are added because of this damage. "The evidence suggests that quality, productivity, and customer service often decline over time," Cameron argues, "and financial performance—while frequently improving in the short run after downsizing due to promised savings and lower costs—erodes over the long run."

Cameron is by no means alone in this view. Studies suggesting that layoffs are counterproductive appear regularly, although they draw less and less attention, now that layoffs have become so embedded in corporate practice. Jason Jennings, a consultant and frequent speaker at corporate conferences, for example, found in a study of four thousand companies that the ten most productive rarely laid off workers. "Layoffs create more problems than they solve," he wrote in his book *Less Is More*, published in 2002. Frederick F. Reichheld, a management consultant at Bain & Company, argues that companies with the highest customer satisfaction are the least likely to engage in layoffs. So are companies that invest in worker training, avoiding layoffs, and the prices of their stocks do better than average. Some companies resorted to layoffs in the 1980s and 1990s, found them to be counterproductive, and have avoided them since. Haas Automation, Inc., a big machine-tool manufacturer, and Harley-Davidson, the motorcycle maker, are prominent on this list.

John A. Challenger, a management consultant in Chicago, notes that companies rarely include in their cost-benefit analyses the cost of fighting wrongful dismissal suits or rising absenteeism among discouraged survivors or the cost of adding foremen and supervisors to monitor the work of the survivors, whose commitment and motivation have been diluted by a layoff. There is also the cost of a misconceived downsizing. Nitin Nohria, a Harvard Business School professor who studied layoffs over more than a decade at a hundred large companies, discovered that very often too many people were laid off, or the wrong ones, and those who survived weren't retrained to pick up the workload in a shrunken company.

The survivors, in addition, are frequently shell-shocked. Some experts argue that fear—fear that they, too, will be laid off—drives survivors to work well. But consider the case of the twelve Xerox software engineers who worked together in product development in the mid-1990s at a Xerox office near Rochester, New York, where the company is headquartered. Before Xerox laid off people in the Rochester area, the twelve engineers spent their mornings doing what they were paid to do: inventing software. In the postlayoff atmosphere, they did not get down to that essential, innovative task until after 5 p.m. Unnerved by the layoffs, they felt compelled to show off their prowess, which they did in meetings and crisis sessions with peers and bosses. These gatherings took up much of the day and often served as little more than stages for the engineers to advertise their individual abilities. Leslie Perlow, then a professor of organizational behavior at the University of Michigan business school, observed the shift in behavior during the weeks she spent with the engineers as part of a study. "They felt they were rewarded for individual heroics, and their crisis meetings [as deadlines approached] gave them an outlet for heroics," she said. "The layoff atmosphere exacerbated this need to 'show' performance."

The Xerox engineers still had their jobs, of course. The vast majority of laid-off workers never get back to where they were, either in income or in self-respect or in the social relationships that develop over years of employment at the same company or in the same calling. "People choose a career," says Dr. Pedro Ruiz, a professor of psychiatry at the University of Texas in Houston and a vice president of the American Psychiatric Association, "and then when they are forced to change, they lose their network system, they are isolated, and they lose confidence in themselves. Young people still in their twenties do manage to make the adjustment, but after the mid-thirties, that is unusual."

It certainly was for Stephen Holthausen, the former Connecticut banker who spent the last decade of his working life trying futilely to re-create for himself, as the supervisor of a tourist information center, the prestige and way of life he had enjoyed as a successful loan officer, until his employer laid him off at age forty-five. After more than a decade, his salary climbed back to the $50,000 he had earned in his last year as a loan officer. But he never allowed himself to step mentally from banking into tourism, although he seemed to work well in that field. Even in his private life, he linked himself to banking. He met the woman who eventually became his companion when both were bank loan officers in southern Connecticut in the mid-sixties. They got together after his divorce and hers, and after he landed in tourism. She had continued in banking, was never laid off, and she helped to sustain his image of himself as a banker. "When Sandy goes to banking functions and my name comes up," Holthausen said, "you never hear, 'That son of a bitch.' You hear positive things like how he was fair and how he was diligent, the nice things you want to be remembered for, and she relates these back to me." As they entered their sixties, Holthausen decided that he would time his retirement from tourism to coincide with hers from banking. He would then move thirty miles to the town where she lived, so that he could settle down near her if not with her. And in retirement at least he would once again be a banker, associated with bankers.

His children were achievers. He mentioned them often and their success bolstered his own self-esteem. Any banker and community elder, as he had been, would be proud to be their father. His son, Christian, joined a big corporation not long after graduating from college and earned regular promotions. Christian told me politely that he did not want to revisit his father's experience. Holthausen's daughter, Gretchen, while very open, was also determined not to let what happened to her father happen to her. She married a young man who earned a living as a carpenter and electrician. They purchased and renovated a home together, and she continued to work as a research assistant at Yale while going to school at night to qualify as a school psychologist. "I am able to separate my self-worth from my worth as a worker," she told me. "If what happened to him ever happens to me—and I'm saying this in the hypothetical because I've never been through that experience—I would be able to separate self from situation."

Kenneth Halajian, the lawyer and publishing executive, held on to his sense of self, or tried to, in a much different way. He declared himself retired at age fifty-three and turned retirement into what he insisted was a satisfying career. Halajian had spent his entire working life going up the hierarchy at Matthew Bender & Company. "When I was made editor in chief in 1988," he said, "I remember thinking this is a great position to attain and to have for a long time." That was not to be. As described earlier, as editor in chief and in other executive jobs Halajian had played a role himself in reorganizations and layoffs to accommodate new technology and new owners. And then, shortly before he retired, realizing that his own $160,000-a-year job had become superfluous, he had recommended his own layoff, doing so before the bosses of the company that had just acquired Matthew Bender came to the same conclusion and laid him off or shunted him to a post not of his choosing, which in fact they tried to do. That was Halajian's explanation of his exodus in 2000: a dignified departure that he controlled, after which he wrapped himself in retirement pursuits, elevating those pursuits to spiritual satisfaction, all in the service of incorporating importance, identity, and self-esteem back into his life.

Fly-fishing was one of those pursuits. "I am putting all my energy into understanding where that trout is and what that trout is interested in," he told me. "There are all these variables you need to pay attention to. It's like a project at work, where you have to accomplish X. What are all the variables you need to consider to get you from here to there? It's very similar; it's just different types of things you're looking into."

He told me he had been elected senior warden of his church. The senior warden is the top officer of the vestry, a sort of chief executive; the position requires Halajian to exercise skills and judgment not unlike those he used in his former working life. "I go over the budget of the church," he said. "Talk about flashbacks to corporate life! And there are other things like that for which I'm getting tapped. I'm running the pancake supper. I'm part of a group that's looking into the rummage sale this year; how we're going to do it. . . . We have a new rector and one of the things we started assessing yesterday is the mission statement. Hasn't been looked at in years. Time to engage the whole parish into revising the mission statement. Well, you know, taking an organization through the process of getting everyone engaged in stating a mission and goals that support the mission, I was reminded how many times I did that in corporate life, and those skills still find use outside of corporate life. I find myself using those skills again."

Every so often Halajian acknowledged that he probably would have stayed on as an executive at Matthew Bender if the company had not gone through so many unnerving and threatening changes—four major reorganizations, he counted, and also new owners. "I just got tired of the process and it seemed to be accelerating," he said. So he created substitutes for corporate life and kept away from the emotional battering by insisting on an impossible condition for reentering the workforce as a paid executive. "It would have to be the right offer from the right people," he said. "There would have to be a really inspiring executive at the top, one who had the right vision and used layoffs only as a last resort. Either that or close the doors."

Erin Brown, I suppose, came closest to the sort of aberrant behavior that cries out for therapy. But Halajian and Holthausen and Tim Dewey also suffered from "a state of brokenness," a description that in Maureen Moorhead's view applies to all laid-off workers. Moorhead, intense and energetic, started out as a social worker in Cincinnati and from there moved into counseling. She conducted focus sessions in that city for men and women who had lost white-collar jobs and who came for help to the Hyde Park Community United Methodist Church, which in the early 1990s had formed a support group to help the growing number of white-collar job losers in the congregation and later from anywhere in the city. Her message essentially was a pep talk. She embraced the view that getting back into the workforce was really a matter of willpower, of focusing on a job goal and then passionately pursuing that goal. "It is taking control of your job hunt instead of being at the mercy of just answering job postings," Moorhead explained. "Employers are drawn to people who have energy and drive and very often they will create a position to accommodate them."

She was Say's law in action. But even for her, that gospel of mainstream economic theory had cracks. Four hundred people had come through her workshops over a two-year period, each paying $90 for four all-day sessions, and despite her upbeat message, she noticed that virtually all of her clients were subdued, dispirited, grieving, feeling alone. "There is a brokenness in them," Moorhead said, coining a term that captures more aptly than psychiatric language the damage from layoffs in the United States today. Moorhead gave her clients one-on-one tutoring in how to take control of their lives. But if they were too angry and saddened to respond to her message—too broken, as she put it—then she referred them to a minister for help or to a former executive who had suffered through a severe depression himself after losing his job and now counseled others trying to get through the same experience. "He went back to school to learn how to do this," she said.

Every so often, the concern over layoffs, particularly during political campaigns, provokes a conference on the subject. The Federal Reserve Bank of Chicago convened such a conference in November 2004, two weeks after the presidential election. More than one hundred experts, some of them economists who had worked in Washington as labor policy advisers, gathered for a day and a half of presentations at the bank's stately pillared building on LaSalle Street in the center of the city. Seating themselves at long, narrow tables arranged in rows in the richly lighted conference room, they listened to speaker after speaker document the significant wage loss that most laid-off workers experience in their next jobs.

A phenomenon still in doubt in the Clinton years, and never explicitly acknowledged by President Clinton or President Bush, was now abundantly documented. A number of the invited experts ran federally subsidized job-training programs, and they confirmed what the speakers and panel members demonstrated in their statistical studies. The wage loss for men and women who were working again two or three years after a layoff—and roughly half of all those laid off were working again—had crept up to an average of 14 percent by 2004, or so the statistical evidence suggested. That meant someone earning $500 or $1,000 a week before being laid off earned on average $425 or $850 a week two or three years later.

The speakers insisted that the primary remedy lay in education and training. In this, they embraced the common stance of both Democrats and Republicans. But they also acknowledged that training alone would not solve the problem; the loss too often consisted of income that had accumulated from raises, promotions, experience, effectiveness, and reputation built up over years spent at the companies that laid them off. Only the same sort of tenure and endeavor at the new employer could replace the pay that went with it. "When you sever the connection to a long-held job, you are destroying something that you can't restore, not quickly," said

Louis S. Jacobson, a senior economist at Westat, a research firm that studies the costs of layoffs and the effectiveness of worker assistance programs.

None of the speakers identified the wage loss as evidence of the destruction of social capital, but that was the issue. And for the first time, I heard academics and a sprinkling of current and former public officials openly proposing income support to offset the wage shortfall until the social capital embedded in a worker's years of endeavor could be restored.

Their chief proposal was federal wage insurance, a concept that Clinton's advisers briefly considered among themselves and discarded, and that Bush actually instituted in 2002, although on a minuscule scale, covering fewer than three hundred people by 2005. Wage insurance under the Trade Act of 2002 is packed with restrictions. It pays a reemployed worker half the difference between the lost wage and the new one, up to a maximum of $10,000 over two years. But to qualify, the worker has to be at least fifty years of age, with a prelayoff salary of less than $50,000. In addition, participation in a job-training program is a must, and the layoff has to be a result of imports replacing the product the worker helped to make. Service-sector workers affected by trade don't qualify, not even call center operators whose jobs are transferred to India or Ireland or some other English-speaking country. With so many obstacles, wage insurance during the Bush presidency was never likely to be a safety net. But it is public recognition, however reluctant and unpublicized, that the cache of self-respect, social relationships, and reputation acquired over years at a company or in a profession has value and cannot easily be replaced. Certainly the wage portion does not come back easily. As Robert LaLonde, a University of Chicago economist, put it: "The earnings loss in the next job is often permanent."

Erin Brown did not try to rebuild his lost status and income, which had reached $70,000 in his final years at United Airlines. Days before the birth of his second son, Luke, in March 2005, he took a job as a maintenance worker in the Indianapolis public schools, at $18 an hour, or $37,500 a year. "It is not a custodial job; it is just above that," Erin said. "It is not the sort of position that most people would want." Still, the hourly wage was a few dollars more than he could make as an air-conditioner repairman for a private company—the other option he was considering—and, working for the public schools, he would have health insurance, a pension, job security, and enough free time to renovate the home he and his wife had purchased down the street. As for Stacy, maintenance work in the public schools fell far short of the reengagement that she wanted for her husband. Nevertheless, she was glad to have him working again. "It has improved our relationship," she said.

With Luke's birth, she started a six-month maternity leave and told her employer that she would return, although with Erin reemployed and plainly enjoying his status as the breadwinner, she did not want to go back. When the leave ended she announced her intention not to return, and to her surprise her firm proposed that she work at home, part-time, for $85 an hour, which she did, getting up at four a.m. and doing most of the work before her children awoke. Erin objected; he felt the family could live on his $18 an hour. But Stacy insisted. The remodeling of the house they had purchased was going slowly, postponing any payoff from their investment in housing, and with two children their expenses were rising. "The reality is that we need the money," Stacy said. "Erin did not want to need the money, but I did not want to be restricted in what we could do."

Craig Imperio never lost a taste for success. Unlike Brown, he went at the task of rebuilding income and career almost immediately, his self-esteem sufficiently intact to keep him going. In the fifteen months after United Airlines put him on the street in Indianapolis, he completed his schooling for an engineering degree and, unable to get work as an engineer, as noted earlier, took a job as an aircraft mechanic again, this time repairing jet engines for Pratt & Whitney in Columbus, Georgia. His wife, Sarah, and their two sons soon joined him, trading home ownership in Indianapolis for a rented apartment in Columbus.

At Pratt & Whitney, Craig's sense of himself as a valued employee soon began to come back. The company sent him to school to be certified as an inspector of repaired engine parts and also paid his tuition to study for an MBA degree in his off-hours. His skill gradually drew the attention of the plant's general manager, who invited Craig to play golf with him several times and encouraged his young subordinate (Imperio turned thirty-one during his first year at Pratt & Whitney) to apply for a slot as a shift supervisor when one came open. Trading on the respect that he was gradually acquiring, Craig helped three colleagues from Indianapolis land jobs as mechanics at Pratt & Whitney. One was his brother-in-law,

Brad Sanger, who also moved his family to Columbus. And soon the Imperios and the Sangers purchased homes.

But Imperio's wage remained stuck at $17 an hour—less than 60 percent of his final pay at United—and Sarah estimated that four or five years would pass before her husband's salary climbed back to its former level. Craig doubted that he would ever earn more than $20 an hour as an aircraft mechanic, no matter how much seniority he accumulated at Pratt & Whitney. There were simply too many unemployed aircraft mechanics seeking jobs and no employer had to pay more than $20 an hour to get them, he reasoned. He would have to move up into engineering or management to earn more, and if that did not happen, then he would have to move on, using his MBA degree to get work in some other industry, a career change that would force him once again to rebuild his reputation and value from scratch. "I don't think I've taken a step back by coming to work for Pratt & Whitney," Craig told me. "I am still inching forward. There are people out there who feel a lot more offended by what is happening to them than I do."

The inching forward worked. Imperio gradually formed relationships with nearly every manager in the facility. "I made sure they knew who I was," he said, "and that made them more willing to interview me when I applied for a job opening." The payoff came in spring 2005; he was promoted to quality engineer, with a big jump in salary, to $27 an hour. Imperio now supervised the repair work, "making sure that everything gets adhered to that has to be adhered to." He saw the promotion as a step up the ladder, with more to come. "My goal is to finish school and get my MBA," he said, "and the goal before that was to get promoted, which I did. You can only have one goal at a time."

Getting back on the ladder eluded Elizabeth Nash, the former Procter & Gamble executive in Cincinnati who had been pushed into retirement in 2002 at age forty-seven. Over twenty-five years at Procter, Nash had come to think of herself as a highly skilled and effective professional and she tried to transfer this value—this sense of herself—to another company. The first attempt failed when she joined F+W Publications, making $82,000 a year, far less than the $150,000 she had once earned. After that experience, her salary expectations shrank. She concluded that she would probably never get above $100,000 again. By the end of 2004, she was competing to be hired as the human resources manager for a small Midwest hotel chain, at a salary of $90,000. "I told them that was doable," she said. But months passed and the job did not materialize.

Nash was also discovering that her years at Procter could work against her. In her various job interviews, she had learned to be careful about how she described her Procter connection. The huge and successful consumer products company has its headquarters in Cincinnati, where it has a reputation for employing the city's smartest, most skilled people. If you work for Procter you must be among the very best. Otherwise, Procter would not have hired you and kept you, any more than Harvard would accept and tolerate a second-rate student. "But you don't come right out and say that in a job interview," Nash explained. "You don't want to throw it in people's faces. I slip it in. People say, What can you do for me, what do you have to show for your experience? And I say twenty-five years at Procter and since then independent consulting, including consulting for Procter."

Those last four words have become, in Nash's mind, the most important. "People in Cincinnati have the impression," she said, "that if you leave a company like Procter after so many years, as I did, there must be something wrong with you." Here was evidence that although Procter had forced her out, it valued her work. If that were not the case, she would not have been called back as a consultant in the summer and fall of 2004. True, the consulting fee of $75 an hour was less than half what she had asked for and the work soon disappeared in yet another reorganization of a Procter operation. Still, she clung to Procter's belated and halfhearted affirmation of her value. It bolstered her résumé and kept up her spirits as she hunted for a job that would give her reentry into a corporate organization. Once inside, she would be able to contribute to the new employer's success and in doing so rebuild her own self-esteem. Meanwhile, she became a sales representative, strictly on commission, for a software company that was trying to sell its product to Procter and counted on her contacts at her old employer to make the sale, which would bring her a $5,000 commission if the many hours invested in the effort actually paid off. The whole endeavor made her realize how thoroughly her forced retirement had made her an outsider. "I am not betting my future on a relationship with Procter," she told me. "That would be pitiful."

Like Tim Dewey, she yearned for a slot in a company. Until that happened, she networked with consultants who might offer her work, cared for her parents—her father died during this difficult period and her mother, suffering from Alzheimer's, entered a nursing facility near Nash's home—and made an extra effort to keep in contact with her numerous friends, who became a partial substitute for the lost satisfactions of work. "I am rich with friends," Nash said, "and most of them are right here in Cincinnati." She attributed her sanity to those friends, and also to what she described as her own solid upbringing, in particular her relationship with her father, who had given her support and advice and had himself been forced out as an AT&T executive a few years before he wanted to retire.

More than many laid-off workers, Nash managed to maintain her spirits. Or so she convinced herself. But occasionally something happened that made her realize how starved she was for affirmation and how much damage had been done to her self-esteem. She is a pro bono speaker for a network of vocational schools that offers skills training to adults. These schools also sponsor talks by experts like Nash and the invited audiences are businesspeople whom Nash considers her peers. One of her talks, in January 2005, went especially well. Her subject was "effective remote teams," which means the best techniques for managing workers stationed elsewhere—an expertise she acquired at Procter, with its numerous offices in the United States and abroad.

Despite snowy weather, the turnout for her talk was large and Nash said she got a lot of positive feedback, which surprised her and pleased her very much. "People have told me, Gosh, you've been through a lot the last few years, Liz, but you seem to be pretty upbeat about it, and I'm glad that I give that impression," Nash said. "But I was so excited after that presentation and that positive feedback. I was so hungry for that feedback. I couldn't go to sleep that night. I must have called ten people who have asked, 'Have you had any job offers lately?' to tell them the presentation went really well. You have to remind yourself, when you are not working, how good you are. You don't get the daily reinforcement and the sense of accomplishment that a job provides. You apply for a lot of jobs and you get no feedback, or negative feedback. No feedback is negative feedback. It is just a black hole out there."

CHAPTER NINE

Solutions

Layoffs are not going to go away, but they don't have to be as numerous as they now are. Shrinking the number is possible, but before we can make it happen, we have to address a philosophical issue: Are we going to once again be a community of people who feel obligated to take care of one another, or are we going to continue as a collection of individuals, each one increasingly concerned only with his or her well-being? If we can band together again, as we did during a forty-year stretch that started in the Depression and ended with the Vietnam War, then job security will gradually return to the United States—not to the degree that once existed, but more than we have today.

Banding together does not mean propping up every telephone call center, software operation, and factory simply to save the jobs. The global economy is not to be denied. But it does mean assessing the costs involved in layoffs, all the costs, and having the will to act on what we learn. We do this now in other areas. We band together to assess damage to the environment, and insist on limiting the damage. During the Social Security debate, millions of people questioned the efficacy of personal retirement accounts. Public opinion polls captured their doubt, and President Bush backed down. In the matter of layoffs, however, we give employers a nearly free hand and resign ourselves to the results. Neither Democrats nor Republicans call for a debate that might arouse people to act in unison or out of concern for one another. And on a personal level, we are inundated with self-help books that urge individuals to create, from within themselves, their own job security.

One of the all-time best-sellers in this genre, a fairy tale entitled *Who Moved My Cheese?*, features two mice and two miniature humans who, with "their complex brains," are far less suited to the layoff era than the mice are, although in this tale the mice and the humans are equally reliant on cheese. When the cheese disappears—i.e., the jobs—the humans passively wait for the cheese to reappear somehow while the mice quickly hunt for a new supply and find one even tastier than the last. The humans eventually get the message, and in the happy ending, Spencer Johnson, the author, drives home his point: Set forth right away, as the mice do, in search of that new supply, and when you find it, be ready, as the mice are, to energetically repeat the search, once the new supply also disappears, which it surely will. Johnson, a medical doctor and writer of inspirational books, calls this healthy change. "Enjoy change," he urges his readers, simplifying a message about job loss that runs through the self-help literature.

The aircraft mechanics who lost their jobs at United Airlines in Indianapolis were offered free copies of *Who Moved My Cheese?* when they showed up at the federally funded reemployment center, seeking help in getting new work. There was even a class—not mandatory like the classes in résumé writing and job interviewing—at which the book was discussed, the message being that the mechanics should move on, too, in good spirits. Not many bothered with the book or the class. The ones I knew sneered at this attempt at emotional uplift. They were realistically skeptical about landing on their feet through their own efforts alone. But they did not band together in a campaign to keep the maintenance center open once United gave up. Nor did they take their cause to the community through their union, the International Association of Machinists, attempting to enlist the support of civic organizations, churches, student groups, and small-business owners who benefited from the presence of more than two thousand well-paid mechanics and their families. The community, and the nation, would have been well served if the mechanics and their union had taken this route.

United was inspired to build the imaginatively conceived and super-efficient maintenance center by the promise in the early nineties of expanding airline travel. Once in operation, however, the huge facility took a prominent place in America's industrial structure. It was a step forward in airline safety and in cost-effective, state-of-the-art aircraft maintenance. Closing such a publicly valuable facility should not be the prerogative of the private sector, not when so much benefit is lost. And yet the mayor of Indianapolis and the governor of Indiana, like the mechanics, let this happen, although the city and the state put up most of the financing to build and equip the maintenance center and were its principal owners, leasing the facility back to United. Unable to keep the airline in place and unable to substitute another big airline, the city and state sought a smaller tenant and in doing so gave up on operating the maintenance center at anywhere near its full, most efficient capacity.

There were alternatives to that surrender. In the interest of safety—and not as industrial policy—the federal government could have required the airlines to overhaul their aircraft at five or six designated maintenance centers, the very best in the country. The one in Indianapolis would be among those designated. With government guaranteeing a steady flow of maintenance work, United or another big airline might be quite willing to be the proprietor, or a consortium of airlines, with the industry setting the amounts to be charged and unions negotiating wages and job security.

The obstacles to this or to other actions that would diminish the number of layoffs are formidable. Government regulation is held up as counterproductive and inefficient in a society that extols individual endeavor, but regulation is vital when it protects our common interest, as in this case. On another front, city and state governments siphon more than $30 billion a year from potential public investment and spend it instead on tax breaks and other lures to get companies to move from one locale to another, laying off the workers left behind. Congress and the federal courts can put a stop to this practice, and they should. Stepped-up public investment would promote employment and job security, although in this anti-government era there is very little support for a practice that the nation took for granted in the fifties and sixties. A stronger labor movement would also inhibit layoffs. Right now, unions and layoffs are locked in a downward spiral. Layoffs undermine the labor movement, which then becomes less capable of inhibiting layoffs. That destructive dynamic must be reversed.

These solutions will be hard to put in place, but if we do manage to diminish layoffs, we will have taken a big step toward repairing a larger framework. Stable jobs and sufficient incomes in stable communities are powerful equalizers. Restore them—or begin to restore them—and the political influence that wealth now buys and that distorts democracy will be easier to unwind. Today, access to a good education is skewed more than ever toward the offspring of well-to-do families, and that, too, will begin to change. Without these changes, we give up the preconditions of democracy.

The preconditions were achieved in the republic's early days through a large population of self-supporting farmers and in later times through stable wage income and the earnings of small businesses in thriving towns and cities. "There was an implicit understanding forty years ago that if you went to school and did not assault people on the streets and worked in a disciplined way, you could have a good life," notes Joel Rogers, a professor of political science, law, and sociology at the University of Wisconsin. That understanding is breaking up, and the easy and frequent use of layoffs greases the way for it to happen. While many changes are needed to get America back to a better course, reducing the number of layoffs is a good starting point, and that task should begin with small, clearly defined steps that stand a chance of succeeding.

• • •

To set the stage for specific proposals, layoffs must be clearly perceived as a crisis. Policy makers, economists, executives, and politicians undercount the actual number of workers laid off, and in doing so deprive people of the data they need to document how widespread and debilitating the practice is. The Bureau of Labor Statistics has found in its biennial surveys of displaced workers that between 3.3 and 5.9 percent of all full-time workers at least twenty years of age were permanently laid off every two years from 1981 through 2003, or an average biennial rate of 4.3 percent. That is millions of men and women in a full-time workforce that averaged nearly 97 million people in those years, even allowing for double counting and other distortions that surveys of this nature entail. Hidden layoffs—disguised as retirements, buyouts, temp work, and contract work—increase that already significant percentage, and if they were added to the count, it might stir us to action, or at the very least bury the myth that nothing all that out of the ordinary is happening that can't be cured through a concerted effort at education and training.

The bureau comes up with its layoff count on the basis of a biennial survey of sixty thousand representative households, done by the Census Bureau, in which people are asked whether they lost or left a job in the previous three years because a factory or company closed or moved, there was insufficient work for them, or their positions were abolished. Only one layoff is counted for those who say they were laid off more than once in that three-year period. The tens of thousands of early retirements and buyouts are not counted either, unless a household member chooses to report this experience as a forced separation, a difficult thing to do since early retirement and buyout do not fall easily into the categories specified in the poll taker's question. That's what they are, however: layoffs. Virginia Gibbs, the Citigroup executive who lost her job through early retirement, has no doubt on that score. "If the message is that you don't have value and we therefore want you to retire, then early retirements are layoffs," she said.

Contract workers whose contracts end and are not renewed also do not appear in the bureau's layoff count. Neither do temps whose assignments end, even when these assignments lasted for several years. Granted, some temps and contract workers choose this form of employment. It fits their lifestyle. But a large number say they are temps and contract workers because employers won't hire them in regular jobs. Whatever the reasons, the growing presence of temps and contract workers—they constitute more than 10 percent of the nation's workforce, up from 2 or 3 percent thirty years ago—is evidence of a reorganization of the workplace to accommodate layoffs without having to call them that.

The list of hidden layoffs continues. Many companies outsource food service or building maintenance or computer services or payroll preparation or sales or some other function, and the employees who did this work in-house are transferred to the payrolls of the outsourcing companies. An unknown number then quit rather than accept the lower pay and reduced benefits so often forced on them by their new employers. They lay themselves off, in effect. The Educational Testing Service in Princeton, New Jersey, the company that prepares the SAT college entrance exams, shifted more than six hundred employees to other companies through outsourcing: first the outsourcing of building and grounds maintenance, then human resources, and after that computer maintenance. "They went to work for the contractors at slightly less pay, although it really was more than slightly less because they were not likely to get raises," Anthony Carnevale, then chief economist at the testing service, explained. No one tracked how many subsequently quit.

Several young people told me they had resigned from promising jobs after their bosses explained that layoffs were coming. Many went on to new employment. Economists often describe this as "voluntary mobility," a healthy job churning as opportunities come and go in a dynamic economy. What happened to Jessica Welch meets this description, but not in her eyes. She was a senior account executive in the New York office of Ogilvy Public Relations Worldwide when she left in 2002 at age twenty-six and took a similar job at Manning Selvage & Lee, also in public relations. She had not intended to leave. She was doing well at Ogilvy, where she had worked for three and a half years. "We had regular performance reviews and those worked fine," Welch told me. "They were saying, You are one of our valued employees. But they were also beginning to say, You might want to look beyond this company; I don't know how long we can keep you."

Her clients at Ogilvy were mostly high-tech companies, including Sun Microsystems, and in the dot-com bust billings dropped. There were layoffs, and on top of the layoffs, salary freezes, and promotion freezes, Welch said, "I did not know from one day to the next whether I would be let go or not." Shortly before she left, her bosses transferred her to corporate practices, an operation relatively immune to layoffs. "I still did not feel safe," she said. Back in Colorado, her home state, her father and two aunts had gone through layoffs and their experiences added to her uneasiness. Just then, an executive at Manning Selvage called. He had seen her name on a press release that impressed him and he recruited her, miraculously at $58,000 a year, or $9,000 above her Ogilvy pay. She accepted the offer the day it was made.

Then there is the netherworld of jobs that are so poorly paid and so stripped of opportunity (no promotions, no raises, no training) that quitting them and being laid off are roughly the same. The message from management is that your value is minimal, not worth preserving. The people in these jobs are drawn mostly from the 25 percent of the workforce earning $9 an hour or less in 2004 at fast-food restaurants, discount stores, supermarkets, telephone call centers, and elsewhere. Turnover is frequently 100 percent a year or more; indeed, the jobs are designed for turnover. People lay themselves off out of discouragement and exhaustion. "The distinction between quits and layoffs is not always clear," Henry S. Farber, a labor economist at Princeton University, acknowledges.

A higher minimum wage would separate the two. It would also force employers to value their workers more and, valuing them more, they would be more likely to invest in training—which raises commitment on the part of the employer, inhibiting layoffs—and in automation, to get a better return from more expensive workers. For all this to happen, however, the minimum wage, at $5.15 an hour in 2005, would probably have to go up to $12 an hour, although not right away. That would be too big a raise for many employers to adjust to all at once. But a law that recognized $12 an hour as the goal to be achieved in nine or ten years and moved toward that goal in 50- or 75-cent increments would gradually eliminate low-wage work as a form of layoff.

Proposing a significant rise in the minimum wage in this day and age of resistance in Congress to any increase at all sounds like pie in the sky, but by earlier standards, $12 an hour is reasonable. Back in 1968, the purchasing power of the minimum wage reached a record $8 an hour in today's dollars, and thereafter dwindled, particularly in the eighties and nineties, when Congress no longer tried to keep the minimum in step with inflation. Restoring the lost inflation adjustment and incorporating gains in labor productivity since the late sixties more than justifies a $12-an-hour minimum. That wage for a full-time worker would have been enough in 2004 to lift a family of four well above the official poverty line. Nine or ten years from now, it will probably no longer be enough. But raising the minimum in prescribed steps would pressure employers to make their employees more efficient, largely through training. The additional revenue generated by the greater efficiency and by higher productivity would allow companies to recover their greater wage cost.

Moving in this direction is not easy, not without an accurate head count of laid-off workers as a prod. Among economists, Farber is well known for his detailed analyses of the worker-displacement data issued biennially by the Bureau of Labor Statistics. Like other economists, he wonders why "fear of job loss is on everyone's lips" when the government's count of displaced workers does not statistically constitute an epidemic. The bureau commissioned the surveys in the early eighties when layoffs were limited mainly to blue-collar factory workers. The question asked then and unchanged to this day—did you lose your job because a plant or office closed, your position was abolished, or you had insufficient work?—was designed to fit the experience then. The numerous hidden layoffs did not appear until the nineties, and to capture more accurately what was happening, the bureau in the final years of that decade considered rewording the survey question to broaden it. After much discussion, however, redesign was rejected. The decision not to act was mainly out of concern that a change would cancel the usefulness of nearly twenty years of data from the previous surveys, Thomas J. Nardone, an associate commissioner at the bureau, said. "We would have had a break in a series that a lot of people used to examine job displacement."

Farber was among the numerous outside experts consulted by the bureau. He favored redesign. "If you ask people, 'Did your job end against your wishes and if so why?' you would get better answers," he said. Farber's more comprehensive survey—issued annually instead of biennially, a frequency the bureau did favor—might easily produce a biennial layoff rate averaging 7 or 8 percent of the nation's full-time workers, who totaled 114 million in 2004. That is far more alarming than the 4.3 percent from 1981 through 2003 that the bureau now reports. It is high enough so that over a fifteen- or twenty-year period the majority of workers are likely to go through an experience that barely existed thirty-five years ago. The bureau's count hides that, and, in doing so, suppresses the alarm that would prompt us to pull back from such damaging behavior.

Apart from an accurate count, there is another statistical obstacle to full recognition that layoffs are overwhelming us. If they are, many mainstream economists argue, then why don't the statistics show a decline in job tenure?—that is, a decline in the number of years that workers spend with the same employers. The bureau's tenure surveys, in their current format, date only from 1983, when the age of the layoff was already under way, making comparisons with prelayoff years difficult. In addition, the growing number of women who have stayed in the workforce after childbirth has lengthened average tenure for the entire workforce, even allowing for layoffs. The baby boom generation also influences the data. Older workers generally have more years at a job than younger workers, and as the baby boomers have aged their large presence among workers in their middle forties to late fifties has bolstered tenure in this age group. Despite these counterweights, tenure has clearly begun to decline. The percentage of employed wage and salary workers in their thirties and early forties—the post–baby boom generation—who have ten years or more with the same employer has fallen 3 to 4 points since 1998, according to the bureau's 2004 survey. There were declines as well for older workers in the baby boom generation, although those declines were smaller.

The message from the numbers is beginning to win converts even among mainstream economists like David Neumark, a senior fellow at the Public Policy Institute of California. In 1996 he insisted that the statistical evidence then available gave no support to the media's perception of widespread layoffs. Four years later, as the editor of a collection of research papers on job stability, Neumark gave a little ground. "My reading of the evidence is that the 1990s have witnessed some changes in the employment relationship consistent with weakened bonds between workers and firms," he wrote. By January 2005, he was en route to an about-face. "I think there are a lot of indications that say the employment situation has changed," he said. "We are finding that the people who used to be in the most secure jobs are experiencing less stability."

•   •   •

Once the existing statistics are brought into line with reality, an additional layer of data should be added, this one supplied by the corporations themselves. The public disclosure involved would add to the pressure on companies to refrain from layoffs.

Public disclosure does that. Just as environmental impact statements inhibit polluting, similar corporate accounting might very well improve job security. The time seems ripe. The Enron scandal and the subsequent corporate debacles have resulted in laws and regulations that insist on accurate, honest accounting to protect investors and shareholders. The new byword—professed, at least—is corporate responsibility. That standard should be extended to layoffs, which are as damaging to the laid-off as a bankruptcy and the collapse of a company's stock price are to investors and shareholders. And yet the accounting needed to enforce corporate responsibility does not exist for layoffs. "There have been some attempts to look at the economic consequences of these things," says Sanford Jacoby, the economic historian at the University of California, Los Angeles. "But it is very hard to get numbers from companies and companies very often do not collect numbers."

Every company in the country with one hundred or more employees should be required to file annually with the government, perhaps the

Labor Department, a certified document not unlike the certified earnings reports and balance sheets that publicly traded companies regularly file with the Securities and Exchange Commission. This new document would specify the number of people who left the company over the previous twelve months, the wage of each, the number of hours each worked, and the reasons for departure: layoff, resignation, early retirement, standard retirement, buyout, transfer to the payroll of an outside contractor who took over a service previously performed in-house, temps whose assignments ended, contractors whose contracts were not renewed.

Where the reasons for departure are ambiguous, the employer would specify whether the employee left voluntarily or against his or her wishes or, in the case of early retirement, to avoid a threatened layoff. As a final requirement, the employer would file an impact statement that estimated the savings from involuntary separations and also the losses, insofar as the latter can be measured in such things as additional sick days among the survivors, additional defects in the goods and services the survivors produced, and additional outlays for temps and contract workers brought in to do some of the work the laid-off once performed. None of this is radical. Publicly traded companies now must disclose the compensation for each of their five highest paid executives. Shareholders have a stake in the huge sums they earn, and society has a stake in how companies dispose of employees—a stake some states are beginning to recognize. Five states, for example, passed laws in 2004 that restrict outsourcing, particularly if a company does business with the state. And the California legislature passed a bill that requires a company with more than 250 employees to report annually the breakdown of people working directly for the company or providing services to the company as temps or in some other outsider arrangement. Governor Arnold Schwarzenegger vetoed the bill.

Whatever the final format, the corporate documents would be subject to audit, just as tax returns are, and to penalties for false statements. Before they were submitted, outside accountants would have to certify their accuracy, just as they certify corporate earnings reports. They would be made available to the public within, say, three months of the annual filing deadline. Academics would undoubtedly swoop down to analyze data never before available to them.

The public would have two levels of information. One would be the worker-displacement surveys currently produced by the Bureau of Labor Statistics, issued annually instead of biennially and redesigned to capture hidden as well as straightforward layoffs. That would be the headline gauge of layoffs in America. The second level would be the much more detailed information about corporate behavior with regard to employment and layoffs that the certified reports would provide and that academics and researchers would then collate and analyze. "You could find out what the good actors do and set standards that way," says Charles Sabel, a political scientist at Columbia University whose research ranges into this sort of issue.

Turnover among Silicon Valley firms, for instance, is high. The average may be 60 percent a year; that is, six out of every ten employees leave within a year. The certified filings would tell us for sure. The 60 percent becomes the norm, then, and companies on the high end, say at 90 percent a year, become targets of media attention and public inquiry. Did they engage in more layoffs than others in the Valley? If so, did the high-layoff companies outshine those that kept layoffs below the norm? "The only thing you can do is obligate companies to file comparable data" and then draw conclusions from the results, Sabel argues.

Different norms would emerge for insurance companies, Wall Street brokerage houses, telephone companies, airlines, auto parts manufacturers, chemical companies, retail stores, and commercial banking. In each industry, the outliers could be singled out and targeted, and the norms themselves studied, to determine whether the norm in, say, retailing should be as high as it is. Knowing they were vulnerable to public scrutiny, many chief executives, concerned about their companies' reputations—and their own—would attempt to keep layoffs within the norms for their industries, or avoid them altogether if they were not likely to produce certifiably good results. One hopes that would happen. "Companies don't like to be inhibited, and this would do that a little bit," says Michael Piore, an economist and management expert at MIT.

* * *

Once the data are in place, then pressure can build for other changes. City and state governments compete fiercely to lure companies and jobs to their locales, offering not only tax breaks but free land, free training for workers, and wage subsidies. These lures are rarely a deciding factor.

Companies pick one city rather than another, or migrate from one city to another, mainly in pursuit of lower labor costs and to escape unions, but the subsidies are an additional lure, and in the case of migration, the workers left behind are laid off. Sometimes the companies get the subsidies to stay put, as Sears, Roebuck & Company did in 1989. It received more than $250 million from the State of Illinois (mainly in tax breaks) after announcing that it would move its headquarters to either Texas or North Carolina. Congress can put a stop to this war of the states, invoking its constitutional power to regulate interstate commerce. So can the federal courts. Indeed, the U.S. Court of Appeals for the Sixth Circuit ruled in September 2004 that a subsidy given to the DaimlerChrysler Corporation to put a plant in Ohio, not Michigan, constituted interference in interstate commerce. The ruling was appealed, and if it is upheld by the Supreme Court, it would be a big step toward ending the war of the states.

The states themselves cannot really stop the practice. "If a state were to withdraw unilaterally from the bidding war, that would be economic suicide," says Arthur Rolnick, the director of research at the Federal Reserve Bank of Minnesota and a longtime opponent of dueling subsidies. But if the practice were banned at the federal level, that would almost certainly cut back the frequency of corporate migration, and in doing so reduce the number of layoffs. The $30 billion in taxpayer money that now goes into these corporate lures could be diverted to spending on public projects that increase the number of jobs, a worthier goal than encouraging companies to put jobs in one state rather than another, a zero-sum game.

The war of the states takes place on a global scale, too. The president of Intel, Paul S. Otellini, told the President's Advisory Panel on Federal Tax Reform in the spring of 2005 that because of high tax rates in the United States, his company may build its next $3 billion semiconductor factory overseas, in a country where tax rates are lower. Instead of laying people off, Intel would simply not add to the nation's workforce. For other companies, however, the tax lure encourages them to shift production abroad, laying off workers at home. Otellini argued that Intel's tax bill is several times higher in the United States, where it has twelve semiconductor factories, than it is overseas, where it has four factories. "The problem that we have and that the industry has is that it costs us $1 billion more [a year] to operate inside the U.S. than outside the country," he said. "It's not wages and capital; it's almost all attributed to tax benefits—or the lack thereof—in the United States compared to what is offered elsewhere."

The answer is not tax breaks in the United States, but no tax concessions overseas. That is a tough goal to achieve, but not out of line with the efforts of Democratic and Republican administrations alike to get European governments to reduce subsidies that give their farmers and their aircraft manufacturers, for example, an advantage over ours. Uniformity in tax rates should be a high priority in trade negotiations. So should enforcing environmental standards and raising wages, particularly the latter. As various economists are increasingly pointing out, when two countries—let's say China and the United States—make a product or produce a service with equal skill, efficiency, and technology, then the advantage goes to the low-wage country, assuming distance isn't an issue—and it seldom is anymore, even for China. That country is approaching the United States in productivity and sophistication in some industries while paying very low wages to workers in those industries. All else being equal, the adjustment has to come in wages: if China's do not rise to our level, ours have to drop toward their level.

Creating the conditions that allow these workers to move toward the American level should be written into trade agreements and enforced. The AFL-CIO proposal is the right approach. Require countries, as a condition of free trade, to permit their workers the right to organize and bargain collectively, and if that does not take place then under the rules of a trade agreement an action can be brought and the offending country's goods and services can be blocked from entry into the United States. As of 2005, these requirements have been written into only one trade agreement involving the United States, the one negotiated with Jordan during Bill Clinton's second term. We insist that other countries honor our patents on innovative products: the iPod, for example. That is called protecting intellectual capital and it is written into all our trade agreements. We should do the same for human capital.

•   •   •

Official recognition of the layoff phenomenon, through far more accurate data, would undermine another flawed thesis: that markets on their own can generate full employment without a helping hand from government. Full employment has happened in only three of the last thirty years—not enough years to make a dent in layoffs. The problem is that the private sector is primarily interested in meeting those national needs that promise a sufficient profit, and therefore its appetite for workers is limited, except in unusual moments like the late nineties, when a bubble in stock prices and in housing prices helped to produce a frenzy of private-sector activity and hiring. Most of the time, government must step in, much more than it has since the seventies, to satisfy needs that markets do not.

The vehicle should be public investment, and by public investment I do not mean a temporary Keynesian stimulus to end a recession or revive a weak economy, but constant outlays to satisfy legitimate needs and to lift well-being. Public transportation has deteriorated, for example. So have schools, drinking water systems, parks and libraries, and low-income housing. The rise of two-earner families cries out for quality day care that does not exist in the private sector for families unable to afford $800 to $1,000 a month per child—the going market price for quality care. For those who cannot afford this much, and most families cannot, government should subsidize the cost of quality care, which means subsidizing the wages of thousands of trained and skilled people, even employing some in government-owned centers. Along these lines, an expanded Head Start program for preschool youngsters and health clinics in poor neighborhoods would be sources of steady, useful employment for skilled people. All of these proposals harness public investment to move the nation toward full employment at decent pay in ways that benefit all of us.

On a larger stage, government should once again take the lead in developing technologies that the private sector, on its own, shies away from as too risky. Alternative energy is an obvious candidate. Flat-panel screens for computers and television, as well as for military use, are an example of a missed opportunity, a technology invented in the United States but developed by Japanese companies working with their government and then manufactured in Japan, although production gradually shifted to other Asian countries. IBM in the early eighties asked the federal government for help in building a flat-panel plant in the United States. The request was rejected and IBM put the plant in Japan instead, in partnership with Fujitsu. In motor vehicles, American manufacturers rushed to produce a hybrid car powered by a gasoline-electric engine only after the popularity of the Toyota Prius demonstrated the commercial viability of this new, fuel-saving Japanese technology. By 2005, Toyota was shipping seven thousand Priuses a month to the United States from factories in Japan, generating job security there, but not here. We could be enjoying those jobs if the American government had stepped in years ago to support the development of this potentially promising but not yet commercially viable technology, doing so in the interest of fuel conservation. The resulting exports would have been a shot in the arm for American auto manufacturers. Several factories, instead of closing, would have remained open, with their employees in place, to produce hybrid cars, and that would have continued until the technology was fully exploited and some production inevitably shifted out of the country.

In an earlier era of much more faith in the payoff from public investment, President Eisenhower and Congress, to take one famous example, did not hesitate in the late fifties to authorize huge sums to get the United States into space in competition with the Soviet Union. The Cold War drove that investment; job security and full employment should move us now. The Eisenhower investment, continued by subsequent administrations, produced not only jobs but careers, and these very often in the private sector, which benefited from the contracts to get us into space. The private sector also benefited from new technologies that were developed for the space program. Miniaturized electronic circuitry came out of this research, for example, and this circuitry went into radios, recording devices, watches, and computers.

Public investment of this sort invariably expands private-sector activity. Its importance is fundamental and has been since the early nineteenth century. Even now we resort to it, despite all the emphasis on markets rather than government. The Human Genome Project, which mapped the human genetic blueprint at a cost to the government of $3 billion, is spawning many new products and jobs, and is likely to do so for years to come. The Erie Canal and the transcontinental railroad in the nineteenth century, and rural electrification, radar, and nuclear power in the twentieth all contributed to successes in the private sector. To this day, patents filed for new medicines, chemicals, electronic devices, and communications equipment invariably list publicly funded research. The National Science Foundation, for example, financed some of the research incorporated in such breakthrough Internet tools as Netscape,

Internet Explorer, and Google. Public investment, in sum, raises the odds of steady employment and takes some of the sting out of layoffs, in part through the message—implicit in a recognition of the importance of public investment—that generating jobs is a shared responsibility.

All this has to be paid for, of course, and that requires much more tax revenue. The best and fairest way to raise money is to restore an income tax that is more progressive than our current tax rates—one in which the highest earners pay over to the Internal Revenue Service most of their income above, say, $150,000 a year. That is a high marginal tax rate, to be sure, but not out in left field. Within the lifetime of everyone over twenty-five years of age, the marginal rate was above 50 percent. That was the case until 1979, shortly before Ronald Reagan became president and altered the tax structure. Going back to a higher level from the present 34 percent will by no means be easy. Doing so flies in the face of the prevailing wisdom, first embraced by Reagan and solidly reaffirmed in the presidency of George W. Bush. This wisdom hews to the thesis that tax cuts have a supply-side effect; people keep more of their income, and that is an incentive to work harder and invest more. It is a doubtful, unproven proposition. In any case, there was plenty of work and investment in the heyday of the progressive income tax, which has two other advantages.

Richard Layard, the British economist, lays them out. When it comes to "happiness," he wrote in a recent book by that title, each additional dollar of income adds less to the happiness of a rich person than it does to the happiness of a lower-income person, who uses the dollar to meet real needs. We are a happier people, then, as a result of the progressive income tax. What's more, Layard argues, spending on luxuries tends to be addictive and a progressive income tax curbs that addiction. "The current pursuit of self-realization will not work," he writes. "If your sole duty is to achieve the best for yourself, life becomes just too stressful, too lonely—you are set up to fail. Instead, you need to feel you exist for something larger, and that very thought takes off some of the pressure."

•   •   •   •

In various small, peripheral ways layoffs can be reduced, or at least made less painful. Congress or a regulatory agency should require call center operators to identify the city and country in which they are located, the purpose being to embarrass companies into keeping this work in the United States more than they now do. Just as manufacturers label the source of their merchandise, so should service providers, a requirement the California legislature adopted in 2004 and the governor vetoed. We should tax overseas profits of American corporations in the year they are earned, canceling the current deferment of this taxation until the profits are repatriated, if they ever are. Immediate taxation would raise the cost of shifting production to China, Europe, or Mexico, not by a lot but by enough to discourage managers from going ahead with some of these shifts, and the layoffs at home that they entail. Similarly, companies that shift production abroad should no longer be allowed to deduct from their taxable income the expenses involved in the transfer. Along the same lines, CEO salaries should be limited to cash payments (seven-figure payments if necessary), eliminating the stock options, special stock grants, and other performance bonuses that now serve as an incentive to cut labor costs and thus improve short-term profits.

All this is preventive medicine. Under the rubric of helping the victims, Congress should establish a minimum severance package, just as it establishes a minimum wage. Companies would have to pay that minimum to employees who are laid off. The amount should be at least two weeks of pay for every six months of employment, so that workers who have invested thirteen years at a company, building a career, qualify for a year's pay to tide them over while they try to get started in another job.

The message in such legislation is that layoffs cannot be avoided in a global economy, but that in response our communal society (including our corporations) has pitched in to protect the victims from the consequences of an event that is not their fault. In the same vein, the federal government, or a combination of federal and state governments, should subsidize the wages of those who do find new jobs, but then spend several years in the new jobs before their pay finally rises to what they earned before they were laid off. Since the pay loss is a common occurrence, the response should be wage insurance on a broader scale than the program initiated by the Bush administration and described in chapter 8, in which a small number of workers qualify for a federal wage subsidy that lasts no more than two years and makes up only some of the difference between their old and new pay. In expanding wage insurance, however, we implicitly give a green light to layoffs and settle for helping the victims. National health insurance and larger Social Security pensions, not smaller ones, would also help the victims while implicitly accepting the layoffs, treating the symptoms, as it were, without attacking the disease.

• • •

Layoffs won't decline until workers—and whole communities—regain bargaining power. Unions in the fifties and sixties enjoyed considerable public support and that helped them in their bargaining for wages and job security. As a matter of principle, many Americans did not cross picket lines; they viewed a union's struggle as helpful in their own dealings with nonunion employers. That public support had dissipated by the nineties, although there was still hope in that decade that unions could exercise sufficient bargaining power on their own, and they sometimes did.

After a sixty-nine-day strike in 1995, for example, Boeing and the International Association of Machinists, representing the company's factory workers in Seattle, Wichita, and Portland, Oregon, agreed to a clause in their new contract that required Boeing to give workers a say in the outsourcing of work. The clause gave the union ninety days to come up with alternative ways to save the desired amount of money without resorting to outsourcing and layoffs. If work was outsourced, Boeing obligated itself to reassign the affected employees to other work, retraining them for that work if necessary. The clause was hailed as a model in labor's struggle to reduce layoffs. It made them a last resort, not a first one, and the restriction stayed in subsequent contracts, although it was watered down in the 2002 agreement, and outsourcing increased.

Such failures beg for alternative solutions to the bargaining weakness. One lies in persuading state legislatures to act, and some just might be persuaded, the labor lawyer Thomas Geoghegan argues in his book *Which Side Are You On? Trying to Be for Labor When It's Flat on Its Back.* His reasoning is straightforward and caustic. American legal precedent permits "employment at will," which means an employer can fire an employee without giving a reason, unless the employer is prevented from doing so by a specific law (civil rights legislation, for example) or through union agreements, of which there are fewer every year, or through employment contracts, such as chief executives often have, or by other written material that specifies cause for dismissal. Geoghegan would undo employment at will by having each state pass a law saying that layoffs must have a just cause.

Geoghegan is more satirist and realist than preacher. But he means this proposal. If only two or three states acted, a standard would begin to form against which layoffs would be judged. A worker out on strike whose job went to a permanently hired replacement could sue to get the job back, citing the state law. So could the ex-workers at a company that had laid them off on the seemingly just ground that it needed the savings to survive, if the workers could offer evidence that the savings were really used to bloat executive pay or to help pay down debt floated to finance a wasteful acquisition. If the courts agreed, the company would have to rehire the workers or indemnify them. More to the point, the publicity from such cases would begin to revive the resistance that layoffs provoked twenty-five years ago. The barriers that were dismantled through the eighties and nineties would begin to come back. The acquiescence to layoffs would unwind.

Geoghegan's state law is not without antecedents. Montana enacted an unlawful discharge law in 1987, and several other states have attempted to pass similar laws. None of these actions deals with layoffs; instead, they address protection for individuals from unjust dismissal for such activities as being a whistleblower. Layoffs are an entirely different matter. State laws challenging them would give workers the right to second-guess business judgment, an intrusion that when you add up all the damage from layoffs, particularly the damage to a company's own performance, seems justified, and even in the nation's best interest.

The National Conference of Commissioners on Uniform State Laws favors the intrusion and wants legislatures to authorize them. The conference draws its members from bar associations around the country. These representative lawyers meet periodically, and at one of their meetings, in early August 1991 in Naples, Florida, they approved a statute they had been drafting for several years. The Model Employment Termination Act, as it was called, was a template for states to use in adopting their own laws. It would give workers the right to challenge layoffs. They were not outlawed, not by any means. The model act would still allow managers to shed workers, move operations, and outsource, as long as this was done for legitimate business reasons. Laid-off workers could challenge the reasons given for the loss of their jobs and if an arbitrator found that the layoffs were not justified, remedies would be specified, among them reinstatement. "Adoption of a 'good cause' standard," the National Conference of Commissioners said in a summary statement, "would not put this country at a disadvantage in global competition by imposing constraints not borne by firms overseas. . . . The United States is the last major industrial democracy in the world" without laws specifically directed at job security. Nevertheless, in the nearly fifteen years that the model act has existed, no state legislature has embraced its principles.

That is a mistake and it is likely to remain one until public pressure forces action. Absent that pressure, how many state legislators would withstand corporate threats to move their operations elsewhere if the legislators contemplated such a law? Forcing action requires the year-in, year-out efforts of coalitions more deeply rooted in communities than unions are today, even unions like the Service Employees International Union (SEIU), with its knack for arousing public support on behalf of its members, many of them janitors who clean office buildings and get into terrible disputes with the landlords and cleaning companies that employ them.

SEIU is the nation's largest union, growing quickly and very much in the headlines. Community-based coalitions are also multiplying but their growth is less noticed. They are tortoises in this race, proceeding on a couple of tiers. On one tier is the Jobs with Justice movement, a network of coalitions, funded by unions, that enlist support in a community—from churches, politicians, and civic organizations, among others—to help workers at a particular company form a union or bargain successfully. "We are weaker than we used to be and we need these allies," said Ronald Blackwell, the AFL-CIO's chief economist. On another tier, coalitions of a different sort bring together churches, civic organizations, neighborhood groups, schools, and unions—a range of people and institutions that, working together, have the power to influence the behavior of elected officials and corporate managers. Unions are one constituency in these coalitions, whose goals are broader than those of Jobs with Justice and potentially more effective.

Many of these broader coalitions were organized by the Industrial Areas Foundation, or IAF, established in Chicago in 1969 by Saul Alinsky, a social activist who developed some organizing techniques and trained several generations of community organizers, including Cesar Chavez. Three other similar groups came into existence not long after, inspired in part by the civil rights movement and the women's movement, but also by Alinsky. His great concern, when he started in the thirties, was to improve living conditions in Chicago's ghettos and challenge the anti-labor practices of the stockyard operators who employed ghetto residents. The Catholic Church was a big ally then, and often still is.

The coalitions bring together a community's institutions in what Ernesto Cortes Jr., an IAF leader, describes as "a thick network of rela-tionships embedded within and between them." The IAF organizers achieve this by concentrating their efforts on developing local leaders who learn to relate their personal concerns, and anger, to the concerns and anger of others and who then commit the necessary time and energy to the work of the coalitions. "What we're trying to do," Cortes said, "is to draw people out of their private pain, out of their cynicism and passivity, and get them connected with other people in collective action." The result, when this happens, is a broad-based, durable alliance that acts as a political force in favor of projects that embody what the various member groups consider important and are within the coalition's reach.

Living wage ordinances have been a high priority. In only eleven years, starting with Baltimore in 1995, the coalitions pushed the legislative bodies in 130 cities and metropolitan areas to adopt these ordinances. They require companies doing business with a city, or in one way or another benefiting from a subsidy furnished by the city, to pay a mini-mum wage to their employees that is considerably higher than the federal minimum of $5.15 an hour, in some cases more than double it. If employ-ers benefit from an outlay of taxpayer dollars, then employees should, too. That is the logic that the coalitions insist upon in their lobbying efforts. At the very high end, as a result, Fairfax, California, adopted a living wage that was $13 an hour in 2005, plus health benefits.

In recent years, some of the coalitions have ventured for the first time into organizing employee associations. These associations are not to be confused with unions or bargaining units. They represent a cross section of all the workers in a community, union and nonunion alike. Because an employee association is intertwined with other groups in a coalition, it brings political leverage and public pressure to bear in dealing with corporate managers—more leverage and public pressure than unions often muster.

Paul Osterman, an economist at MIT's Sloan School of Management, has spent years studying the work of the coalitions, including the oldest of them all, Communities Organized for Public Service, or COPS, organized by the IAF in San Antonio, Texas, in 1974. Osterman recognizes that the newly emerging employee associations within the coalitions must deal with layoffs. "As a realistic matter," he says, "when a company like Levi Strauss decides to close a plant in San Antonio, which it did do, an employee association is not likely to have any impact. The company is gone; what does it care? On the other hand, if a company lays off five hundred people but stays in the community, then you can imagine an employee association having some influence. If the company sells products in the local market, then it cares what the community thinks. And it has to worry whether its remaining employees will unionize with the help of the association, which would be in a position to enlist community support for the workers to unionize."

Given the downside, a company might agree, in negotiations with an employee association, to lay off four hundred people instead of five hundred, or it might agree, as Boeing once did, to give employees ninety days to come up with alternative ways to save the money without resorting to layoffs—by reducing waste in a factory, for example. Each job saved is a victory and each victory brings people together in the mutual task of resurrecting the obstacles to layoffs that once protected us and lifted our dignity.

Layoffs are a very public topic in America, but the experience itself of being laid off is reluctantly plumbed. The men and women portrayed in this book were hesitant to reveal their feelings, even to themselves, yet they felt impelled to do so to gain some relief from the trauma that had disrupted and skewed their lives. Their stories resonated and, after publication, a broader dialogue began with a number of men and women who found recognition of their own ordeals in *The Disposable American*.

Not everyone who responded had read the book. Some heard me describe its contents in radio and television interviews or in presentations to live audiences. After one such appearance, at City University of New York, a young graduate student in sociology explained that she had purchased the book for her father, although she was not sure she wanted him to read it and put himself through the wrenching experience of reliving his layoff. A reader in Arizona whose husband had lost his job as a computer systems analyst e-mailed, "It seems to us no one is listening . . . I pray someone listens."

In the initial stages of this dialogue, I did not pay a lot of attention to these personal reactions, these appeals for relief. I emphasized instead the book's broader themes—the rise of job security in America over a ninety-year period, starting in the late nineteenth century, its contribution to our industrial success and to our sense of well-being, the unwinding that began in the 1970s, and then, as the barriers to layoffs gradually came down, our acquiescence. Having lost the memory of resistance, we submitted to layoffs.

Absorbing this history strikes me as essential. It should give us back sufficient perspective to shake off acquiescence and to once again mount a resistance. I relearned this history myself as I researched and wrote this book, and I still count on its curative power to restore public challenges to layoffs. But in the dialogue that developed after publication, history and context turned out to be of secondary interest. What touched people were those chapters that reawakened and explained their own experiences. Or, as one reader put it, *The Disposable American* was "personally meaningful." Another who had not yet gone through a layoff but was bracing for one, called me and in the course of the conversation said: "No matter how much you tell yourself you are going to be fine, there is a soft part in you that is crushed."

As the messages and encounters piled up, I found myself focusing more and more in my presentations on three findings in this book. First, that people blame themselves for their own layoffs and our society encourages this self-blame. Second, that the trauma of a layoff—of being told one does not have value—undermines self-esteem and mental health. And, third, that a laid-off worker, no matter how skilled and educated, cannot easily land another well-paying job. Skilled jobs do not exist in sufficient numbers, despite the assertions of our leaders, Democrats and Republicans alike, that they are there for the taking for those willing to get themselves more education and training. The failure to land one becomes, once again, the laid-off worker's fault.

These were the findings that have drawn the most attention in the dialogue that has developed since publication. They are also the least challenged; even critics of other aspects of the book nod in agreement. Of the three findings, the damage to mental health seemed particularly important to those who saw themselves in this book. Certainly the laid-off seek therapy more often than the public realizes. Two dozen psychoanalysts whom I addressed during a conference of the American Psychoanalytic Association last summer acknowledged, almost unanimously, that traumas triggered by layoffs showed up in their patients during therapy. The patients came for other reasons—depression or family conflict or insomnia or an inability to work as well as they had in the past—and, in the course of treatment, layoffs surfaced as a contributing factor.

I reported as much in *The Disposable American,* and after publication the evidence kept coming, not just at the psychoanalytic conference, but from individual psychiatrists. One who sought me out, Dr. Edward Hallowell, who practices in Sudbury, Massachusetts, described the damage as "a loss of confidence that you can deal with what life throws at you. The loss of confidence is self-fulfilling. You render yourself helpless."

"As a clinician," he went on, "I know the antidote to this sort of anxiety: never worry alone. The goal is to connect."

But how does one do this in a society that personalizes layoffs so persistently? In my presentations since publication, I have found myself increasingly embracing the hope that out of a desire to protect their own health, people will finally connect with one another to publicize successfully the fact that layoffs carry great risks. Only then might the dialogue move on to a second stage, one in which our political leaders and corporate managers, constrained by public pressure, find ways to minimize layoffs and the resulting damage to public health.

Dr. Theodore J. Jacobs, a prominent New York psychoanalyst who appears in *The Disposable American,* tried to jump-start this healthier dialogue. Dr. Jacobs introduced me at the American Psychoanalytic Association's conference. He had written a five-page introduction in which he tried to nudge his colleagues into issuing a formal warning that layoffs were harmful to mental health. "It is time," he said, referring to the organization's reluctance to speak out officially on any public issue, "to raise our voices and to actively oppose policies here and abroad that result in pain, suffering, mental anguish, and, indeed, frank mental illness in so many people in this country."

Putting a warning label on layoffs should be roughly similar to the process of putting a warning label on cigarettes. The damage to those laid off would be flagged, and a stigma would attach to the managers and executives who do the laying off. They would be under more public pressure than they are today to limit layoffs and to justify those that are carried out as necessary for corporate survival despite the damage to mental health. The warning label, one hopes, would encourage companies to find ways to cut labor costs short of engaging in layoffs, as they so often found ways in the years before we acquiesced.

These days, economists, corporate executives, management experts, and politicians insist that there are no alternatives: layoffs are inevitable—indeed, desirable—if America is to be successful in today's global market system. Robert M. Solow, a Nobel laureate in Economics, made this point in a letter to me after reading *The Disposable American*. "You sometimes give the impression that firms have alternatives," he wrote, referring to the United Airlines decision to close its maintenance center in Indianapolis and outsource heavy maintenance to contractors with much lower labor costs. "I am skeptical," Solow added, "that this was ever a situation that could have been handled better if only the social norms governing layoffs were different."

Fair point. I raised it with Ben Nunnally, the union leader at the United facility in Indianapolis, and he replied that all the costs of outsourcing had not been adequately considered. The quality of the work done by the contractors, for example, was not as good, Nunnally said, and that meant more repairs between flights once the planes were back in service. Then, too, the contractors took more days to perform the maintenance. The aircraft were out of service longer and United, as a result, needed more planes in its fleet to maintain flight schedules, or eliminate flights and give up passenger revenue. And, in fact, the airline in time quietly took some maintenance back in-house.

So who is right, Solow or Nunnally? That question cannot be answered without much more public accounting. The cost of closing the maintenance center and of outsourcing the work—all of the costs—were not publicly thrashed out, and they should have been. Only then can we know if the situation "could have been handled better," as Solow put it.

It is that thrashing out that is missing in America. When it does finally begin, the damage to mental health must be part of the cost calculation. Perhaps that damage, increasingly evident, might finally force us into a public weighing of all the layered costs of layoffs, which we now too passively accept. Just having this debate would be a balm for the damaged souls who engaged me after publication of this book, trying alone to break through the silence.

NOTES

Myths That Blind

ix *In exchange for:* The 30 million figure is derived from the worker-displacement
surveys conducted biennially by the Bureau of Labor Statistics since the
early 1980s, when the bureau first began them. They are the only government
count of laid-off workers. The twelve surveys conducted so far, covering the
years from 1981 through 2003, attempt to count the people who have been
laid off against their wishes with no expectation of recall in the three years
prior to each survey. Adding together totals from each survey after eliminating overlapping years produces an overall tally of 49 million full-time workers, but that does not allow for double counting, inaccurate recall among the
people surveyed, or the shortcomings of a survey that attempts to project
national totals from interviews with sixty thousand households. Nor does it
include hidden layoffs, particularly the multitude of early retirements and
untimely buyouts that masquerade as voluntary but are in fact forced departures. The 30 million is my estimate, arrived at in discussion with bureau
economists. The bureau declines to produce a total because of the unknown
margin of error. What the bureau does supply are the total layoffs for each
two-year period from 1981 through 2002 and a separate number for 2003.
The two-year totals range from a low of 3,045,000 laid-off workers in
1987–88 to a high of 6,096,000 in 2001–2. These are considered by the
bureau to be accurate counts of the number of displaced workers in each
two-year period. What the bureau cannot determine is how much duplication there is from one survey to the next.

xi *Without the easy:* In 2004, 21 percent of all consumer spending, not counting
petroleum and petroleum products, went for the purchase of imported goods
and services, double the percentage in 1980. The import-share numbers were
furnished by Mark M. Zandi, chief economist at Economy.com, based on
data from the National Income and Product Accounts, which are compiled
by the Commerce Department's Bureau of Economic Analysis.

CHAPTER ONE

The Stanley Works

4 *He was running:* Davis lectured in a special program at MIT's Sloan School of Management that had been funded by twelve corporations, which contributed $5 million apiece. Stanley was not one of them. The goal of the program was to improve the technical and management skills of young people already in manufacturing.

4 *Descriptions of labor:* Peter Cappelli, *The New Deal at Work* (Harvard Business School Press, 1999), pp. 49–50.

5 *And then, starting:* The phrase is borrowed from Bennett Harrison and Barry Bluestone, whose book *The Great U-Turn* (Basic Books, 1988) spotlighted the income inequality then developing, simultaneously with the onset of layoffs. Most economists either challenged their data or argued that the inequality was a temporary phenomenon that would soon correct itself. It did not; the inequality worsened and so did the layoffs that were a cause of it. By 2002, the average annual income of families in the top 20 percent of the income scale was 11.4 times the average for the bottom 20 percent, according to the Census Bureau. The ratio had barely changed from 1966, when the Census Bureau first started to keep this data, until 1978, when it was 7.61, and then the ratio moved steadily upward, except for the late 1990s, when it leveled off and even dropped a bit, only to resume climbing in 2001.

5 *By 2004, the bureau:* The bureau's biennial surveys are conducted in January or February of each even-numbered year. If an individual reports having been laid off more than once, only one layoff is counted. The bureau counts as "worker displacement" each occurrence in which those interviewed said they had permanently lost their jobs because a plant or a company closed or moved, there was insufficient work for them to do, or their position or shift had been abolished. Dismissal for cause is not included in the job-displacement count. See chapter 9 for a detailed discussion of the layoff rate, actual and hidden.

5 *Once-shoddy socket wrenches:* Interview with Donald Davis, October 10, 2002. Davis was not alone in failing to anticipate the Asian onslaught. Jack Welch, in his autobiography, *Jack: Straight from the Gut,* written with John A. Byrne (Warner Books, 2001), pp. 108–9, said that he found a similar complacency when he became chairman of General Electric in December 1981. "At that time, no one in or outside the company perceived a crisis," he wrote. While Davis tried to make Stanley's traditional businesses more competitive and profitable, Welch early on embraced the strategy that in time would become the standard for most of corporate America. What Welch could not fix, which was a lot, he closed or sold. At the same time, he either expanded existing divisions that could excel, or bought new businesses that would.

6 *Community groups, for example:* That was particularly true in the communities that depended for employment on the steel mills in the Youngstown,

Ohio, area. The closing of these mills in the late 1970s reintroduced the public to mass layoffs, a phenomenon that most Americans thought had become extinct after the Depression.

6   *The Roman Catholic Church:* November 11, 1984, and November 13, 1986.

6   *Government regulation had protected:* Statistical Abstract of the United States, 2003 (Hoovers, Inc.), p. 404, Employment by Industry, 1980.

6   *Organized labor:* According to the Bureau of Labor Statistics, work stoppages involving 1,000 workers or more fell from 187 in 1980 to 145 in 1981, to 69 in 1986, to 51 in 1989, and to 45 or fewer each year thereafter through 2004. During the 1970s, by comparison, the number of strikes involving at least 1,000 workers ranged from a low of 219 in 1978 to a high of 424 in 1974.

7   *And the argument:* Sanford M. Jacoby, *Modern Manors: Welfare Capitalism Since the New Deal* (Princeton University Press, 1997), p. 258.

7   *It is like acid rain:* Interview with Dr. Theodore Jacobs, March 13, 2004. Chapter 8 elaborates on the psychological and social damage from layoffs and cites the various sources on which this summary paragraph is based.

8   *Seniority rights continued:* In recent years, several studies have found that permanent layoffs have largely replaced the temporary furlough followed by recall. Henry Farber, a Princeton University economist, and Paul Osterman, an economist at MIT's Sloan School of Management, are the authors of two of these research papers, in 2001 and 1999, respectively.

10   *"I looked at":* Interview with Richard Ayers, December 12, 2002.

10   *But Stanley's directors:* This was Ayers's view. Telephone interviews, November 5, 7, 13, and December 16, 2002.

10   *So in 1997:* Trani's pay averaged $3.5 million a year in his final four years. At the end of 2002, he held options to purchase 3.6 million shares of Stanley stock. He owned outright 250,000 shares worth about $9 million at the end of 2002.

11   *And Trani, who had won:* Before joining Stanley, Trani was president and CEO of GE Medical Systems for ten years under Jack Welch, who praised him as an executive who excelled in the Welch approach. *Jack: Straight from the Gut,* p. 318.

11   *Over the next six years:* By comparison, Welch closed or sold 98 of the 228 factories that General Electric operated in the United States from 1980, the year before Welch took over as chairman and chief executive, until the late 1990s. Thomas F. O'Boyle, *At Any Cost: Jack Welch, General Electric and the Pursuit of Profit* (Alfred A. Knopf, 1998), p. 33.

13   *Ayers, like Trani:* The Richmond factory served a second purpose in Ayers's strategy. By shifting some production to the nonunion plant, he diluted the potential damage to production from a strike in New Britain.

14   *By the late nineties:* When retailers ran special Made in America promotions in the early 1990s, sales rose more than 25 percent, according to Robert Swift of the Crafted with Pride in the USA Council (*San Francisco Chronicle,* February 25, 1992). By the late 1990s, however, the Commerce Department no longer campaigned, as it had in the early 1990s, to increase the domestic

content of products sold in the United States. And companies like Wal-Mart, which claimed in the early 1990s to have repatriated more than 100,000 jobs as a result of its Buy America policy, by the late 1990s no longer concerned itself with the origin of its merchandise.

19 *Stanley's three-year contract:* Of the 442 workers still on the job in the spring of 2003, 160 worked at a Stanley factory in nearby Farmington where the company manufactured remotely controlled entrance doors and 282 worked at the tape measure plant in New Britain. Six hundred of the 800 blue-collar jobs that had been lost since Trani's arrival in 1997 were in the factory complex that made door hinges (400 people) and specialty hinges for oven doors (200). Trani had eliminated these 600 workers in a big layoff in 2001 as production shifted to China and the plants in New Britain were closed. The remaining 200 had been laid off a few at a time, mostly at the tape measure plant.

20 *In his announcement:* Dan Haar, *Hartford Courant,* January 4, 2004, page D1.

20 *He had nearly completed:* Trani said he would engage in the purchase of equity stakes in companies and then participate in the management of the companies until they were improved, as Trani had improved the Stanley Works. This active management would raise the value of the equity stake, or so Trani calculated. "I decided that if some operating expertise were put into this arena there would be much higher returns that could be elicited," he said.

21 *The just-completed fourth quarter:* All the direct quotes from Trani and the paraphrased comments attributed to him in the rest of this chapter come from my interview with him on January 16, 2004, in New Britain.

21 *Revenues and net income:* Net income increased to $34.7 million, or 42 cents a share, from $18.1 million, or 20 cents a share, in the fourth quarter a year earlier. Sales climbed to $727.7 million from $614.3 million. These were the first double-digit percentage increases for a single quarter in Trani's tenure, and the stock price, which was $27 a share when he came aboard in 1997, moved above $37 in January 2004. The stock had traded in the $40–$50 range in the Davis and Ayers eras, and Trani gave himself credit for finally making it move back up again. By the spring of 2004, Stanley stock traded on the New York Stock Exchange above $40 a share.

21 *He had left behind:* One of the executives was John D. Opie, interim chairman of Stanley's board of directors. Opie played a key role in choosing Trani's successor, John F. Lundgren, fifty-two, who took over at Stanley on March 1, 2004, and continued to implement Trani's strategy. Telephone interview with Gerald Gould, a Stanley spokesman, April 1, 2004.

22 *That meant three hundred:* In Indianapolis, the administration of Mayor Bart Peterson, concerned that Trani would move Best away from the city, laying off everyone, negotiated a tax abatement agreement with the Stanley Works. In exchange for a reduction in city tax payments for at least five years, Stanley would keep the Best operation in Indianapolis. If it moved out short of the agreed-upon years, the penalty would be payment of the forgiven taxes.

Interview, April 21, 2004, with Melina Kennedy, who, as Mayor Peterson's director of economic development, negotiated the agreement with the Stanley Works.

22 *Over the next seven months:* The acquisitions were Blick PLC, a British company that provides software for security functions; Frisco Bay Industries, Ltd., a Canadian company that designs, installs, and services integrated security systems; and Senior Technologies, a Nebraska company that sells and services personal security systems for assisted living residences. Interview with Gerald Gould, April 1, 2004, and Dow Jones/Associated Press, *Hartford Courant,* January 29, 2004.

CHAPTER TWO

The Rise of Steady Work

25 *The* Argus *itself:* On October 12, 1998, Gannett closed all eight dailies, replacing them with a single daily newspaper, the *Journal News,* that circulated throughout Westchester County.

26 *Since then, the economy:* From 1870 through 1973, the long-term annual growth rate for the American economy was 3.4 percent, adjusted for inflation. From 1973 to 1993, that slowed to 2.3 percent a year, and even the boom in the late 1990s failed to lift economic growth back to the historical norm. The average annual growth rate in the nineties was 3.11 percent, according to the Commerce Department's Bureau of Economic Analysis. The historical growth rates are from Jeffrey Madrick, *The End of Affluence* (Random House, 1995), pp. 4–6. Madrick, in turn, drew on long-term growth data from the economic historian Angus Maddison and, for more recent years, the published data of the Bureau of Economic Analysis.

26 *A company with one hundred workers:* The actual productivity growth rate, measuring the increase in output per hour worked, averaged 2.8 percent a year from 1948 through 1973, according to the Bureau of Labor Statistics. That slowed to an average of only 1.4 percent a year from 1974 through 1995. Rising productivity is a key source of prosperity. From 1948 through 1973, the revenue from the steady increases in output per hour worked was distributed to owners and workers through rising profits and regular wage increases, raising living standards.

26 *To raise output:* Peter F. Drucker, *The Practice of Management* (Harper & Row, 1954), p. 267. Italics in original.

26 *IBM had embraced:* Ibid., pp. 259–61.

27 *People lost their jobs:* Such reasoning dated from the early days of the Industrial Revolution, to the writings of Robert Thomas Malthus, David Ricardo, and John Stuart Mill. Through most of the nineteenth century, working-age men without jobs and unable to support themselves and their families were blamed for their indigence. In Britain, the Poor Law of 1834, authorizing a network of workhouses, was intended not to relieve poverty, but to force idle

adults to find work, or the state would find work for them as inmates of workhouses. Let the idle laborer understand, Parliament said, "that the parish is the hardest taskmaster and the worst paymaster he can find, and thus induce him to make his application to the parish his last and not his first resource."

27 *Faced with this evidence:* Sanford M. Jacoby, *Employing Bureaucracy: Managers, Unions, and the Transformation of Work in American Industry* (Columbia University Press, 1985), p. 105.

27 *He still considered full employment:* Marshall's disciple and successor as professor of political economy at Cambridge, Arthur Cecil Pigou, was similarly reluctant to recognize unemployment as a dynamic of capitalism beyond a worker's control. Theoretically, he argued, if a worker accepted lower wages, he would remain employed. His boss, responding to lower labor costs, would lower the prices of his merchandise or services. Demand would then rise and so would output and sales, to meet the demand. With sales rising, the downward pressure on wages would ease up. Full employment was simply a question of workers agreeing to lower the price of their labor sufficiently to make them affordable. Versions of this thinking still prevail among mainstream economists and in government and corporate policy. Wage givebacks and cuts in pension benefits and health insurance are examples of the pressure on labor to lower its price to a competitive level.

27 *"People moved around a lot":* Telephone interview with Sanford Jacoby, July 16, 2002.

27 *The economic historian:* Telephone interviews with Robert Margo at Vanderbilt University, September 17 and November 8, 2002. Also, Margo's "The Labor Force in the Nineteenth Century," which is chapter 5 in *The Cambridge Economic History of the United States,* volume 2, edited by Stanley I. Engerman and Robert E. Gallman (Cambridge University Press, 2000). Agriculture's share of the labor force fell to 26 percent in 1900 from 50 percent in 1870 (p. 213).

28 *Men who had once:* John A. Garraty, *Unemployment in History* (Harper Colophon Books, 1978), p. 108.

28 *And in the East:* Telephone interview, Sanford Jacoby, July 16, 2002.

28 *Their jobs were often:* Telephone interview, Peter Cappelli, October 31, 2002. Cappelli is a professor of management at the University of Pennsylvania's Wharton School.

28 *Membership in unions:* Union membership rose to about 16 percent of all workers outside agriculture in 1920 from about 5 percent in 1900. Cited in "Can Increased Organizing Reverse the Decline of Unions in the U.S.? Lesson from the Last Quarter Century," Henry S. Farber and Bruce Western, of Princeton University, a research paper, April 11, 2002.

28 *With steady work:* David Brody, *Workers in Industrial America: Essays on the Twentieth Century Struggle* (Oxford University Press, 1980), pp. 62–65.

28 *By the late 1880s:* Madrick, *End of Affluence,* pp. 38–63. No other nation, Madrick writes, had a large enough population to match the mass market

that came into existence in the United States. It "enabled American businessmen to take fullest advantage of the new mass-production technologies of the time, reducing costs to a fraction of what they once had been for a great variety of consumer and industrial goods" (p. 46).

29 *"A crucial skill":* Peter Cappelli, *The New Deal at Work* (Harvard Business School Press, 1999), p. 4.

29 *The railroads were the first:* Alfred D. Chandler Jr., *The Visible Hand: The Managerial Revolution in American Business* (Belknap Press of Harvard University Press, 1977).

29 *So did a dozen:* Kevin Phillips, *Wealth and Democracy* (Broadway Books, 2002), p. 305.

30 *Here in America:* Peter F. Drucker, "Drucker on Management: The Network Society," *Wall Street Journal,* March 29, 1995, p. A12, and Drucker, *Management Challenges for the 21st Century* (HarperBusiness, 1999), p. 157.

30 *The extension was partly:* Sanford Jacoby, "Melting into Air? Downsizing, Job Stability and the Future of Work," *Chicago-Kent Law Review* 76 (2000), pp. 1195–1234. Also Jacoby, *Modern Manors,* chapter 1.

30 *Personnel departments made:* Jacoby, *Modern Manors,* p. 18; Jacoby, *Employing Bureaucracy,* p. 137.

30 *The personnel departments gradually:* Jacoby, *Modern Manors,* chapter 1.

31 *"The objectives of this search":* Howell John Harris, *The Right to Manage: Industrial Relations Policies of American Business in the 1940s* (University of Wisconsin Press, 1982), p. 17.

31 *The new system:* Peter Cappelli describes the evolution in *The New Deal at Work,* chapter 2.

32 *By 1916:* Patrick W. Seburn, "Evolution of Employer-Provided Defined Benefit Pensions," *Monthly Labor Review,* December 1991, pp. 16–23.

31 *In 1921, the Metropolitan:* American Council of Life Insurance, 1987 Pension Facts.

32 *And they retained:* Seburn, "Evolution of Employer-Provided Defined Benefit Pensions," pp. 16–23.

32 *The new railroad pensions:* Steven A. Sass, *The Promise of Private Pensions* (Harvard University Press, 1997), p. 29.

32 *Procter & Gamble fielded:* Most of this account is based on a telephone interview on April 17, 2003, with Thomas Mess, a director of global business services for Procter & Gamble at the company's Cincinnati headquarters.

32 *Concerned that labor unrest:* The Haymarket Square violence in Chicago on May 4, 1886, was still very much in the public's mind. Anarchists had called for a demonstration in the square to agitate for an eight-hour working day, a major labor issue in the 1880s. Police attempted to disperse the demonstrators. A bomb exploded, and there was rioting. Seven policemen and four other persons died and a hundred people were injured.

33 *World War I solidified:* Welfare capitalism actually had a broader meaning. Job stability was a major element, but as Howell John Harris wrote in *The Right to Manage,* welfare capitalism rested on the premise that in a represen-

tative democracy with an egalitarian political creed, "owners' and managers' power and privilege had to rest on public support to be safe." Managers, therefore, had to win the consent of their workers by demonstrating their "social responsibility" in operating a company in the general interest. In *Risk and the Labor Market: Societal Past as Economic Prologue*, Sanford Jacoby wrote: "Welfare capitalism consisted of a simple precept: that the business corporation rather than government (as in Europe) or mutual organizations should be the primary source of security and stability in modern society."

33 *"Before the war":* Telephone interview with Alfred D. Chandler Jr., November 7, 2002.

34 *They recognized good behavior:* An observation of Sumner Slichter, an economist, in 1919, cited in Sanford Jacoby, *Employing Bureaucracy,* p. 155.

34 *By the 1920s:* Brody, *Workers in Industrial America,* pp. 53–57.

34 *It was the stripping away:* Michael J. Sandel, *Democracy's Discontent: America in Search of a Public Philosophy* (Harvard University Press, 1996), and telephone interview with Sandel, December 18, 2002.

35 *"People feel as if":* Richard Price is also the senior research scientist at the University of Michigan's Institute for Social Research and director of the institute's Michigan Prevention Research Center.

35 *Because workers had taken:* Jacoby, *Modern Manors,* p. 32. Jacoby cites Lizabeth Cohen, *Making a New Deal: Industrial Workers in Chicago, 1919–1939* (Cambridge University Press, 1990), chapter 4.

36 *By the start of the war:* Alan Brinkley, *The End of Reform* (Alfred A. Knopf, 1995), chapter 9. Also, Sanford Jacoby, *Employing Bureaucracy,* p. 241.

36 *Few did, and union membership:* Jacoby, *Modern Manors,* p. 35.

36 *Sometimes unions:* Ibid., p. 36.

37 *Fares, in fact, did fall:* See Air Transport Association, annual passenger yields, 1926–2002, at www.airlines.org/econ/d.aspx?nid=1035. Robert Kuttner makes this point in *Everything for Sale: The Virtues and Limits of Markets* (Alfred A. Knopf, 1996). So does James Crotty, an economist at the University of Massachusetts, Amherst, in *Challenge* magazine (November–December 2002), pp. 34–35.

37 *That happened without people:* Juliet Schor, *The Overworked American* (Basic Books, 1991), p. 167. The annual hours worked by each labor force participant averaged 1,968 in 1948 and 1,944 in 1969. The big decline in time spent at work came in the decades before World War II, and mostly as a result of legislation. The strong postwar gains in productivity were converted, in effect, into higher pay, not more leisure.

37 *By the early seventies:* Bureau of Labor Statistics pension data at www.bls.gov.

39 *Taft-Hartley amended or qualified:* Taft-Hartley, formally the Labor-Management Relations Act of 1947, authorized the federal government to intervene in a labor dispute if a looming strike was deemed likely to imperil national health or safety. The president could decree a sixty-day cooling-off period during which the Federal Mediation and Conciliation Service would step in to help settle the dispute. If the cooling-off period failed to produce

a settlement, the president could report to Congress with recommendations for appropriate action. This national emergency provision of Taft-Hartley, still very much in place, came into immediate use. It was invoked seventeen times between 1947 and 1959. Harold G. Vatter, *U.S. Economy in the 1950s* (University of Chicago Press, 1963), pp. 237–39.

39 *Gradually these local uprisings:* These rank-and-file revolts persisted until the early 1970s. "Almost without exception the revolts were conducted primarily to improve the conditions on the job" and not for increases in wages and benefits, Stanley Weir wrote in "USA—the Labor Revolt," published in the *International Socialist Journal.* From the mid-1950s to the mid-1960s, for example, various locals of the United Auto Workers struck to protest industry-wide agreements signed by the UAW that did not address speed-ups on assembly lines and other local grievances.

39 *Perhaps the most damaging:* While outlawing the closed shop, Taft-Hartley permitted the union shop, which meant that a newly hired worker had to join a union within a specified period of time. For a union shop to exist, a majority of the workers at a business site had to vote approval in secret ballot. A 1951 amendment allowed union shops without a membership vote. In response, about one-third of the states, particularly southern states, enacted right-to-work laws, permitted by Taft-Hartley, and these laws effectively made union shops illegal.

39 *Southern states in particular:* The specific provision in Taft-Hartley that allowed right-to-work laws was section 14(b), which said: "Nothing in this Act shall be construed as authorizing the execution or application of agreements requiring membership in a labor organization as a condition of employment in any State or Territory in which such execution or application is prohibited by State or Territorial Law."

39 *The organizing efforts failed:* Barry Bluestone and Bennett Harrison, *The Deindustrialization of America* (Basic Books, 1982), p. 136.

40 *"In a sense," wrote Thomas Geoghegan:* Thomas Geoghegan, *Which Side Are You On? Trying to Be for Labor When It's Flat on Its Back* (New Press, 2004), p. 53.

40 *"As EHFA grew more national":* Jordan A. Schwarz, *The New Dealers: Power Politics in the Age of Roosevelt* (Alfred A. Knopf, 1993), p. 240.

41 *"In the Depression," Margo says:* Telephone interview, November 8, 2002.

41 *So with government loosely supervising:* The National Industrial Recovery Act of 1933 authorized the creation of the NRA. In essence, the NRA would oversee a system of cooperation among business, labor, and government.

41 *The hope was that through a harmony:* Much of the material in this paragraph and the next is drawn from Alan Brinkley, *The End of Reform.*

42 *The business community:* Michael A. Bernstein, *The Great Depression: Delayed Recovery and Economic Change in America, 1929–1939* (Cambridge University Press, 1987).

42 *There would also be:* Brinkley, *End of Reform*, chapter 2, describes both the "popular and congressional opposition to the liberal vision of a strengthened state."

42 *The unions signed on:* The working-class agenda began to "resemble the lib-

eral agenda of what remained of the New Deal: a belief in the capacity of American abundance to smooth over questions of class and power by creating a nation of consumers." Brinkley, *End of Reform*, p. 226.

43 *The full employment, in turn:* The GI Bill of Rights—the Serviceman's Readjustment Act of 1944—grew out of this thinking. Congress in effect enacted full employment support for veterans. Brinkley, *End of Reform*, p. 259.

43 *In the 1944 presidential campaign:* Quoted in Michael J. Sandel, *Democracy's Discontent* (Harvard University Press, 1996), pp. 260–61.

43 *The new law gave:* The President's Council of Economic Advisers and the Joint Economic Committee in Congress were created to monitor growth and advise on steps to be taken to keep growth on track.

43 *But if that did not happen:* There was disagreement in those days over the definition of full employment. Should it mean employment for everyone seeking a job, or everyone able and willing to work? The former meant putting the unemployed to work; the latter covered the unemployed plus the millions more who wanted to work but were not actively seeking jobs. If the goal was to put the unemployed back to work, did that mean all the unemployed or should an unemployment rate of, say, 4 percent be considered full employment? John Maynard Keynes, the great British economist, favored the latter approach. He saw full employment as a reduction in unemployment to a "frictional" level, the friction coming from a relatively small number of people between jobs. That was the working definition of full employment in the drafting of the 1946 law. William H. Beveridge, a contemporary of Keynes's and a renowned British economist in his own right, disagreed. He defined full employment as "more vacant jobs than unemployed men, not slightly fewer jobs." See *Full Employment in a Free Society* (W. W. Norton & Company, 1945), p. 18. In Beveridge's view, the cost to a company of having unfilled vacancies was much less than the cost to a worker without a job and not enough openings to choose from. It was a point of view that failed to find backing among American economists.

44 *In their classic work:* Charles A. Myers and George P. Shultz, *The Dynamics of a Labor Market: A Study of the Impact of Employment Changes on Labor Mobility, Job Satisfaction, and Company and Union Policies* (Prentice-Hall, Inc., 1951). Shultz later served as secretary of the treasury, from 1972 to 1974, and secretary of state, from 1982 to 1989.

45 *A group of social scientists: Labor Mobility in Six Cities: A Report on the Survey of Patterns and Factors in Labor Mobility, 1940–1950,* prepared by Gladys L. Palmer for the Committee on Labor Market Research (New York Social Science Research Council, 1954), p. 131.

45 *"The kind of job shifts":* Ibid., p. 134.

45 *J. J. Servan-Schreiber, a French journalist:* The English translation was published by Atheneum in 1968.

45 *But even before that:* Bluestone and Harrison, *Deindustrialization of America,* pp. 112–14. Bretton Woods required the Europeans to keep the value of their

currencies almost on a par with the dollar. They did this by using their currencies to purchase excess dollars that the United States generated by running deficits in its international payments.

46 *Several things undid:* This paragraph and the next draw in particular on Robert Brenner, *The Boom and the Bubble* (Verso, 2002), and two books by Barry Bluestone and Bennett Harrison: *The Deindustrialization of America* (Basic Books, 1982) and *The Great U-Turn* (Basic Books, 1988). David Halberstam, *The Reckoning* (William Morrow and Company, 1986), also served as a source, as did *The End of Affluence* by Jeffrey Madrick.

CHAPTER THREE

Retraining the Mechanics—But for What?

49 *It brought fewer of its airliners:* Under FAA regulations, every five years an airliner must go through an overhaul in which it is dismantled down to the metal skin. Every part, every bit of wiring, every bolt, every cockpit device, every fastener and weld is inspected. Whatever is defective or worn is either repaired or replaced. The outer skin is also examined, inch by inch, and repaired where necessary. United operated three such maintenance centers in the 1990s.

50 *After all, no airline in the United States:* The maintenance center was mainly designed to overhaul narrow-bodied airliners, or airliners with only a center aisle in the passenger cabin. The A319 and A320, although larger than the 737, were narrow-bodied, single-aisle aircraft. In the late nineties one bay had been expanded and equipped to overhaul the 767, a wide-bodied, or two-aisle, plane that United, until then, had overhauled only at its maintenance centers in San Francisco and Oakland.

51 *The glimpse that she offered:* What she did not tell the mechanics, and told me only days later in a telephone interview, was that she herself had worked for Ameritech, the telephone company, for thirty-two uninterrupted years, unmarred by layoff. That second income, from the phone company, had gotten the family through her husband's layoffs. She had retired in 1999, at age fifty-six, her last post being office manager. Soon after, she took the job as a credit counselor, working part-time to supplement her phone company pension and her husband's shrinking wage.

51 *"Our name follows the part":* Interview with Craig Imperio, Indianapolis, January 18, 2003.

52 *They were unlikely to match:* Under the contract that United and the machinists' union signed in March 2002, the top was $35 an hour. Later that year, the machinists agreed to a pay reduction to help United, then in bankruptcy, weather its financial crisis. The $35 became $31 an hour. For eight years, until March 2002, the top scale had stayed at $26 an hour. In 1994, at the start of those eight years, an employee stock ownership plan, or ESOP, was created and United's employees got stock in the airline. The stock was payment, in

effect, for the wage concessions the employees had accepted. As the stock rose in value in the nineties, it gave the mechanics a nest egg that in some cases totaled several hundred thousand dollars. These savings disappeared when United went into bankruptcy in the aftermath of 9/11. In the case of the sixty mechanics at the Days Inn, almost none had enough seniority to earn more than $26 an hour.

53 *Outsourcing had won:* Only seven mechanics remained as dues-paying members, including Nunnally, and only one of those seven still worked as an aircraft mechanic, employed by US Airways at the Indianapolis airport. But Lodge 2294 also represented five hundred customer service personnel, reservation agents, and baggage handlers employed in Indiana by United, Northwest Airlines, and Southwest Airlines. In its heyday in the late 1990s, Lodge 2294 had three thousand members, most of them mechanics.

54 *When that failed:* The Indianapolis Airport Authority, an autonomous agency, formally owns the maintenance center, but the city and state also have an ownership interest. The mayor, in addition, had a political stake in getting the center up and running again, and for that reason played a big role in the hunt for a new tenant. He also appointed a majority of the Authority's board of directors.

55 *He thought then:* United's contract with the IAM had a no-layoff clause for any mechanic in the system hired before 1994. That included Nunnally. In the airline crisis after 9/11, however, United went into Chapter 11 bankruptcy, and the court allowed United to nullify the job guarantee clause.

55 *That had been:* This information came partly from Nunnally, but mainly in telephone interviews with Andrew P. Studdert, former chief operating officer at United, with responsibility for maintenance, and with Frederick L. Mohr, chief of maintenance at the Indianapolis maintenance center from 1997 to 2002. The Studdert interview was on February 13, 2003, and the Mohr interview on April 2, 2003. The eleven-day turnaround time was achieved in 1998 and 1999 for 737s that had been in service five years and were undergoing their first overhaul. For the second "heavy maintenance," when a 737 was ten years old, requiring more work, the best turnaround time was just under twenty days, still faster than anywhere else.

55 *"We had overhaul bays":* Telephone interview with Frederick Mohr, April 2, 2003.

56 *But Andrew P. Studdert:* The state's lawyers also brought pressure. They encouraged United to bring the Airbus maintenance to the Indianapolis facility as a means of meeting its commitment to employ five thousand mechanics. If United had not brought the Airbuses, the state might have taken legal action to force this to happen, according to Mark S. Moore, who was then the State of Indiana's director of public finance. Interview with Moore, August 16, 2005.

56 *"The mechanics loved":* Telephone interview with Andrew Studdert, February 13, 2003.

56 *The rapid turnaround time:* As Fred Mohr explained in a telephone interview (April 2, 2003), rapid turnaround time was one leg of the cost-saving.

Another leg was the indirect savings from quality work in heavy maintenance. The better the quality, the less likely it is that defects will appear in the weeks and months after heavy maintenance. These defects are costly if a plane must be taken out of passenger service for a day or two, or even a few hours, to be repaired.

56 *It was outsourcing: Indianapolis News,* June 6, 1998.

58 *What drove away America West:* Even without the labor trouble, the America West maintenance would have required months of adjustment. That airline's maintenance procedures were too different from United's for the mechanics to make the transition easily from one set of planes to another, according to Andrew Studdert in a telephone interview on May 5, 2003. But without the labor trouble, the two airlines could have standardized maintenance practices, doing so in the interest of cost savings and the efficiencies that would be gained from economies of scale and rapid turnaround time.

59 *The uproar over vacations:* The account that follows is based on interviews with Studdert, Mohr, Nunnally, Doucey, and several of the mechanics.

59 *They were partisans of:* That happened in July 2003, two months after the closing of the maintenance center in Indianapolis. In a representation election, AMFA ousted the IAM as the union representing United's remaining mechanics throughout the airline. In addition, AMFA, which was not affiliated with the AFL-CIO, was the union that represented mechanics at Northwest Airlines and several smaller carriers. A summary of AMFA's history, published on its Web site, declares that in thirty years of existence, it "has never accepted concessions, give-backs, two-tier pay scales, or 'B' rated mechanics."

59 *They should not be lumped:* Deborah Caulfield Rybak and Tony Kennedy, "Below the Radar," *Star-Tribune,* Minneapolis–St. Paul, Minnesota, March 11, 2001, p. 10.

60 *"In heavy maintenance":* Telephone interviews with Frederick Mohr, April 2 and May 21, 2003.

60 *Turnaround time inched up:* Telephone interviews with Andrew Studdert, February 13 and May 14, 2003.

60 *Then in July 2000:* The old, three-year agreement, which covered mechanics everywhere in the United system expired on July 12, 2000. The new one was not signed until March 2002. During the dragged-out contract negotiations, the slowdown in Indianapolis spread to United maintenance operations in other cities, so much so that in November 2000, United asked the United States District Court for the Northern District of Illinois for a restraining order. The airline's brief in support of its request cited Local Lodge 2294 in Indianapolis half a dozen times, including this citation: "The cycle times for both 'light' and 'heavy' checks at United's Indianapolis maintenance center have been steadily increasing since July 2000, and during September–November 2000 were more than double their historical average."

62 *When I pointed this out:* Telephone interview with Tori Bucko, February 6, 2003.

63 *But in the winter:* The aircraft mechanics at United Airlines were the biggest

single group. However, reservation clerks, baggage handlers, pilots, and others were also laid off, mostly at United, but also at other airlines with operations in Indianapolis.

64 *In the end, Goodwill:* The initial $3.1 million grant awarded by Congress as a direct result of 9/11 funded the AIR Project until the fall of 2003. After that, the state appropriated nearly $1.5 million from its pool of federal money earmarked for job retraining. That kept the AIR Project alive until the summer of 2005.

64 *Their failure to land:* The theory had an escape clause: if the necessary jobs fail to materialize in the short run, they will in the long run. "The long run" is never defined. It is sometimes thought of as the time needed for an economy to adjust to a new set of circumstances and to generate a new set of necessary, well-paid jobs. The adjustment process can continue beyond a worker's lifetime. But this caveat is rarely invoked to relieve a laid-off worker of blame for failing to move on to the next job.

65 *"When large numbers":* Beyond the airline industry, only 15,000 of the 53,000 unemployed men and women who sought help in Indianapolis from Goodwill Industries in 2001 managed to land employment that year at any wage, according to Goodwill. That was a better year for the local economy than 2002. Only 9,300 of the 55,000 people outside the airline industry who went through the Goodwill recycling centers in 2002 landed jobs.

65 *Most of the unfilled jobs:* See, for example, *Workforce Intermediaries for the Twenty-first Century,* a briefing book edited by Robert Giloth and consisting of twelve essays and studies prepared for a February 2003 conference sponsored by the American Assembly of Columbia University. Seventy percent of the jobs that result from these programs pay less than $11 an hour.

65 *The vehicle for doing this:* The Comprehensive Employment and Training Act (CETA) replaced the Manpower Development and Training Act (MDTA), enacted in 1962 during the Kennedy administration. MDTA, like CETA, provided both training and public service employment.

65 *But thanks to CETA:* In addition to CETA, there were also several small, publicly funded job-creation programs, usually serving local or regional populations. These included the Supported Work Program and the Youth Incentive Entitlement Pilot Projects, as well as the New Hope program in Milwaukee in the 1990s. These programs were mainly for women coming from welfare.

65 *Most of the jobs:* As originally enacted in 1973, anyone unemployed for seven days or more was eligible for a public service job funded through CETA. There were no income restrictions. In 1978, however, amid charges of cronyism, fraud, and the wasting of taxpayer money on middle-class beneficiaries, the CETA rules were amended by Congress to limit job slots to those with incomes below the poverty line. As a result, full-time adult jobs funded under CETA fell to 400,000 by the time Reagan took office in 1981, at a budgeted cost of $3.1 billion. In addition to the adult jobs, CETA funded a million summer jobs for teenagers. Gordon Lafer, *The Job Training Charade*

(Cornell University Press, 2002), p. 171. Lafer, a political scientist at the University of Oregon, furnished additional data from his research in a June 10, 2004, e-mail to me.

65 *CETA also paid:* At the height of the public service job creation, in 1978, the unemployment rate averaged 6.1 percent. It would have been roughly 7 percent without the CETA-funded jobs. Put another way, CETA jobs soaked up 43 percent of the unemployment over a 4 percent unemployment rate, which is considered full employment. CETA, in other words, got the nation nearly halfway to full employment. Sar Levitan, Frank Gallo, and Isaac Shapiro, *Working but Poor* (John Hopkins University Press, 1993), p. 95.

66 *Saying we should solve:* For an account of the swing from job creation under CETA to job training under JTPA, and the politics involved, see Lafer, *The Job Training Charade,* chapter 5, particularly pp. 168–84.

66 *They often find:* See Louis Uchitelle, "College Still Counts, Though Not As Much," *New York Times,* October 2, 2005, section 10, p. 1.

66 *The number of jobs:* The percentage of college graduates twenty-five and over who were employed fell below 76 percent in 2003 and 2004, the lowest level since 1979, according to a calculation by the Economic Policy Institute based on Bureau of Labor Statistics data. The bureau itself, in a 1992 study, found that 19 to 20 percent of all college graduates in the labor force in the 1980s were either "educationally underutilized or underemployed." That was up from 11 percent in 1970, nearly 17 percent in 1975, and nearly 18 percent in 1979. Daniel E. Hecker, "Reconciling Conflicting Data on Jobs for College Graduates," *Monthly Labor Review,* July 1992, p. 3. The Hecker study updated an analysis that had been done periodically since the 1960s by the bureau's Office of Occupational Statistics and Employment Projections. The updating ceased after Hecker's 1992 work.

66 *"The average college graduate":* Katz, who served as the Labor Department's chief economist during the first two years of the Clinton presidency, put the matter this way during an interview on March 10, 2004: "As the nation becomes more education-intensive, college-educated workers don't work in a small group of elite jobs anymore. They work in things like production, software programming, basic communications, middle management, retail store buyer. Those are core jobs not much different than core blue-collar jobs of the past, in the sense that they are subject to the vagaries of the economy and firms are going to find ways to reduce cost on them, whether it is through new technologies or lower-cost locations."

66 *On average, there were:* The Job Openings and Labor Turnover monthly survey, also known as JOLTS, is available on the Bureau of Labor Statistics Web site (www.bls.gov).

66 *So the demand for jobs:* Using Labor Department data, Bartik calculated how many additional full-time jobs would be needed to give each household, particularly households below the poverty line, enough hours in 1998 to equal one full-time job. "Poverty, Jobs and Subsidized Employment," *Challenge,* May–June 2002, p. 100.

66 *From the spring of 2003:* Calculation by the Economic Policy Institute, analyzing data from the Bureau of Labor Statistics.

67 *Seven of the ten occupations:* The report is available from the Labor Department. It is also cited in Steven Greenhouse, "Retraining for What? If You're a Waiter, the Future Is Rosy," *New York Times,* March 7, 2004, section 4, p. 5.

67 *More than 45 percent:* The Economic Policy Institute provided this wage tabulation using data from the Bureau of Labor Statistics.

67 *That is roughly the income:* The National Academy of Science and the Census Bureau have developed an experimental "basic-needs" budget as a potential substitute for the current official poverty measure. The basic-needs budget declared that a family of four was impoverished in 2003 if its income fell below $25,000, or nearly $6,200 above the official poverty threshold of $18,810 for the same family. In Indiana, the Economic Development Council produced a similar "basic-needs" budget for a family of four in that state. The council calculated the budget as a guideline for the use of public subsidies. There was no point, the study in effect argued, in spending taxpayer money on subsidies as an incentive to get companies to locate in Indiana, or expand in the state, if the jobs involved in the location or expansion paid less than $13 to $14 an hour. For a discussion of this issue, see Louis Uchitelle, "How to Define Poverty? Let Us Count the Ways," *New York Times,* May 26, 2001, p. B7.

67 *By the spring of 2004:* The data in this paragraph and the next two are from a performance analysis, furnished by the AIR Project, for the 369 former airline employees, half of them mechanics, who had obtained work as of March 31, 2004, after having gone through Bucko's recycling program. Over the next fifteen months, seventy-six more former airline employees, both mechanics and nonmechanics, who went through the AIR Project program had landed in jobs, Goodwill Industries reported, without providing a breakdown of the jobs taken, or the pay of each. The average wage for the seventy-six was $15.36 an hour, according to the Goodwill summary, furnished by Cindy L. Graham, Goodwill's vice president for marketing for central Indiana. E-mail, April 18, 2005.

67 *Of the 185 mechanics:* Because of its central location, Indianapolis is the home city of many trucking companies. In Bucko's experience, the demand for cross-country drivers is second only to the demand for restaurant and hotel workers and hospital housekeepers. Those are low-wage jobs, while the laid-off who take the two-week course to get a commercial truck driver's license can in most cases quickly land driving jobs that start at $35,000 to $40,000 a year. The trade-off is days and even weeks on the road away from home, disrupting family life.

68 *The wage loss:* See the worker-displacement surveys issued biennially by the Bureau of Labor Statistics.

69 *Mark Crouch, a professor:* Telephone interview, February 6, 2003.

70 *The mechanics would also be required:* The AIR Project administered the Myers-Briggs test, whose questions are designed to bring out personality types.

71 *"I've worked with":* Interview with Tori Bucko, April 21, 2004.

71 *Her story, leaving out the pain:* Based on a telephone interview with Tori Bucko, February 6, 2003, and an interview in person on April 7, 2003.

74 *But he agreed:* The funding for the Labor Institute for Training in Indiana came from federal and state grants. The Labor Institute and similiar organizations elsewhere in the country operate as not-for-profit corporations whose activities are coordinated by the AFL-CIO's Working for America Institute. Funding, however, does not come from the AFL-CIO.

75 *And the meeting:* Barnes left LIFT in July 2005 after state and federal funding was cut back.

75 *By 2004, municipal and state:* Estimate furnished by Alan Peters, a professor of urban planning at the University of Iowa, and cited in Louis Uchitelle, "States Pay for Jobs but It Doesn't Always Pay Off," *New York Times,* November 10, 2003, p. 1. There is no official calculation of the total subsidies paid. Peters and others base their estimates on their own surveys of state and municipal budget data. Until the 1970s, the federal government funded most job-creation subsidies. The emphasis then was on regional development, the goal being to subsidize job creation in regions with high unemployment.

76 *If the center had gone:* See also Louis Uchitelle, "Shifting Workplace—A Special Report: Renewed Corporate Wanderlust Puts a Quiet Brake on Salaries," *New York Times,* July 24, 2000, p. 1. There is no government tally of the number of times companies move operations from one city to another within the United States or place a new facility in a city where the company has not operated before, responding in part to publicly subsidized bidding wars. The most authoritative private tally comes from *Site Selection* magazine, which estimates that the total rose gradually in the 1980s to nearly 5,700 in 1989, then dropped during the 1990–91 recession, rose gradually again until 1994, and then accelerated as the economy boomed, reaching 12,700 in 1999. Starting in 2000, the total fell as the economy weakened.

76 *To land this plum:* The city and state were stuck with annual debt payments totaling $34 million a year until 2019 to service the $320 million in bonds that had been floated to build the maintenance center, only now the jobs no longer existed to justify this outlay in tax revenue. In addition, the Indianapolis Airport Authority, a municipal corporation, took over more than $3.5 million of the $14 to $16 million a year in maintenance costs that United had paid, laying out the money to keep the now-empty center on "warm idle," its complex systems free of deterioration.

76 *"If it had paid":* Interview with Arthur Rolnick, October 29, 2003.

76 *"I think the way":* Interview with Peter McDonald, June 23, 2004. By then, United did no heavy maintenance in-house. In addition to Indianapolis, the Oakland maintenance center was also closed, leaving only the one in San Francisco, which focused on overhauling jet engines and avionics gear. "We're very capable at that," McDonald said. "But we have outsourced our heavy maintenance. We don't see that growing. That's done." The number of aircraft mechanics employed by United fell to 5,300 in 2004 from 12,000 in 1998, according to Rich Nelson, a United spokesman.

77 *"I would say to the airlines"*: Interviews with Mark Moore, April 21, May 27, and July 14, 2004. Alan Degner, then commissioner of Indiana's Department of Workforce Development, made the same general point in a telephone interview, October 28, 2003. "To me it would make a lot of sense," Degner said, "for the airlines to come together as a consortium and use it as a facility for any carrier's planes to be serviced. To do it solely with one company becomes more challenging."

77 *Mayor Bart Peterson finally:* The AAR Corporation, a public company whose stock is traded on the New York Stock Exchange, provides various services for commercial airlines and for government and military aircraft. These include the sale or lease of used aircraft and jet engines, the sale of parts, and aircraft maintenance. AAR operates at fourteen centers, including the one in Indianapolis. The company's revenues were $652 million in 2004. It employs 2,300 people and is headquartered in Wood Dale, Illinois, near Chicago.

78 *"The last guy":* Telephone interview with Ben Nunnally, July 13, 2004.

79 *Now to have AAR:* Mary Beth Schneider, "Dems See Hope in New Facility," *Indianapolis Star*, June 18, 2004.

CHAPTER FOUR

The Shock, Part 1

80 *What is striking:* The stories in this chapter are based on numerous interviews, in person and by telephone. I spoke or met with Craig Imperio eleven times between January 18, 2003, and July 11, 2005. His wife, Sarah, participated in some of the conversations. There were eight interviews with Tim Dewey from April 8, 2003, to August 2, 2005, and eleven with or about Erin Brown from April 9, 2003, to October 25, 2005. Erin's wife, Stacy, was present for some of these conversations and they include two in which I spoke only with Stacy. There were also e-mail exchanges with people in this chapter.

82 *He was only twenty-nine:* In the AIR Project program, the maximum education/retraining grant for any individual was $6,500.

83 *The second semester:* The $180 monthly premium covered the parents. The children qualified for publicly subsidized health insurance.

84 *They also used unlicensed:* To be a licensed mechanic, the candidate had to successfully complete two years of college-level schooling, or its equivalent, and pass qualifying examinations specified by the Federal Aviation Administration. United employed only licensed mechanics. But the FAA allowed the contractors to use unlicensed mechanics, as long as they were supervised by a licensed mechanic who signed off on their work.

84 *As for job security:* Telephone interview with Craig Imperio, April 14, 2004.

CHAPTER FIVE

The Shock, Part 2

98 *She was in her early forties:* The stories in this chapter, like those in chapter 4, are based on numerous interviews, in person and by telephone. There were eight conversations with Virginia Gibbs between November 23, 2002, and late August 2005, including a group session at Right Management in New York. The eleven conversations with Kenneth Halajian extended from November 23, 2002, through August 1, 2005. Two of those contacts were at group sessions at Right Management. The ten conversations with Stephen Holthausen or his daughter, Gretchen, took place between January 8, 2003, and August 5, 2005. These were in addition to my interviews with Holthausen in earlier years, particularly in 1995 and 1996, when I was doing the reporting for Louis Uchitelle and N. R. Kleinfield, "On the Battlefields of Business, Millions of Casualties," *New York Times*, March 2, 1996, section 1, p. 1. The fifteen conversations with Elizabeth Nash took place from April 4, 2003, to September 15, 2005. There were in addition e-mail exchanges with most of the people in this chapter.

100 *Sanford I. Weill, the new chairman:* For a while, Weill shared the chairmanship with John Reed, the chairman and chief executive of Citicorp at the time of the merger. Reed was chairman when Gibbs joined Citibank, and while layoffs certainly accelerated under him, she considered Reed more committed to his employees than Weill.

101 *Along the way, Lipp:* Carol J. Loomis, "Citigroup: Scenes from a Merger," *Fortune*, January 11, 1999.

105 *The family lived:* The Halajians sold the house in the spring of 2005 and moved to a three-bedroom town house in nearby Ossining.

108 *The $15 million in loans:* Holthausen said that in 1989 and 1990 his clients defaulted on a total of $150,000 in loans, or 1 percent of all his outstanding loans.

109 *They had made too many:* The New England Savings Bank also failed, in 1993, because of bad real estate loans.

110 *Feeling panicky, Diane:* Stephen Holthausen told this story in our interviews and also in a pretrial memorandum filed on May 29, 1992, in state superior court as part of the divorce proceedings.

115 *"We built up tons":* Interview with Richard Pease, April 25, 2003.

117 *Her pension savings:* See chapter 2 for a description of Procter's unusual pension plan.

118 *There was even alimony:* In the fall of 2003, Verizon and FedEx created incentive packages to leave that included full pensions years ahead of schedule, company-paid health insurance, and severance equal to a year or more of pay. At FedEx, 3,600 workers took the offer and left; at Verizon, 21,600. Ezra D. Singer, then Verizon's executive vice president for human resources, said: "The incremental cost of these packages is not significantly greater

than the cost of a layoff." Louis Uchitelle, "Incentives Lure Many to Quit, Even with a Lean Job Market," *New York Times*, January 11, 2004, section 1, p. 1.

118 *If transfer to another department:* The rationale for outsourcing IT to Hewlett-Packard, the company that eventually got the contract, was that HP, handling information technology for many companies, could take advantage of economies of scale to keep the cost below what each individual corporate client could achieve on its own.

120 *It is most common:* See, for example, the work of Jacob S. Hacker, a political scientist at Yale University, including these articles: "False Positive," The New Republic Online, August 6, 2004, and "Call It the Family Risk Factory," *New York Times*, January 11, 2004, op-ed page.

120 *"The downwardly mobile":* Katherine S. Newman, *Falling from Grace: Downward Mobility in the Age of Affluence* (Vintage Books, 1989), pp. 9–10.

CHAPTER SIX

Dismantling Job Security, 1977 to 1997

124 *The original bill:* Helen Ginsburg, *Full Employment and Public Policy: The United States and Sweden* (Lexington Books, 1983), chapter 3. Most of the material in this account of the Humphrey-Hawkins Act is taken from Ginsburg's book, from *The Annals of the American Academy of Political and Social Science*, volume 418, March 1975, and from conversations with Stanley Moses, professor emeritus in the Department of Urban Affairs, Hunter College of the City University of New York. Moses played a role in the drafting of full-employment provisions in early versions of the legislation.

124 *It was "stripped of its orginal":* 1978 *Congressional Quarterly Almanac,* p. 272.

125 *It will "increase the nation's":* Article by Hawkins in *The Annals of the American Academy of Political and Social Science*, volume 418, March 1975, pp. 13–16. Okun's law is a reference to the late Arthur M. Okun, a professor of economics at Yale in the 1950s and a chairman of the President's Council of Economic Advisers in the Lyndon Johnson administration.

125 *But it did not:* The unemployment rate in 1983, as measured by the Bureau of Labor Statistics in its monthly employment reports, averaged 9.6 percent, even higher than it had been in 1978. Not until 2000 did unemployment finally average only 4 percent and then only because a bubble economy generated an unusual demand for workers. By 2001, with the bubble gone, unemployment was rising again, reaching 5.8 percent by December of that year.

125 *The act also spoke:* The Federal Reserve defined zero inflation as an inflation rate of 2 percent or less as measured by the Consumer Price Index. That would not happen until 2001, and then it was the result of an excess supply of goods, services, and workers, a strong dollar that held down import prices, and recession. All of this held down prices despite very low interest rates.

125 *This the Fed under:* President Carter named Volcker as chairman of the Federal Reserve in 1979. Greenspan succeeded Volcker in 1987.

125 *So each time:* By raising interest rates to discourage spending on credit, the Fed reduced inflation. But higher interest rates slowed the economy and unemployment rose. The trade-off found its way into mainstream economic theory, helping to justify unemployment as an antiinflation tool, and by extension the layoffs that helped to raise the unemployment rate. Many economists declared that the "natural rate" of unemployment, the rate that would keep inflation roughly in check, was 5 or 6 percent, substantially above the Humphrey-Hawkins definition of full employment. In the 1950s and 1960s, the unemployment rate was often 2 percentage points lower, without pushing up inflation. Similarly, in the late 1990s, when unemployment fell into the 4 percent range, inflation was mild. In the view of Robert Eisner, a Northwestern University economist, the natural rate of unemployment thesis, known as NAIRU, justified a modern-day version of Karl Marx's reserve army of the unemployed, the goal being to dampen wage pressures. What Volcker and Greenspan and the advocates of NAIRU ignored, Eisner argued, was that employers often respond to tight labor markets not by raising prices but by getting more output from their workers, either without paying them more or in exchange for higher wages. See Robert Eisner, "Viewpoint: Who's Afraid of Jobs and Growth," *New York Times*, March 31, 1996, section 3, p. 14.

125 *Not surprisingly:* From 1975 through 1996, the average annual unemployment rate, as measured by the Bureau of Labor Statistics, fell below 6 percent in only six years and below 5.5 percent in only two, 1989 and 1996. The late 1990s produced a booming economy, a stock market bubble, and the dot-com frenzy, a period of unusually strong demand for labor. The average annual unemployment rate, as a result, dropped below 5 percent from 1997 through 2001. Rather than cut this off, Greenspan, changing tactics, held down interest rates, arguing that improvments in productivity were sufficient for employers to cover the cost of higher wages without having to raise prices. Inflation did not rise. By 2002, however, unemployment was back above 5.5 percent, and it stayed in that range until 2005. In the 1950s and 1960s, by comparison, an average annual unemployment rate above 5.5 percent was the exception, occurring only five times in twenty years.

125 *They could ignore:* Richard Layard, *Happiness: Lessons from a New Science* (Penguin, 2005), p. 26.

126 *It should do so: The Annals of the American Academy of Political and Social Science*, volume 418, March 1975, pp. 13–16.

126 *That meant community job creation:* This was already happening on a very small scale as a result of the Comprehensive Employment and Training Act, or CETA, passed by Congress and signed by President Richard Nixon in 1973. See chapter 3.

127 *Government would "respond directly": The Annals of the American Academy of Political and Social Science*, volume 418, March 1975, p. 14.

127   *Partly in response:* The act set the unemployment goal at 4 percent for the entire labor force, ages sixteen to sixty-five, and 3 percent for adults twenty-one and over.

127   *The unemployment rate:* The unemployment rate in 1976 averaged 7.7 percent.

127   *Humphrey did not run:* Humphrey died in January 1978.

127   *"You needed much higher":* Telephone interview with Stanley Moses, June 20, 2004.

128   *The oil price shocks:* Until 1973, steady increases in productivity meant rising sales revenue per worker. Split between owners and workers, the increases were enough to sustain healthy profits and also healthy raises, which unions demanded and companies paid. By producing more in a given period of time, workers in effect paid for their own raises. After 1973, however, the productivity growth rate fell back, but not the pressure from unions for healthy raises, which increasingly shrank profits. That made labor cost-cutting through layoffs increasingly attractive, and acceptable.

128   *Neoclassical economics came back:* New classical, or neoclassical, economics denied that a shortfall in demand for goods, services, or workers could exist in a properly functioning market system, a shortfall that government would have to offset through public investment and other stimulative spending. Markets balance on their own at robust levels, the neoclassicists insisted. By their very nature, demand equals supply. Supply even generates demand. People who produce goods and services earn wages and profits that they use to buy all the output of goods and services, carrying out these transactions either directly from wages or through the investment of saved earnings. What gets made is sold and everyone who wants to work, or makes an effort to qualify for a job, ends up employed—except perhaps during recessions and crashes. If there is no full employment, then it must be because government is distorting the market's healthy mechanisms, by insisting, for example, on wage levels that are above what the market will pay for the particular skills and services of a worker, or groups of workers. Full employment in this view means the wage level that employers are willing to pay to hire the last available workers. In practice that could be close to zero.

129   *Taxes and regulations:* One of the influential leaders of neoclassical economics was Martin Feldstein, a Harvard professor who was president of the National Bureau of Economic Research for many years and, from 1982 to 1984, chairman of President Reagan's Council of Economic Advisers. In a 1993 memoir, *American Economic Policy in the 1980s: A Personal View,* he wrote: "While there is certainly never unanimity among economists, by the late 1970s the combination of Keynesian macroeconomics and interventionist microeconomics that had been widely accepted in the postwar decades was clearly in retreat. In its place, the traditional market-oriented ideas that had previously characterized economics since the time of Adam Smith were having a greater influence on both research and policy conclusions."

129   *"To live for the moment":* Christopher Lasch, *The Culture of Narcissim: American Life in an Age of Diminishing Expectations* (W. W. Norton & Co., 1979), p. 5.

129 *Once the bill:* Thomas Petzinger Jr., *Hard Landing* (Crown, 1995), p. 105.

129 *In the unregulated, freewheeling:* Formed in 1981, People Express disappeared in 1986, absorbed into Continental Airlines.

130 *Regulation had created:* Domestic fares came down to an average of $4.16 to fly one passenger mile in 2004 from $8.49 in 1978, adjusted for inflation, or 51 percent, according to the Air Transport Association, an airline industry group (www.airlines.org/econ/d.aspx?nid=1035). But fares also fell steadily in the twenty-six years prior to airline deregulation—to $8.49 in 1978 from $13.70 in 1952, a decline of 38 percent. The percentage was less but the lower fares under deregulation often came with restrictions: advance purchase, penalty payments for switching flights, Saturday night stay-overs.

130 *Deregulation in airlines:* Statistical Abstract of the United States, 2003, p. 404, Employment by Industry, 1980.

130 *While discount fares:* Despite this advantage, by the late nineties, some of the regional, low-cost airlines, like Southwest, had grown large enough and sufficiently innovative to force major airlines to match their discount fares. In response, the majors cut costs through layoffs, wage concessions, and various other changes, the goal being to offer similar low-cost service on competing routes. Roles thus were reversed. With the discount airlines accounting for 25 percent of all passenger traffic in the United States by 2004, the major airlines found themselves forced by the newcomers—those that survived and prospered—into the same layoffs and hardship they had forced on newcomers in the earlier years.

131 *"I was never able to follow up":* The section above on airline deregulation and Alfred Kahn is drawn from my reporting for Louis Uchitelle, "Off Course," *New York Times Magazine,* September 1, 1991. The Kahn quote in this paragraph is from the 1991 interview and was not previously published.

132 *Eight days after the shutdown:* Staughton Lynd, *The Fight Against Shutdowns: Youngstown's Steel Mill Closings* (Singlejack Books, 1983), p. 27.

132 *Few such community coalitions:* What lives on are employee stock ownership plans, or ESOPs. In most of these plans, employees purchase stock and thus provide financing. That works more or less effectively at companies with fewer than one thousand workers, and most of the eleven thousand ESOPs today are in such companies. But at big corporations, ESOPs give employees only limited representation on boards of directors, often because the employees purchase their ownership stock on credit and, until the loans are paid off, the creditors represent the employee-shareholders on the boards. In this situation, management operates in traditional ways, frequently cutting costs to increase profitability, although that results in laying off the shareholder-owners. United Airlines is a famous example of this dynamic.

132 *Oxygen technology, in contrast:* Coming out of World War II, the steel industry had not anticipated failure and collapse. It had intended to gradually scale back the excessive wartime production capacity and modernize, shifting to new, more efficient technologies that foreign competitors had already

embraced. But the Korean War and the weapons buildup in the early sixties helped to sustain demand, and the aging facilities were still in place in the seventies when the foreign competitors invaded the American market. The steel companies, in response, shrank the business, the closing of the Campbell Works being a first step in this process. Michael A. Bernstein, *The Great Depression* (Cambridge University Press, 1987), pp. 220–21.

132 *Youngstown Sheet & Tube:* Lynd, *The Fight Against Shutdowns,* p. 16.

133 *Instead of using:* Ibid., pp. 24–25.

133 *Two years later:* Welch, *Jack: Straight from the Gut,* pp. 148–50.

134 *There simply wasn't:* In a special issue on June 30, 1980, entitled "The Reindustrialization of America," *Business Week* noted that Japan and West Germany were overtaking the United States in steel, autos, machine tools, consumer electronics, and other basic industries. There was stiff criticism of American management for its shortsighted focus on immediate earnings and its failure to invest sufficiently in modernization, although it had seen the competition coming. The nation's executives were lambasted for their tunnel vision, their nonentrepreneurial behavior, their emphasis on marketing and finance rather than production and quality. But in the end, they were let off the hook. The real villain, *Business Week* declared, was government intervention, dating back to the New Deal.

134 *By the 1980s:* Federal Reserve, Flow of Funds Accounts, January 15, 2004, www.federalreserve.gov

135 *"There had always been":* Interview with Peter Cappelli, January 3, 2004.

135 *That included steel imports:* See Judith Stein, *Running Steel, Running America* (University of North Carolina Press, 1998), pp. 229–50. Carter was reluctant to grant trade relief to the domestic steel industry, although he recognized that the Europeans, for example, did not reduce steelmaking capacity, in contrast to the American industry, which did, doing so through plant shutdowns and layoffs. The Europeans, Stein wrote, "shut down older, inefficient facilities and expanded the new ones built on the coast. The EC subsidized closures, extended loans for new plants, financed research and worker retraining, set minimum prices and negotiated import quotas with nearly every steel exporter in the developed and developing world." Japan took a similar approach. Meanwhile their excess production was exported to the United States, sometimes at prices lower than those charged in Japan and Western Europe.

135 *Basing his decision:* The $525 million would fund the installation of electric furnaces. To put that huge sum in context, Judith Stein notes in *Running Steel, Running America* that the capital expenditure for the entire steel industry in 1978 was $2.5 billion (p. 245).

136 *Contributions would also have to come:* This account draws in part on Judith Stein's *Running Steel, Running America,* chapter 9, and in part on Staughton Lynd's *The Fight Against Shutdowns.*

136 *Pressure also came:* Complicating matters, the LTV Corporation, whose holdings included another big steelmaker, acquired Lykes, a goal being to

become globally competitive by consolidating and modernizing the steel operations. LTV filed for bankruptcy protection in 1986. Later LTV's steel assets were purchased by the International Steel Group.

136 *And, surprisingly:* Telephone interview, December 15, 2003, with Gar Alperovitz, a professor of political economy at the University of Maryland, who participated in the endeavor to reopen the Campbell Works. Also, an interview with Lynn Williams, retired United Steelworkers president, on January 5, 2004.

136 *The reason he offered:* Lynn Williams interview, January 5, 2004.

136 *"Lloyd was much more":* Another explanation of McBride's refusal to endorse community ownership also surfaced in the fall of 1977. Earlier in the year, the United Steelworkers membership had elected McBride president, rejecting Ed Sadlowski, an insurgent candidate who had gotten support from members of the local at the Campbell Works, particularly a group that pushed community ownership of the mill. Then, too, the United Steelworkers leadership might have seen in community ownership a challenge to its own dominant role. Nevertheless, the steelworkers' union eventually supported a scaled-down version of community-worker ownership at Campbell. Instead of the all-at-once $525-million investment, the rolling mill portion of the plant would be upgraded and reopened. It would finish steel that had been made elsewhere, and later there would be installation of an electric furnace and caster to resume the manufacture of raw steel. That less expensive proposal did not fly with the Carter administration.

137 *It encouraged the formation:* Lynn Williams interview, January 5, 2004.

137 *The latter disappeared:* Mini-mills, recycling scrap steel, can produce a ton of steel with approximately 70 percent of the labor required in traditional integrated mills. The mini-mill workers were nonunion, making them easier to lay off than the unionized employees in the integrated plants. Robert Carbaugh and John Olienyk, "U.S. Steelmakers in Continuing Crisis," *Challenge,* January–February 2004.

137 *"We obviously would not":* Lynd, *The Fight Against Shutdowns,* p. 159.

138 *"Everyone is against a shutdown":* Telephone interview, November 14, 2002.

138 *Although he disagreed:* Before Congress acted, several state legislatures enacted laws requiring advance notification of plant closings. Maine, Massachusetts, South Carolina, and Wisconsin were among the states that acted ahead of Congress and President Reagan. Senator Dan Quayle, the Indiana Republican who would soon become Bush's vice presidential running mate, was quoted in the April 15, 1985, edition of *U.S. News & World Report* as saying that layoffs without advance notice were "irresponsible and callous."

138 *"In most cases, companies":* "Job Security v. Labor Market Flexibility: Is There a Tradeoff?" research paper, spring 1994. For a description of WARN's provisions and a study of their impact on workers and companies, see "Advance Notice Provisions in Plant Closing Legislation," by Ronald G. Ehrenberg and George H. Jakubson of Cornell University, 1988. The study was published by the W. E. Upjohn Institute for Employment Research.

139 *As if insufficient demand:* The exchange-rate agreement that was reached came to be known as the Plaza accord, named for the Plaza Hotel in New York, where central bankers and finance ministers from the big industrial nations met in September 1985 to work out a new set of exchange rates.

139 *Starting in 1979:* Economic Report of the President for 2004, Table B-46, p. 338.

139 *Corporate raiders were:* Julie Creswell and Mark Borden, "Raiders Reborn," *Fortune,* July 10, 2000, p. 36. Quoted in Alex Berenson, "Buccaneer, or the Shareholder's Best Friend?" *New York Times,* September 24, 2000, section 3, p. 1.

140 *Pickens agreed in December 1984:* Eric N. Berg, "Pact Ends Mesa's Bid for Phillips," *New York Times,* December 24, 1984, section 1, p. 33.

140 *Steinberg got $325 millon:* Thomas C. Hayes, "Steinberg Sells Stake to Disney," *New York Times,* June 12, 1984, section 4, p. 1.

140 *"What companies gradually discovered":* Interview with Thomas Kochan, January 4, 2004.

141 *In the most talked about deal:* Bryan Burrough and John Helyar, *Barbarians at the Gate* (HarperCollins, 1990), p. 507. Most of the RJR Nabisco account in this chapter is drawn from the book. See also Betsy Morris, "RJR Nabisco Takeover: Defeated RJR Chief Johnson Won't Be Short of Consolation," *Wall Street Journal,* December 2, 1988. Among other items in Johnson's departure package, his most recent annual salary—$1,736,700, including bonuses—was paid to him through 1991, and the final buyout brought him upward of $25 million for the more than 235,000 shares he had accumulated in RJR Nabisco.

141 *They raised most:* By the middle of 1988, corporate debt in the United States totaled $1.78 trillion, up from less than $1 trillion in 1982, according to the Federal Reserve. Leveraged takeovers alone accounted for $300 billion of this total, including $150 billion in bank loans and a similar amount raised through high-risk junk bonds. See Louis Uchitelle, "Pushing the Stakes to New Heights," *New York Times,* October 30, 1988, section 1, p. 1.

141 *At the time, that was:* In June 1989, for example, just four months after Kravis's firm, Kohlberg, Kravis, Roberts & Company, took control of RJR Nabisco, five of its European food businesses were sold to BSN, a big French food company, for $2.5 billion. Steven Greenhouse, "5 RJR Units Sold for $2.5 Billion," *New York Times,* June 7, 1989, section 4, p. 1. See also the 10-K filing by RJR Nabisco on December 31, 1988, and a similar filing from RJR Nabisco Holdings on December 31, 1993.

141 *Faced with such:* The pastoral letters were published on November 11, 1984, and November 13, 1986.

142 *In effect he was:* Years later, many of the fired air traffic controllers still maintained an informal network and a sense of loyalty and camaraderie born of having sacrificed their jobs for what they considered a higher cause. See Newman, *Falling from Grace,* pp. 144–73.

142   *Hiring permanent replacement:* According to Robert B. Reich, the secretary of labor during President Clinton's first term, from the late 1930s until 1981 there were only five cases on record of companies permanently replacing striking workers. By comparison, almost a dozen companies did so over the next decade or so, including Eastern Airlines and Greyhound, and many more threatened to do so. Robert B. Reich, *Locked in the Cabinet* (Alfred A. Knopf, 1997), pp. 93–94.

142   *What reaction there was:* "Harris Poll Finds Most Oppose the Air Strike," United Press International as published in the *New York Times,* August 21, 1981, p. A18.

143   *"Ranking and spanking":* The Economist, March 31, 2001, p. 57.

143   *The upper 20 percent:* Sanford Jacoby, "Melting into Air: Downsizing, Job Stability and the Future of Work," *Chicago-Kent Law Review* 76 (2000), p. 1203.

143   *Their departures, even after:* Temporary workers leave jobs at the end of assignments and go back to the agencies that sent them out, Manpower, for example, or Labor Ready. The agencies are the employers and as long as they can send people on to new assignments, the temps are not counted in government data as laid off. That happens only when Manpower does not come up with a next assignment and the temp's relationship with Manpower ends.

144   *Almost no one:* Fast-food restaurants employ about 3.5 million people, the biggest group of low-wage workers, and the turnover rate is 300 to 400 percent a year, according to Eric Schlosser in *Fast Food Nation* (HarperCollins, 2002), pp. 72–73.

144   *The innovative attempt:* Saul A. Rubinstein and Thomas A. Kochan, *Learning from Saturn* (Cornell University Press, 2001), is a concise account of the Saturn endeavor.

145   *"We are in a position":* Bush Bernard, "Saturn Workers Cast Lot with Rest of GM," *The Tennessean,* December 15, 2003, p. 1E. The agreement ended Saturn's separate status and folded the production of these cars into the rest of the GM operation. After a transition period, the once-separate labor agreement melded into the UAW's master agreement with GM.

145   *Or as Richard Freeman:* Interview, September 28, 2002.

145   *One-fifth soon came:* See Peter Cappelli, *The New Deal at Work* (Harvard Business School Press, 1999), p. 74, and Louis Uchitelle, "More Downsized Workers Are Returning as Rentals," *New York Times,* December 8, 1996, section 1, p. 1.

145   *Fear of layoff:* Interview with Paul Osterman, November 14, 2002.

146   *"It was not merely":* Telephone interview, March 1, 1994. See Louis Uchitelle, "The Humbling of the Harvard Man," *New York Times,* March 6, 1994, section 3, p. 1.

149   *"conservative populism":* Bill Clinton, *My Life* (Alfred A. Knopf, 2004), pp. 144–45.

149   *"What the sixties did":* Interview with Richard Licht, June 5, 2003.

149   *"Americans," Lasch wrote:* Lasch, *The Culture of Narcissism,* p. 5.

CHAPTER SEVEN

A Green Light from Clinton

152 *Patrick Buchanan's early success:* About one-third of Buchanan's support came from white males without college educations, exit polls showed. Michael Moore, in his book *Downsize This!* (Crown, 1996), p. 18, wrote that Buchanan had transformed himself into the great white worker's hope.

152 *"Chainsaw" Al Dunlap:* As chief executive of Scott Paper starting in 1994, Albert J. Dunlap laid off tens of thousands of workers, doing so with considerable fanfare and harshness. Media accounts referred to him as Chainsaw Al and he embraced the sobriquet. Dunlap insisted that the layoffs were necessary to cut costs, and Scott's stock price rose, making Dunlap a star on Wall Street. His memoir, *Mean Business* (Crown, 1996), was a best-seller. He left Scott Paper in 1996 and became chief executive of the Sunbeam Corporation, where he once again engaged in flamboyant layoffs and the stock price rose for a while. But Sunbeam collapsed into bankruptcy. The Securities and Exchange Commission investigated and Dunlap was accused of having engineered a large accounting fraud that artificially inflated Sunbeam's profits. In September 2002, Dunlap agreed to pay a $500,000 fine and to be banned from ever again serving as an officer or director of a public company.

152 *For illustration, there were:* The headshots of four of the ten chief executives pilloried in Sloan's article appeared on the cover, illustrating the headline, "Corporate Killers." Besides Dunlap, they were Robert B. Palmer of Digital Equipment Corporation, Robert E. Allen of AT&T, and Louis V. Gerstner Jr. of IBM. Their photos reappeared inside the magazine, as illustration for the article itself, this time with the police-style captions. The six other chiefs whose photos appeared were Walter Shipley, head of the newly merged Chemical and Chase banks; Charles Lee, GTE Corporation; Ronald Allen, Delta Airlines; John McDonnell, chairman and former CEO of McDonnell Douglas; John Stempel, former CEO of General Motors; and Edward Brenner, former CEO of Sears, Roebuck & Company. The layoffs attributed to them had been announced over a nearly six-year period, starting in July 1990. By 1996, McDonnell, Stempel, and Brenner were no longer CEOs.

153 *"He said these amazing":* Robert Allen's quote is as Sloan remembered it during our interview. The Allen quote printed in the February 26, 1996, issue of *Newsweek* said: "I wouldn't see any value of going on TV and crying" (p. 46).

153 *But rather than boast:* For a broader account of the shift taking place, see Louis Uchitelle, "The New Buzz: Growth Is Good—Latest Strategy for Business Is a Positive Spin on Layoffs," *New York Times,* June 18, 1996, section 4, p. 1. By the summer of 1996, the economic boom of the late nineties was just getting started, and while that did not stop layoffs, which were by then an ingrained practice, it did often generate hiring in one section of a

company even as existing employees were laid off in another. That was one aspect of the new spin on layoffs. I wrote: "The shift reflects a new mantra, still being developed by management consultants, for how to justify corporate reorganizations that still cost jobs. 'The consulting industry is pushing growth much more than in the past,' said William Matassoni, a partner at McKinsey & Company, Inc., the management consulting firm. 'There was too much emphasis on let's cut back, let's get rid of people, and not enough on how to grow once companies become leaner and more efficient.' The new rhetoric features such jargon as 'growing the revenue line,' which means increasing sales so that jobs can be added as business expands. 'Execute growth-capturing actions' appeared on many of the slides that Braxton Associates, a consulting arm of Deloitte & Touche, showed at a 'growth conference' in Chicago in late April. And there is 'corporate anorexia,' increasingly used to mean too few employees left after layoffs to make growth possible."

154 *Or, as Sloan put it:* Sloan cited to me Bernard Ebbers, chief executive of WorldCom, as a vivid example of just how thoroughly the ethos moved on. Ebbers sank WorldCom into bankruptcy in July 2003. He was pilloried for doing so and for deceiving shareholders, employees, and the public. But "no one has been after Bernie Ebbers for layoffs," Sloan noted, although Ebbers laid off thirteen thousand workers, or 15 percent of the employees, in the two years prior to the bankruptcy filing, and there were layoffs before that. See the *Wall Street Journal,* June 6, 2002. In addition, see the *Dallas Morning News* and the *Washington Post,* April 4, 2002, and the *New York Times,* June 29, 2002. When World.com announced in December 1998 that two thousand workers would be laid off, the *Times* carried the announcement as a one-paragraph Company News brief (December 12, 1998, section 3, p. 3). Similarly, the *Times* used a one-paragraph Company News brief on June 6, 2002 (section 3, p. 4), to report a WorldCom announcement of job cuts that some analysts said might total sixteen thousand. WorldCom had employed more than eighty thousand people in the early months of 2001.

154 *In doing so:* See Alison Mitchell, "Clinton Prods Chief Executives to 'Do the Right Thing,' " *New York Times,* May 17, 1996, section 4, p. 1.

155 *When the* New York Times *found:* The *Times* series ran from March 3 through 9, 1996, and was entitled "The Downsizing of America." The reporters involved in the project, including myself, mixed an analysis of "worker displacement" data collected by the Bureau of Labor Statistics with extensive interviewing and found a startling familiarity with layoffs across the population. A *Times*-sponsored poll of 1,500 people, designed to represent a cross section of the adult population, added to the evidence. Twenty percent of those polled said that they had been laid off in the past fifteen years, 14 percent said that they lived in a household where someone had been laid off, and 38 percent said that someone they knew well had been laid off.

155   *the White House responded:* "Job Creation and Employment Opportunities:
The United States Labor Market, 1993–1996, a Report by the Council of
Economic Advisers with the U.S. Department of Labor, Office of the Chief
Economist, April 23, 1996."

155   *It was a bogus claim:* The Bureau of Labor Statistics, the Labor Department's
data-gathering subsidiary, counts layoffs every two years going back to 1981.
See the biennial worker-displacement surveys at www.bls.gov./schedule/
archives/all_nr.htm. The data for 1994 and 1995, collected in a survey conducted in January 1996, would not be published until August. Lacking the
official count for those two years, the *New York Times* constructed an estimate for use in its series of articles on layoffs published in early March. The
estimate was based on a statistical projection that the bureau reviewed. The
Times's estimate turned out to be very close to the actual layoff numbers.
Despite steady economic growth, the layoff rate in 1994 and 1995 was almost
as high as it was during the 1990–91 recession, the worker-displacement survey showed, once it was released in August. In addition, the mid-nineties
layoff rate was higher than it had been during most of the eighties recovery
years.

155   *That number showed a decline:* The white paper did acknowledge that "the
official data on [job] displacement after 1993 are not yet available." But it
said that "an alternative job loss measure has fallen since then." What had
fallen, according to this alternative measure, was the number of people collecting unemployment insurance for five weeks or less after having lost a job.
That narrow subset of all job losers, cited in the white paper as evidence of a
declining layoff rate, fluctuates with the business cycle, rising in recessions
and falling in recoveries as the unemployed get back into a growing workforce. And the workforce was indeed growing in the spring of 1996, strongly
enough to get the recently unemployed back into jobs more quickly than
usual.

155   *"We did not want":* Interview with Michael Ash, October 3, 2002.

156   *The wages for the specific new jobs:* Sales supervisors, electricians, and electronics engineers, for example, were three of the occupation categories that experienced large employment gains, and they were cited in the white paper. For
each of these occupational "cells," the median wage was above the national
median. Ergo, the new jobs paid well. But the particular people hired in 1994
and 1995 as sales supervisors, electricians, and electronics engineers, or a portion of them, may have been hired at the low end of each cell's range of
wages, earning in some cases less than $480 a week.

156   *Some were lower:* See Jared Bernstein, "Anxiety over Wages Still Justified,"
Issue Brief no. 113, Economic Policy Institute, April 30, 1996.

156   *"We in the Labor Department":* Interview with Lisa Lynch, January 4, 2003.
Lynch, a professor of economics at Tufts University, served as chief economist in the Labor Department from October 1995 to February 1997.

156   *"You guys were really":* Interview with Martin Baily, November 11, 2004. Baily
was CEA chairman from August 1999 to January 2001. After the Clinton

administration, Baily joined the Institute for International Economics, a think tank in Washington. His expertise is in productivity and international economics.

156 *At the insistence of Lynch:* The percentage of laid-off workers who earned less in their next jobs has risen steadily over the years, the Bureau of Labor Statistics reports. The bureau measures "median weekly earnings of long-tenured [employment that lasted at least three years] displaced full-time wage and salary workers—on their lost jobs and on jobs held at the time of the survey." The first survey, conducted in January 1984 and covering the 1981–83 period, found that 50.9 percent of the full-time workers laid off in the previous three years and reemployed in full-time work at the time of the survey earned less than in the lost jobs. By the 1994 survey, the portion earning less had risen to 52 percent, and in the January 2004 survey it reached 56.9 percent. In each of the ten biennial surveys, less than 55 percent were reemployed in full-time jobs at the time of the surveys. Of those reemployed, a quarter or more were earning 20 percent less than in their lost jobs.

157 *But subsequent research showed:* Erik Olin Wright and Rachel Dwyer, "The American Jobs Machine," September 2000, unpublished final draft. Wright and Dwyer are sociologists at the University of Wisconsin, Madison, and Ohio State University, respectively. Using the white paper's cell methodology, Wright and Dwyer examined job creation over the eight Clinton years and found that new jobs were bunched at the high and low ends of the wage spectrum.

157 *"We negotiated as hard":* Interview with Robert Reich, February 26, 2003. After leaving the Clinton administration, Reich became a professor of social and economic policy at Brandeis University's Heller School. In December 2005, he switched to the University of California, Berkeley, as a professor at the Graduate School of Public Policy.

157 *"Everyone—the audience, the administration":* Richard W. Stevenson, "Bobbing and Weaving on Issues of Layoffs," *New York Times,* May 18, 1996, section 1, p. 31.

157 *"We must start":* Ibid.

158 *And Clinton did:* Congress in August 1996 made health insurance more "portable" by passing a law, coauthored by Senators Nancy Landon Kassebaum, Republican of Kansas, and Edward M. Kennedy, Democrat of Massachusetts, that said in effect that the next employer of a laid-off worker could not exclude the new hire from health insurance on the ground of a preexisting medical condition; that is, one that existed before the new hire was laid off from his last job or during a period of unemployment between jobs. The same rule applied if the laid-off worker purchased a private individual insurance policy. The bill passed with strong support from both parties and the president signed it on August 21, 1996. The administration also backed legislation and took steps through the Treasury Department to allow workers to transfer savings in 401(k) accounts and other defined contribution pension plans from one employer to the next. Among other problems,

some employers had barred these transfers out of concern that the plan at the old employer failed to meet federal requirements and accepting money from such a plan would automatically disqualify their plans from favorable tax treatment. The administration's measures were intended to protect employers from inadvertent disqualification. See, for example, Robert D. Hershey Jr., "Clinton Announces Steps for More Portable Pensions," *New York Times*, September 18, 1996, section 4, p. 2.

158 *The twelve-page white paper:* A second white paper, very similar to the first in its findings and conclusions, came out in December 1999, on the eve of the president's last year in office. This second white paper, "20 Million Jobs: January 1993–November 1999," was issued by the Council of Economic Advisers and the Office of the Chief Economist at the Labor Department. The head of the CEA then was Martin N. Baily, the economist who, as a member of the CEA in 1996, had helped to draft the first white paper. The Labor Department's chief economist in 1999 was Edward Montgomery, a University of Maryland labor economist who succeeded Lisa Lynch in the job and worked with Labor Secretary Alexis Herman through the rest of the second term, as chief economist at first and later as deputy labor secretary.

158 *Alan Greenspan, the Fed's chairman:* Testimony before the Committee on the Budget, House of Representatives, October 8, 1997. The text of Greenspan's statement at the hearing is available at www.federalreserve.gov.

159 *As Gene Sperling:* Interview with Gene Sperling, September 17, 2003.

159 *The same is true:* Bill Clinton, *My Life,* and Robert E. Rubin and Jacob Weisberg, *In an Uncertain World* (Random House, 2003).

159 *Clinton's memoir refers:* Clinton, *My Life,* pp. 364–65.

159 *There are numerous abstract:* Rubin and Weisberg, *In an Uncertain World,* p. 125.

159 *Reich, who was leery:* Ibid., pp. 152–53.

159 *He had joined Citigroup:* Ibid., p. 304. "What I was really trying to create for myself was some type of consigliere position, or to become a minister without portfolio who lends a hand in many areas."

159 *His name was not yet:* Kerry's platform also included various tax incentives intended to discourage outsourcing and layoffs. His foray into anti-layoff rhetoric came in his references during the 2004 primary campaign to "Benedict Arnold" CEOs who sent jobs overseas. As soon as Kerry secured the Democratic nomination, he dropped the epithet and sought support from corporate executives. See Jacob M. Schlesinger and John Harwood, "Kerry Pitches Pro-Business Side of His Platform—Senator Woos Buffett, Cites Rubin and Offers Proposals to Quell Corporate Skeptics," *Wall Street Journal,* May 3, 2004, p. A1.

161 *For Rubin, however:* For a different view, see Alan S. Blinder and Janet Yellen, *The Fabulous Decade: Macroeconomic Lessons from the 1990s* (Russell Sage Foundation and Century Foundation, 2001), chapter 3.

161 *He shared a Nobel Prize:* George A. Akerlof, at the University of California at Berkeley, and Stiglitz, then at Columbia University, shared the Nobel Prize

in 2001 with a third recipient, A. Michael Spence, of Stanford University, who did similar work in asymmetric or imperfect information. Asymmetric information means that the parties in a transaction are not equally informed, as mainstream economic theory assumes.

161   *"I could always find":* Louis Uchitelle, "The Economics of Intervention: A Prominent but Impolitic Theorist Questions the Worship of Free Markets," *New York Times,* May 31, 1998, section 3, p. 1. Used cars illustrate the point. A used car salesman knows more about the shortcomings of the cars he is selling than his customers do. The marketplace, as a result, will cheat the less informed unless government intervenes, which it does in the case of used car sales through the application of lemon laws that require used car dealers to issue warranties for the cars they sell. Without those warranties, the car buyers stand a good chance of being victimized, and in the long run, the car dealers suffer too. Distrustful customers, once or twice burned, go elsewhere and the car dealers are forced out of business.

161   *Take the auto industry:* Interview with Joseph Stiglitz, February 14, 2003. Stiglitz joined the Clinton administration in 1993, at the age of fifty, coming to Washington from Stanford University. He served as a member of the Council of Economic Advisers until 1995 and then as its chairman, until he left the administration in 1997. After serving as chief economist at the World Bank, he joined Columbia University's faculty.

162   *By the end:* Louis Uchitelle, "College Degree Still Pays, but It's Leveling Off," *New York Times,* January 13, 2005, section 3, p. 1.

163   *Reich laid out:* Robert B. Reich, *The Work of Nations: Preparing Ourselves for 21st Century Capitalism* (Alfred A. Knopf, 1991).

163   *Clinton even carried a copy:* Bob Woodward, *The Agenda* (Simon & Schuster, 1994), p. 20.

163   *"Consider, for example":* Reich, *Work of Nations,* pp. 248–49.

164   *This was the thesis:* During Clinton's eight years as president, Congress authorized and the president signed one increase in the minimum wage. It rose in two steps to $5.15 an hour in 1997 from $4.25 in 1991, when George H. W. Bush was president. (Bush had increased the minimum, in two steps, from $3.35 in 1989.) Clinton also increased the Earned Income Tax Credit (EITC), which gives a cash tax credit to individuals and couples whose taxable earnings, as stated on their annual returns, range between $11,490 and $35,458, the latter for a married couple filing jointly and with two or more children.

164   *"Comfortably integrating":* Reich, *Work of Nations,* p. 248.

164   *That was still Reich's:* Interview with Robert Reich, February 26, 2003. Some of the Reich quotes in this section come from a follow-up interview on December 17, 2004, in which he clarified points he had made during the first interview and elaborated on them.

165   *These ideas were incorporated:* Bill Clinton and Al Gore, *Putting People First: How We Can All Change America* (Times Books, 1992).

165   *There is evidence:* Perhaps the best example of publicly funded training tai-

lored to employer needs took place in San Antonio, Texas, in the 1990s. A coalition of community organizations put together by the Industrial Areas Foundation got companies in the city to agree to give specified "living wage" jobs to residents who demonstrated the necessary skills. "Community organizations and area technical colleges then [worked] together to identify candidates for the reserved positions, [trained] them to the required competencies, and [supported] them during the training period with integrated income and other supports." *Rekindling the Movement: Labor's Quest for Relevance in the 21st Century,* edited by Lowell Turner, Harry C. Katz, and Richard W. Hurd (Cornell University Press, 2001), pp. 269–70. See also Paul Osterman, *Gathering Power: The Future of Progressive Politics in America* (Beacon Press, 2002), chapter 2 and pp. 161–65. City and state government money, some of it economic development funds channeled into human development, funded the project, which was known as Quest and has been replicated in some other cities. Foundation grants also played a role.

166 *As Gene Sperling put it:* Interview with Gene Sperling, October 13, 2003.

166 *"If job applicants did not meet":* Interview with Anthony Carnevale, April 1, 2003. Carnevale also served in the 1990s as chief of research at the Educational Testing Service in Princeton, New Jersey, the organization that produces the Scholastic Aptitude Test, and then went to the National Center on Education and the Economy in Washington.

166 *The standards board:* See "Putting Students and Workers First? Education and Labor Policy in the 1990s," by Alan B. Krueger and Cecilia E. Rouse, Princeton University labor economists, and the comments on that paper from Lawrence Mishel, Roger B. Porter, and Robert B. Reich. The paper and comments appear as chapter 10 in *American Economic Policy in the 1990s,* edited by Jeffrey A. Frankel and Peter R. Orszag (MIT Press, 2002). As Mishel points out in his comment, the 1.5 percent payroll training tax and the school-to-work program were among the proposals put forth in "America's Choice," the 1990 report of a blue ribbon commission—The Commission on the Skills of the American Workforce—chaired by two former labor secretaries, F. Ray Marshall, a Democrat, and William E. Brock, a Republican, and by Ira Magaziner, a consultant.

167 *Come January, Lloyd Bentsen:* Steven Greenhouse, "Better Times May Lead Clinton to Focus on Deficit," *New York Times,* December 7, 1992, section 1, p. 1.

167 *The House passed:* Catherine S. Manegold, "For 2nd Time, Senators Block Bill to Bar Replacement of Strikers," *New York Times,* July 14, 1994, section 4, p. 23. The bill in question was the Workplace Fairness Act.

168 *"Further litigation":* Steven Greenhouse, "Clinton Won't Appeal Court Rebuff on Workers," *New York Times,* September 12, 1996, section 1, p. 15.

169 *"For President Clinton":* Interview with Gene Sperling, September 17, 2003.

170 *Reich took the proposal:* Interview with Alan Krueger, December 10, 2004. Krueger is a labor economist at Princeton University who served as chief economist in the Labor Department in 1994 and 1995.

171 *"The opportunity to have":* Louis Uchitelle, "U.S. Seeks to Ease Friction in Companies," *New York Times,* July 27, 1993 section 4, p. 1.

171 *"The most interesting thing":* From 1994 through 1997, US West employment fell from 55,246 employees to 51,110, and then in 1998, an exceptionally profitable year, employment rebounded to 54,483, according to the company's published financial statements. US West was one of the former Baby Bell operating units. It provided local phone service in fourteen western states. In the summer of 2000, Qwest Communications International acquired US West. The $36 billion acquisition combined Qwest's high-speed communications network with US West's local service as well as its wireless and data-services operations. After the acquisition, Qwest's employment fell from 61,306 in 2001 to 46,876 in 2003.

172 *"The thought was":* Interviews with Ronald Blackwell, February 2 and 4, 2005.

173 *They should be allowed:* The commission's report called for "prompt elections after the NLRB [National Labor Relations Board] determines that sufficient employees have expressed a desire to be represented by a union. Such elections should generally be held within two weeks. To accomplish this objective we propose that challenges to bargaining units and other legal disputes be resolved after the elections are held."

173 *Such dismissals:* The commission would require "by statute that the NLRB obtain prompt injunctions to remedy discriminatory actions against employees that occur during an organizing campaign or negotiations for a first contract." See executive summary, final report, the Dunlop Commission on the Future of Worker-Management Relations.

173 *"I don't think the administration":* Interviews with Richard Freeman, January 4, 2003, and January 7, 2005.

173 *"I don't think Clinton":* Interview with David Bonior, January 8, 2005. Bonior left Congress in 2001 to run for governor of Michigan. He was unsuccessful. He later became chairman of American Rights at Work, an organization that pushes for a stronger union movement.

174 *Freeman even conveyed:* Interviews with Richard Freeman, January 4, 2003, and January 7, 2005.

174 *"It was the last gasp":* Interview with Lawrence Mishel, November 21, 2004.

174 *Clinton, a committed free-trader:* Trade liberalization under Clinton included, in addition to NAFTA, the Uruguay Round of the General Agreement on Tariffs and Trade, which lowered trade barriers for many countries; a decision to emphasize trade with China over human rights in that country; the Asia-Pacific Economic Agreement, which liberalized trade in that region; and the opening rounds of an effort to negotiate a free-trade agreement for the Americas. No president since Harry S. Truman implemented a broader free-trade policy, wrote Robert Z. Lawrence, an international economist at Harvard's Kennedy School of Government, in "International Trade Policy in the 1990s," which was published as chapter 5 of *American Economic Policy in the 1990s,* edited by Jeffrey Frankel and Peter Orszag.

175 *A decade later:* The estimates were based on the United States' trade balance with Mexico. A growing trade surplus, in America's favor, would mean that America was exporting more to Mexico than it was importing from that

country, including the imports from American operations in Mexico. Economists at the Institute for International Economics argued that the existing $9 billion trade deficit with Mexico would turn into a surplus that would grow to between $7 billion and $9 billion a year as American producers sent more and more goods and services south. Producing all the exports would generate the 200,000 jobs. Instead of a trade surplus, however, the deficit grew to $113.3 billion in 2004, and on the basis of that deficit, the Economic Policy Institute estimated a net loss of one million jobs as a result of NAFTA. See EPI issue brief, July 20, 2005. The one million figure may be overstated. Low-cost consumer products imported from Mexico, for example, presumably brought down retail prices. These lower prices hopefully stimulated sales, and retailers added workers to handle the additional activity, thus reducing the net job loss. In a study published in 2005, the Institute for International Economics, which had favored NAFTA, put the net job loss at about 425,000 through 2002, covering trade with Canada as well as Mexico. See Gary C. Hufbauer and Jeffrey J. Schott, *NAFTA Revisited: Achievements and Challenges* (Institute for International Economics), p. 41.

175 *Most of them disappeared:* Some of the jobs disappeared as manufacturing companies shifted assembly operations to Mexico and then shifted production of components as well, instead of shipping them from the United States. Ford Motor Company, for example, made gasoline motors at a factory in Chihuahua, shipping engine blocks from the United States for use in the motors, which were then exported to the United States. After a while, Ford began purchasing the blocks from a supplier in Mexico rather than one in the United States and jobs in this country were lost. Other jobs disappeared as a result of union organizing efforts, which employers countered by shutting plants in the United States and moving the work to Mexico. See "Final Report: The Effects of Plant Closing or Threat of Plant Closing on the Right of Workers to Organize" by Kate Bronfenbrenner, director of labor education research, New York State School of Industrial and Labor Relations, Cornell University. Report submitted to the Labor Secretariat of the North American Commission for Labor Cooperation on September 30, 1996.

175 *There was even a line:* The concept was incorporated into a bill that Clinton signed into law on November 29, 1993. The new law extended unemployment benefits, one rationale being that the extended benefits would be cost-neutral. The savings would be achieved by profiling men and women coming through state unemployment offices who were applying for benefits. Those who seemed likely to benefit from training would be shunted into a two-week course that included résumé writing and job interviewing. A handful of studies showed that this type of assistance got the unemployed back to work faster, thus saving money on unemployment benefits. The extended unemployment benefits would thus pay for themselves. Lawrence Katz, a Harvard professor who was the Labor Department's chief economist in 1993 and 1994, brought these studies to Reich's attention.

176   *"The only time":* Interview with Lawrence Katz, March 7, 2003.

176   *The outlays then fell back:* Measured another way, the funding fell to 7 percent of the gross domestic product in 2000 from 10 percent during Clinton's first term. There were additional outlays of $10 billion for college tuition, in the form of tax credits and scholarships. But they were mostly to help young people defray the cost of schooling. Only a portion of the money—$3 billion or less—went to the education of dislocated workers. The estimated cost of tuition tax credits and subsidized scholarships is from Ray Uhalde, co-director of the Center for Workforce Development in Washington and a former deputy assistant secretary of labor for employment and training in the Clinton and George W. Bush administrations. He retired in the summer of 2002.

176   *This shifted much more:* By 2003, there were more than 1,300 of these "one-stop" centers around the country, most of them housed in the same building as the state unemployment office, so that in one stop a dislocated worker received unemployment benefits and help in landing a new job. State governments often added money of their own to supplement the federal funding.

176   *"We accepted the fact":* Interview with Harry Holzer, December 13, 2002.

CHAPTER EIGHT

The Consequences—Undoing Sanity

178   *The layoff had destroyed:* Interview with Stacy Brown, December 27, 2004.

179   *There is much discussion:* Concerning children, some studies show that children in two-parent families react differently to a father's job loss than to a mother's. In a study of 4,500 school-age children, for example, Ariel Kalil and Kathleen M. Ziol-Guest of the University of Chicago found that "mothers' employment is never significantly associated with children's academic progress. In contrast, we found significant adverse associations between fathers' job losses [and] children's probability of grade repetition and school suspension/expulsion."

180   *One study, for example:* M. Merva and R. Fowles, "Effects of Diminished Economic Opportunities on Social Stress: Heart Attacks, Strokes and Crime," Salt Lake City Economic Policy Institute, University of Utah, 1992. The study covered fifteen metropolises over a twenty-year period. For other studies of the effects of unemployment on health, see "Links in the Chain of Adversity Following Job Loss: How Financial Strain and Loss of Personal Control Lead to Depression, Impaired Functioning and Poor Health," by Richard H. Price, Jin Nam Choi, and Amiram D. Vinokur, *Journal of Occupational Health Psychology* 7 (2002).

180   *"There are many people":* Interview with Dr. Theodore Jacobs, August 5, 2004. In addition to his posts as a clinical professor of psychiatry at New York University School of Medicine and at the Albert Einstein College of Medi-

cine, Dr. Jacobs is also the supervising analyst at the Psychoanalytic Institute at New York University and at the New York Psychoanalytic Institute.

181 *"Fundamental in-the-bones blow":* Interviews with Kim Cameron, January 17, 2005, and February 2, 2005.

181 *"It is subversive":* Interview with Kim Cameron, February 2, 2005.

185 *The president of the association:* Interview with Dr. Steven Sharfstein, January 17, 2005. Dr. Sharfstein's one-year term as president of the APA began in May 2005. He is president and chief executive of Sheppard Pratt Health Care System, a nonprofit organization in Baltimore that provides mental health care for drug addicts and education for mentally disturbed children, among other services. He has a private psychiatric practice in Baltimore and has been a clinical professor of psychiatry at the University of Maryland.

186 *"Our experience in industry":* Job Loss—a Psychiatric Perspective, published by Mental Health Materials Center, New York, 1982.

186 *They distributed that study:* Nick Kates, Barrie S. Grieff, and Duane Hagen, *The Psychosocial Impact of Job Loss* (American Psychiatric Press, 1990).

186 *I asked the doctors why:* The conversation took place on April 8, 2005, during and after a session of the Committee on Psychiatry and Industry at the spring meeting of the Group for the Advancement of Psychiatry.

187 *When I posted a request:* The request was posted at the winter meeting, January 2005, at the Waldorf-Astoria. Dr. Rolde is also on the faculty of the Psychoanalytic Institute of New England East (PINE) and is a member of the Psychoanalytic Society of New England East (PSNE) as well as the Boston Psychoanalytic Society and Institute (BPSI).

188 *With his unemployment insurance:* Bell Tech.logix is a subsidiary of Bell Industries.

188 *Working in cubicles:* Bell Tech's customers were actually telecommunications companies like Comcast and Iowa Telecom that provided Internet access and other network arrangements to their subscribers and contracted with Bell Tech to handle customer service calls from the subscribers.

189 *Nothing about Dewey's circumstances:* We spoke several times by telephone in the early months of Dewey's new job.

191 *Careers, in turn:* Richard Sennett, *The Corrosion of Character: The Personal Consequences of Work in the New Capitalism* (W. W. Norton & Company, 1998), pp. 27, 120.

192 *"All this layoffs destroy":* Interview with Arne Kalleberg, January 22, 2005.

192 *Indeed, the prevailing wisdom:* See Richard B. Freeman and Rebecca M. Blank, "The Connection Between Protection and Flexibility," published as a chapter in *Social Protection Versus Economic Flexibility: Is There a Trade-off?* (University of Chicago Press, 1994). Freeman and Blank, both mainstream economists, cite the evidence in favor of job security and conclude that there has been insufficient research to resolve the issue. That was more than a decade ago, and the issue has still not been conclusively resolved.

192 *"Academics engaged in this":* Interview with Thomas Kochan, January 4, 2004.

193 *One recent attempt:* Jody Hoffer Gittell, *The Southwest Airlines Way: Using the Power of Relationships to Achieve High Performance* (McGraw-Hill, 2003).

193 *"An airline without good":* Interview with Jody Gittell, January 3, 2004.

193 *"Corporate downsizing remains":* Kim Cameron, "Downsizing and the New Work Covenant," *Exchange* magazine, Spring 1997.

194 *"There is this":* Interview with Jerry Jasinowski, February 21, 2003. Jasinowski retired as president in 2004.

194 *"Layoffs create":* Jason Jennings, *Less Is More* (Penguin, 2002), p. 82.

194 *Frederick F. Reichheld:* Interview with Frederick Reichheld, December 8, 2003.

194 *So are companies:* Laurie Bassi and Daniel McMurrer, "Are Skills a Cost or an Asset?" *Milken Institute Review,* third quarter 2004, pp. 24–29.

194 *John A. Challenger:* Challenger is chief executive of Challenger, Gray and Christmas, in Chicago. He made these points during a presentation at a conference on layoffs held at the Federal Reserve Bank of Chicago, November 18 and 19, 2004.

194 *There is also the cost:* See David E. Sanger and Steve Lohr, "Searching for Answers," *New York Times,* March 9, 1996, p. 1.

195 *"They felt they were":* Louis Uchitelle and N. R. Kleinfield, "On the Battlefields of Business, Millions of Casualties," *New York Times,* March 2, 1996, p. 1.

195 *"People choose a career":* Interview with Dr. Pedro Ruiz, February 4, 2005. Dr. Ruiz is a former president of the American College of Psychiatrists, the American Board of Psychiatry and Neurology, and the American Association of Social Psychiatry.

198 *She conducted focus sessions:* Similar support groups appeared everywhere in the country in the nineties, many of them connected to churches and synagogues. Robert Wuthnow, a Princeton University sociologist, described them to me in a 1996 interview. Sometimes they grew out of Bible study meetings at someone's home. Rather than just Bible study, four or five people in a group of, say, fifteen raised the subject of jobs and income, and one or two said they had lost their jobs. The Bible study group soon became a support group.

198 *"It is taking control":* Interview with Maureen Moorhead, March 28, 2003.

199 *The wage loss:* Henry A. Farber, a Princeton University labor economist who has built a reputation in his field for analyzing layoff data, produced this percentage from an analysis of the worker-displacement survey published in August 2004 by the Bureau of Labor Statistics. Others at the Fed conference found similar wage loss in their studies.

199 *That meant someone earning:* There were exceptions. Hispanic factory workers in Chicago who lost jobs that paid $7 to $9 an hour often landed new jobs at similar pay, in different small factories in Chicago, after a period of training, mainly classes in English and mathematics. But the training was not the point. Their wages were already near or at the bottom. Interview with Thomas DuBois, director of Workforce Programs, Instituto del Progreso Latino in Chicago.

199 *"When you sever":* Interview at Fed conference, November 2004. See also "Earnings Losses of Displaced Workers," by Louis Jacobson and two other economists: Robert J. LaLonde of the Graduate School of Business, University of Chicago, and Daniel G. Sullivan, Federal Reserve Bank of Chicago, *American Economic Review,* September 1993, p. 685.

200 *Their chief proposal was:* Gene Sperling, chairman of the National Economic Council in Clinton's second term, and Edward Montgomery, who was chief economist of the Labor Department and then acting deputy secretary, told me in interviews about the wage-insurance discussions. Montgomery, on November 29, 2004, said: "We weren't in our proposals trying to prevent job loss, but to offer people wage insurance, so that if your wage was below what your old job paid, the insurance would take some of the sting out of the job loss."

200 *In addition, participation in:* For a good summary of this and related legislation, see "Honoring the Commitment: Assisting U.S. Workers Hurt by Globalization," by Lori G. Kletzer of the University of California at Santa Cruz and Howard Rosen of the Trade Adjustment Assistance Coalition, November 2004. In a discussion of why so few workers had applied or qualified for wage insurance, the authors of this research paper argued that it did not cover job loss from outsourcing, particularly outsourcing of service industry work, nor did it cover workers employed in export-related industries who lost their jobs because of a drop in exports. And wage insurance was not extended to the millions of workers laid off for reasons unrelated to trade.

204 *"It is just":* Five months later, in the fall of 2005, Nash went to work for the Devine Group, a Cincinnati company that administers personality tests to the employees of corporate clients. Nash assessed test results and did employee development. She earned $89,000 a year, once again far below her Procter & Gamble salary.

CHAPTER NINE

Solutions

206 *"Enjoy change," he urges:* Spencer Johnson, *Who Moved My Cheese? An Amazing Way to Deal with Change in Your Work and in Your Life* (G. P. Putnam's Sons, 1998).

207 *Today, access to:* For a discussion of the skew in education toward the offspring of the wealthy, see David Leonhardt, "The College Dropout Boom," *New York Times,* March 24, 2005, section 1, p. 1.

208 *Without these charges, we give:* For an elaboration of this argument, see Michael J. Sandel, *Democracy's Discontent: America in Search of a Public Philosophy* (Harvard University Press, 1996), and Gar Alperovitz, *America Beyond Capitalism: Reclaiming Our Wealth, Our Liberty and Our Democracy* (John Wiley & Sons, 2005).

208 *"There was an implicit":* Interview with Joel Rogers, August 31, 1995.

208 *The Bureau of Labor Statistics:* I am indebted to Tom Nardone, Ryan Helwig, and Steven Hipple, economists at the Bureau of Labor Statistics, for help in compiling and interpreting this data, which is from the bureau's twelve biennial worker-displacement surveys since the early eighties. The 4.3 percent is calculated by dividing the number of displaced full-time workers in each survey period by the number of adult full-timers in each period, and then averaging the percentages. The bureau considers the percentages more reliable than the actual layoff count. The sixty thousand households surveyed represent a cross section of the national population at the time of each survey. As the population shifts so does the cross section brought together to represent it. In any one survey, some segments of the population, blue-collar auto workers, for example, might be overrepresented or underrepresented in the cross section and in the layoff count.

209 *Whatever the reasons:* The more than 10 percent is from the Contingent and Alternative Work Arrangements Survey, 2001, produced by the Bureau of Labor Statistics.

209 *"They went to work":* Interview with Anthony Carnevale, April 1, 2003.

210 *She accepted the offer:* Interviews with Jessica Welch on December 16, 2002, and April 12, 2005, and e-mails.

210 *"The distinction between":* "Job Loss in the United States, 1981–2001," a paper prepared by Henry Farber for the annual meeting of the American Economic Association in Washington in January 2003. The other Farber material in this section is drawn from interviews on September 12 and October 23, 2002, and January 27, 2003.

211 *Back in 1968:* There is disagreement among economists on how to calculate the inflation adjustment. One school holds that a minimum wage of $7.68 an hour in 2005 would restore the purchasing power of the late sixties; another school sets the number at $8.50 an hour.

211 *Restoring the lost inflation:* Jared Bernstein, a senior economist at the Economic Policy Institute, took the nominal minimum wage of $1.60 in 1968 and increased it by the growth in productivity and inflation each year through 2004. That calculation produced a minimum of $14.79 for 2004, Bernstein reported in a July 20, 2005, e-mail and spreadsheet. In the absence of action at the federal level, a dozen states have enacted minimum wages above $5.15 an hour, with Alaska's $7.15 an hour at the high end in 2004.

211 *But raising the minimum:* Many economists, even those who favor a higher minimum wage, argue that if it gets too high, employers won't hire as many people, particularly people they deem lacking in sufficient skills to be worth the higher minimum. One hundred people employed at $5.15 an hour would drop to ninety-four at, say, $8 an hour. Other economists argue that fewer people at $8 an hour pumps more income into total wages. This view holds that it is better to have ninety-four people earning a passable wage than one hundred earning an inadequate one.

212 *The decision not to act:* Interview with Thomas J. Nardone, April 15, 2005.

212 *Farber's more comprehensive survey:* The Bush administration's initial budget proposal for the 2004 fiscal year included funds for an annual worker-displacement survey, Nardone said, but the allocation did not survive in the final budget.

212 *It is high enough:* The John J. Heldrich Center for Workplace Development at Rutgers University, for example, concluded from a survey of 1,015 adult workers in June 2003 that "nearly one-fifth of American workers were laid off from their jobs during the last three years."

212 *The bureau's tenure surveys:* Until 1983, wage and salary workers were asked "When did you start working at your present job?" Too often, the bureau explains, the question was taken to mean when did you start in your present position within the company that employs you and not when did you start at your present employer. Since 1983, the question has been "How long have you worked continuously for your present employer?"

213 *"My reading of the evidence":* David Neumark, *On the Job: Is Long-Term Employment a Thing of the Past?* (Russell Sage Foundation, 2000), p. 23.

213 *"I think there are":* Interview with David Neumark, January 7, 2005.

213 *"There have been some":* Interview with Sanford Jacoby, July 16, 2002.

214 *Five states, for example:* Tamara Hrivnak and Andrew Smith, "View from Here: Offshore Backlash," *Legal Week,* June 30, 2005.

214 *And the California legislature:* California Employment and Legislative Update, October 2004, p. 2.

215 *"You could find out":* Interview with Charles Sabel, April 12, 2005.

216 *The ruling was appealed:* The case was brought by Peter Enrich, a professor of law at Northeastern University, and Ralph Nader, the consumer advocate and presidential candidate. The appeals court found that an investment tax credit awarded by the City of Toledo to DaimlerChrysler Corporation violated the Constitution's interstate commerce clause. The city gave the tax credit to the automaker as an incentive to locate a new plant in Toledo rather than a city in Michigan. On appeal, the Supreme Court accepted the case for the 2005–2006 session.

216 *"If a state were":* Interview with Arthur Rolnick, April 4, 2005.

216 *The president of Intel:* John Markoff, "Intel Officer Says High Taxes Could Send Plant Overseas," *New York Times,* April 1, 2005, section 3, p. 12.

217 *All else being equal:* For a technical explanation see Paul Samuelson, "Where Ricardo and Mill Rebut and Confirm Arguments of Mainstream Economists Supporting Globalization," *Journal of Economic Perspectives,* summer 2004, pp. 135–46.

219 *Several factories, instead of closing:* I am indebted to George C. Lodge, professor emeritus of business administration at Harvard Business School, and the late Seymour Melman, professor emeritus of engineering at Columbia University, for help in gathering material reported in this paragraph.

219 *The National Science Foundation:* CHI Research, a consulting firm, looked at the volume of United States patents granted in 1993 and 1994 and found that a large percentage of the research cited in the patent applications was pub-

licly funded in one form or another. The CHI finding is cited in Daniel Alt-
man, *Neoconomy: George Bush's Revolutionary Gamble with America's Future*
(PublicAffairs, 2004), pp. 63–64. The reference to Netscape, Internet
Explorer, and Google is from Robert Pear, "Science Trims Money for Science Agency," *New York Times*, November 30, 2004, section 1, p. 16.

220 *It is a doubtful:* The longest test came in the eighties, during the Reagan
presidency. The Reagan tax cuts were supposed to generate so much work
and investment that they would pay for themselves. That would happen
because there would be more wages and profits to tax, and this extra income
would raise as much tax revenue as before, even at lower tax rates. Economic
growth in the eighties turned out to be slower than in the seventies and the
sixties, and wages stagnated during most of that period. Economic growth in
the first five years of George W. Bush's presidency, another testing period for
supply-side tax cuts, has also been, on average, less than robust.

220 *We are a happier people:* Layard is not the first to make this point. It was a
Thorstein Veblen theme in the early twentieth century. In those years, Walter Weyl, an economist and journalist who helped to found *The New Republic* magazine and promoted progressive causes championed by Theodore
Roosevelt, wrote: "A million dollars of commodities consumed by one over-
rich man gives less pleasure than would the same sum added to the expendi-
ture of 10,000 people." Quoted in Sandel, *Democracy's Discontent,* p. 225.

220 *"The current pursuit":* Richard Layard, *Happiness: Lessons from a New Science*
(Penguin Press, 2005), p. 234; also chapter 10.

221 *Immediate taxation would raise:* As the Democratic candidate for president in
2004, John F. Kerry included in his platform a proposal that would have
ended the deferral of taxes on overseas earnings.

221 *Companies would have to pay:* Germany, France, and Belgium require
minimum severance payments to workers who are laid off, as well as advance
notice of layoffs. These measures reduced layoffs during "the adjustment
of employment to changes in output," two American labor economists,
Katherine G. Abraham, of the University of Maryland and Susan N. Houseman, of the W.E. Upjohn Institute for Employment Research, reported in a
1993 research paper, "Does Employment Protection Inhibit Labor Market
Flexibility? Lessons from Germany, France and Belgium," published by the
Upjohn Institute. Rather than layoffs, the adjustment was made by cutting
back hours or through work sharing. These are forms of layoffs, but they are
shared by an entire staff rather than concentrated in a relatively small group
of workers who are dismissed, and the hours are restored when and if a company's output rises. Meanwhile benefits are preserved.

222 *It made them: Monthly Labor Review,* January 11, 1996. See also the *Tacoma
(Wash.) News Tribune,* December 28, 2001, p. D1; *Business Week,* August 12,
2002, p. 74; and *Business Week,* August 9, 2004, p. 33.

222 *One lies in persuading:* Thomas Geoghegan, *Which Side Are You On? Trying to
Be for Labor When It's Flat on Its Back* (paperback ed., New Press, 2004).
Geoghegan's proposal concerning state legislatures appears in the afterword,

p. 352. The book was first published in hardcover by Farrar, Straus & Giroux in 1991. The afterword was written in 2004.

223 *The model act would:* The text of the model act is available on the Westlaw Web site, www.westlaw.com.

224 *Forcing action requires:* Janitors in Los Angeles, for example, most of them Hispanic immigrants represented by the Service Employees International Union, marched in the streets during a three-week strike in the spring of 2000, and as they passed the huge office buildings they normally cleaned at night, office workers streamed onto the sidewalks in open support. Cardinal Roger Mahony said a special mass for the strikers and Rabbi Steven Jacobs honored them at a labor-oriented Passover seder. With all this support, the janitors, who earned in the $6-to-$7.50-an-hour range, won a 27 percent raise over three years instead of the 18 percent offered by their employers.

224 *"We are weaker":* Interview with Ronald Blackwell, April 18, 2005.

224 *Many of these broader:* Paul Osterman, *Gathering Power: The Future of Progressive Politics in America* (Beacon Press, 2002), p. 23. Osterman is an economist and the deputy dean at the Sloan School of Management, Massachusetts Institute of Technology.

225 *Three other similar groups:* The three others were the Association of Community Organizations for Reform Now (ACORN), Citizen's Action, and National People's Action.

225 *The coalitions bring together:* Ernesto Cortes, "Reclaiming Our Birthright," Shelterforce Online, no. 101, September–October 1998.

225 *The IAF organizers:* Osterman, *Gathering Power,* pp. 44–46.

225 *"What we're trying to do":* William Greider, *Who Will Tell the People: The Betrayal of American Democracy* (Simon & Schuster, 1992), p. 226.

226 *"As a realistic matter":* Interview with Paul Osterman, April 10, 2005.

ACKNOWLEDGMENTS

So many people made this book possible. At the top of the list are the editors of the *New York Times,* who encouraged me to write about layoffs and sharpened my reporting in the endless, challenging discussions that each story entailed. When I finally undertook this book, the *Times* granted me a leave of absence and then, when the leave ran out and the book wasn't finished, gave me the leeway to get the job done. Glenn Kramon, Tom Redburn, and Bill Schmidt were particularly supportive, but there were many others over the years who, as friends and editors, brought me along as a writer and reporter.

Apart from the *Times,* the midwife for this book was Eric Wanner, president of the Russell Sage Foundation in New York. Eric encouraged me to apply for a visiting scholarship at the foundation, submitting as my application the proposal that became *The Disposable American.* I did much of the research and reporting during the ten months that I spent at Russell Sage's pleasant quarters on East Sixty-fourth Street, and I benefited greatly from the research assistance that the Russell Sage staff furnished as well as the frequent discussions with other visiting scholars, most of them economists and social scientists. They mulled over and challenged my findings in most helpful ways. Sheldon and Sandra Danziger of the University of Michigan, Henry Farber and Avinash Dixit at Princeton, and Michael Burawoy of the University of California at Berkeley were especially giving of their time.

Jeff Madrick, a first-rate economics writer and the author of *The End of Affluence* and *Why Economies Grow,* among other books, talked over with me material in this book, and flagged organizational problems in early drafts of several chapters. I am indebted to Jeff for the dialogue we maintained and for his frank criticisms. Marie Winn, the wonderful author of *Red-Tails in Love* and *The Plug-In Drug,* read the manuscript in progress and her running commentary was immensely helpful. Others read all or parts of the book and their critiques improved the final product. I am especially indebted to Jared Bernstein, Mark S. Moore, R. Alan Hunter, Teresa Ghilarducci, Dr. Theodore Jacobs, Edward Klagsbrun, Betsy Wade, and my brother Ben Uchitelle.

They were the readers. Others helped along the way. Many appear in the text or in the endnotes, often briefly, belying the time and commitment generously given. I feel particularly close to the men and women who were laid off and who shared their stories as they struggled, and still struggle, to rebuild or just hold on to their lives. They are brave and resilient people. Still others, unmentioned in this book, to whom I am grateful include Phyllis Antush, Joel

Beaubien, Truman Bewley, Richard Bruder, John Colburn, Glenn Collins, James Corcoran, Judy Davis, Margaret Emerick, Neil Fligstein, Nancy Folbre, Lawrence Gigerich, Cindy Graham, Carol Heim, Richard Lauf, Frank Levy, Norman Levy, Tom Mess, Immanuel Ness, Suzanne Nichols, Carl H. Pforzheimer, Hannah Pierce, Diana Polak, Robert Pollin, Richard Rampley, William M. Rodgers, Robert Shapiro, Mark R. Thierman, Linda Williamson, Rhoda Wright, and John Zinner.

Donna Anderson, a librarian at the *Times*, is a master at locating source material and she blessed me frequently with her skills. Jonathan Segal, my excellent editor at Alfred A. Knopf, kept me on track when I faltered and helped me resolve difficult organizational problems. His deft editing greatly improved the final draft. Toward the end, Richard Leone, president of the Century Foundation, gave me financial support that paid for essential reporting trips.

This book would not exist without my wife, Joan Uchitelle. We have been companions in a long and very satisfying marriage, and I cannot imagine undertaking this project, and then completing it, without that companionship and her support. I am grateful also to my friends, who cheered me on, and to my grown daughters, Isabel and Jennifer, who in the nicest way set a pace for me. When I began this book, in the fall of 2002, neither was married. Now both are, to wonderful young men, and each has a child—grandchildren awaiting the arrival of this book.

Acknowledgments

DURING THE SIX YEARS I worked on this book, many people encouraged and supported me. I am grateful to them all. Nina Goldman, Cindy Shearer and John Curtis talked, listened and sustained me when I first began to write. The University of Minnesota Creative Writing Program, The Loft Mentorship Program and the Fishtrap Imnaha Writers' Retreat provided strong writing communities. Thanks to John Witte, editor of the *Northwest Review*, for originally publishing portions of chapter nineteen (in a different form).

Patricia Hampl coaxed me to care about every word. Charlie Baxter told me it was done when I needed to hear it. Julie Schumacher, Madelon Sprengnether, and Patricia Weaver Francisco gave critical feedback, advice, and encouragement. Readers and writing companions Rachel Moritz, Amanda Coplin, Brian Malloy, Jennine Crucet, Ann McDuffie and Sari Fordham spurred me on. Special thanks to Joni Tevis for riding to the rescue, along with David Bernardy, at the eleventh hour.

I am indebted to Maria Massie for confidently shepherding this book into the publishing world, to Amy Scheibe for beautiful editing under difficult circumstances, to Beth Partin for painstaking care of the manuscript, and to Nicole Caputo for the gorgeous cover. Thanks to everyone at Counterpoint for believing in good books, and for their enthusiasm and hard work on behalf of this one, especially Jack Shoemaker, Charlie Winton, Roxanna Aliaga, Sharon Donovan, and Abbye Simkowitz.

I could not have written this book without the love and support of my family. To Jeni Flynn I am grateful for many years of excellent step-mothering—and especially for putting a roof over my head during the first nine months of writing. Thanks to Joe Keith for telling me stories about Paris, Lisa Adelson for standing by me all those years, and Lee Flynn for unflagging enthusiasm for this project.

My father, Russell Flynn read drafts even when it pained him, made sure I got all the dates and numbers right, and always, always believed I was a writer. My sisters, Sara and Amy, have given me a lifetime of solidarity. I am grateful beyond words to all three of them for sharing their memories, letting me tell this story, and for tolerating with grace this appalling invasion into their privacy.

And finally, to my husband Mike Rollin who raised my spirits for the final push, and suggested the title—everything is better when you are here.

INDEX